Success Academy

To Nettie Lesters,
With deepest thanks for your help
with the book and for your
continuing scholarship involving
underrepresented students and
college access.

Margo

Brookings SD
December 2014

Joseph L. DeVitis & Linda Irwin-DeVitis
GENERAL EDITORS

Vol. 65

The Adolescent Cultures, School & Society series
is part of the Peter Lang Education list.
Every volume is peer reviewed and meets
the highest quality standards for content and production.

PETER LANG
New York • Washington, D.C./Baltimore • Bern
Frankfurt • Berlin • Brussels • Vienna • Oxford

MARYJO BENTON LEE

Success Academy

How Native American Students Prepare for College (and How Colleges Can Prepare for Them)

PETER LANG
New York • Washington, D.C./Baltimore • Bern
Frankfurt • Berlin • Brussels • Vienna • Oxford

Library of Congress Cataloging-in-Publication Data

Lee, MaryJo Benton.
Success academy: how native American students prepare for college
(and how colleges can prepare for them) / MaryJo Benton Lee.
pages cm. — (Adolescent cultures, school and society; vol. 65.)
Includes bibliographical references and index.
1. Indians of North America—Education (Higher)—United States.
2. College preparation programs—United States. I. Title.
E97.L46   378.1'98297—dc23   2013018177
ISBN 978-1-4331-1946-0 (hardcover)
ISBN 978-1-4331-1945-3 (paperback)
ISBN 978-1-4539-1167-9 (e-book)
ISSN 1091-1464

Bibliographic information published by **Die Deutsche Nationalbibliothek**.
Die Deutsche Nationalbibliothek lists this publication in the "Deutsche
Nationalbibliografie"; detailed bibliographic data is available
on the Internet at http://dnb.d-nb.de/.

The paper in this book meets the guidelines for permanence and durability
of the Committee on Production Guidelines for Book Longevity
of the Council of Library Resources.

© 2013 Peter Lang Publishing, Inc., New York
29 Broadway, 18th floor, New York, NY 10006
www.peterlang.com

Printed in the United States of America

This book is dedicated with love to

The Success Academy Scholars
2000–2012

Dino, Alaina, Cat, Tia, Marsha, Dan, Daisy, Robert, Jordan, Randi, Fawn, Brennon, Vanessa, Jillian, Josie, Sammone, Giles, Stephanie, Christopher, Dani, Jovi, Rylin, Kelly, Maria, Kaleb, Aly, Santee, Ariana, Dalta, Christina, Jasonya, Cassie, Leah, Jaymee, Jasmine, Josalyn, Shantayah, Donnie, Shafawn, Hepi, Anna, Marialan, Chris, Jody, Jared, Robyn, Rae Dawn, Jinte, Butterfly, Aaron, DiVonne, and Shaina

You unveil opportunities for hope. You help us
learn, unlearn, and relearn what is possible.

Whatever you can do,
or dream you can,
begin it.
Boldness has genius,
power and magic in it.

—Goethe

Contents

Acknowledgments

For all that has been—Thanks. For all that will be—Yes!

These words of the great peacemaker Dag Hammarskjöld resonate with me, having been given the opportunity to tell a story about a project close to my heart. The Flandreau Indian School-South Dakota State University Success Academy has filled my life and the lives of those around me for more than a decade.

For all that has been—my thanks are boundless.

I would first like to thank my Success Academy students. Thank you for sharing a part of your life with me. Together we have learned that there are no failures, only early attempts at success. I love you all. This book is for you.

To the visionary educators from the Flandreau Indian School—Superintendent Betty Belkham, Principal Stuart Zephier, Success Academy Principal Sandra Koester Elenkiwich, and Librarian/Teacher Susan Mendelsohn—who asked South Dakota State University to partner with them in a bold, new endeavor that was to become Success Academy—thank you for 12 years of being both giving and forgiving.

Thank you to the generous South Dakota State University administrators who said "yes" and made Success Academy a reality with their unwavering support for so many years. Marcus Dahn, director of diversity enhancement, drafted the first Memorandum of Understanding, and President Peggy Gordon Miller signed it into being. Executive Vice President for Administration Michael P. Reger provided the initial funding. For many years, Acting Director of Diversity Enhancement Allen Branum nurtured the program not only with the resources of his office but also with his own wisdom and caring.

The groundwork was laid for the creation of Success Academy at SDSU by three special people. So many of us at SDSU learned how to collaborate respectfully with Native communities through the work of Honors College Dean Tim Nichols and Provost and Vice President for Academic Affairs Laurie Stenberg Nichols. Their extraordinary 2+2+2 program led the way for all future college access and systemic change initiatives at South Dakota State University. For almost 40 years, the work of Distinguished Professor of English Charles L. Woodard has shaped American Indian Studies at SDSU and, by so doing, has shaped the conscience of the university. To these three individuals I express my deepest appreciation. I have grown so much from your leadership, your scholarship, and your friendship.

I offer my heartfelt thanks to the College of Engineering, Success Academy's SDSU "home" for its first 10 years. A special thank you goes from me to former Dean Duane Sander and to former Dean Virgil Ellerbruch and to Assistant Dean Rich Reid and to Dean Lewis Brown. Dean Brown once said, "If everyone else leaves us, we will still support Success Academy because it's the right thing to do." I have never forgotten those words—or what they have meant to the longevity of the program. Former Dean of the College of Arts and Sciences Jerry Jorgensen made possible the expansion of freshman Success Academy into a sophomore-year program, and I owe him a huge thank you for that.

About 300 SDSU faculty and staff members and about 4,000 SDSU students have served as Success Academy planners and presenters since 2000. I remember every one of your contributions, and I will always be thankful for what you gave to the Success Academy students. A special thanks is extended to Success Academy's "academic parents," retired SDSU faculty and community volunteers who mentored numerous cohorts of juniors through the college preparatory process. Four enormously devoted individuals—Physics Professor Larry Browning, Math Professor Christine Larson, English Professor Darla Bielfeldt, and Distinguished Professor of Geography Charles "Fritz" Gritzner—introduced the Success Academy seniors to their first college classes. A hugely supportive network of Student Affairs professionals from many offices throughout SDSU made the transition from high school to college a smooth one for our Success Academy scholars. I would like to especially thank SDSU Financial Aid Director Jay Larsen for always believing in our program and our students. To all of those mentioned, the students and I stand forever in your debt.

Thank you from the bottom of my heart to the SDSU Native American Club, its advisers and its students, for being strong, positive role models for our Success Academy participants. Staff at SDSU's American Indian Education and Cultural Center have contributed so much to Success Academy, and I would like to thank Valerian Three Irons, Joseph Brewer, Nanabah Allison-Brewer, Doris Giago, and Charlotte Davidson for all they have taught me throughout my years at SDSU. I also extend my deepest thanks to "success coaches" Jill Kessler, April Eastman, and Eliza Yellow Bird Johns for their work with the Success Academy scholars. Funding from the Citi Foundation and the South Dakota Space Grant Consortium made possible the culture-based classes for Success Academy seniors, and I thank Jerry Nachtigal of Citi and Kevin Dalsted of SDSGC for their assistance in securing that support.

The true joy of Success Academy has been in the partnership forged between South Dakota State University and the Flandreau Indian School. The commitment of FIS administrators, faculty, and staff to their students' futures and to the Success Academy program is monumental and greatly appreciated by me and others at SDSU. Thank you, Zonya Tantype and Derek Burshiem, for so ably counseling FIS students throughout your long careers. Thank you especially to Ronna and Dick Gould, Robin and Roger Fodness, Danelle and Ron McKinney, and Colleen and Art Cartwright—you exemplify all that is good in the profession of teaching.

For all that has been—in the FIS-SDSU Success Academy program of the past 12 years—thanks.

For all that will be—in this book that tells Success Academy's story—I also offer thanks.

Thank you to my editor, Joseph DeVitis, for believing in this project and then so ably seeing it through to completion. Thank you also to Chris Myers and Bernadette Shade at Peter Lang for working with me so kindly and patiently once again.

South Dakota State University was an extremely supportive environment in which to work on this book. I am most appreciative of the time granted to me by the university and Chief Diversity Officer Jaime Nolan-Andrino to complete the manuscript. The staff at the Hilton M. Briggs Library spent endless hours answering my questions and directing me to resources. My sincere thanks go to librarians Mary Kraljic, Vickie Mix, and Elizabeth Fox. Rachel Manzer of the interlibrary loan department was a godsend, tracking down hundreds of articles and books on critical theory and American Indian education from around the country. Senior secretary Betty Nelson, together with daughter Sarah Nelson, created the Success Academy enrollment chart, another key aspect of the project. Program Assistant Kim Steineke and Senior Secretary Tammy Loban made invaluable contributions in sustaining Success Academy throughout its time in the College of Engineering and in maintaining meticulous records that made the writing of this book possible. Professor Emerita of Journalism and Mass Communication Mary Perpich was an important source of information on the history of Success Academy and faculty involvement in it.

The manuscript benefited from the careful editing of individual chapters by Tim Nichols, Charles L. Woodard, and Betty Belkham (Chapter 1), Sandra Koester Elenkiwich (Chapter 2), Jerry Jorgensen (Chapter 3), SDSU Admissions Counselor Kate Stock (Chapter 4), Darla Bielfeldt (Chapter 5), and Tim Nichols (Chapter 6). Nettie Legters, research scientist at The Johns Hopkins University Center for the Social Organization of Schools, helped me better understand the Talent Development High Schools approach discussed in Chapter 1, and for that I am very grateful.

Good scholarship, by necessity, must build on the work of others. I wish to especially acknowledge William G. Tierney, the Wilbur-Kieffer Professor of Higher Education at the Rossier School of Education at the University of Southern California, for his work on Native Americans in academe. Professor Tierney introduced me to Julia E. Colyar, now of the Graduate School of Education at the University of Buffalo, whose writings on college preparation for underrepresented students have informed both my scholarship and my practice. I am also indebted to colleague Terry E. Huffman, professor of education at George Fox University, the author of several books on American Indian education. Enrique (Henry) T. Trueba—teacher, mentor, and friend who passed on to the next life nearly a decade ago—will continue to guide me in all I do.

The great Brazilian educator Paulo Freire once described schools as places where people struggle for justice with "critical hope." My life in schools has now spanned some 50 years—and I have been blessed to know some truly inspiring teachers during that time. I end these acknowledgments and start this book by extending my thanks to them.

To Professor Mary Moeller of the SDSU Teaching, Learning and Leadership Department: I was so fortunate to know you first in your role as an amazing Success Academy workshop presenter. I was thrilled when you agreed to be an editor of this manuscript. Our many hours of discussion about critical theory in education have benefitted me and my text in innumerable ways. Thank you for all you have done.

To Professor Diane Kayongo-Male of the SDSU Sociology and Rural Studies Department: Thank you for being first my teacher and adviser, then my colleague and writing partner, now and always my dear friend. What inspiration you have brought to my life! I am so grateful for our exciting discussions over lunch, your meticulous reviews of the manuscript, and your constant encouragement of my work. In sharing with me your passion for social justice, you always give me hope.

To Professor Emeritus Richard W. Lee of the SDSU Journalism and Mass Communication Department—teacher, activist, husband, and most cherished friend: You bring joy to my heart. Thank you for always being there for me, through 12 years of Success Academy and through the telling of its story.

For all that has been—Thanks. For all that will be—Yes!

Systemic Change and the Birth of Success Academy

Picture a federal Indian boarding school, 125 years old, where vocational training was emphasized, and few graduates attended college.

Picture an overwhelmingly white, land-grant university, having little to no contact with this boarding school, despite being its next-door neighbor in Indian country for more than a century.

Now picture an initiative that turned this situation on its head. In fall 2000 the Flandreau Indian School began an educational reform effort called Success Academy, aimed at preparing *all* of its students for postsecondary education. Over the next decade South Dakota State University responded by committing 300 of its faculty and staff and $85,000 of its annual budget to opening the doors of higher education to Indian students previously excluded.

Twelve years later, about 85 percent of all Flandreau Indian School (FIS) graduates plan to continue on to postsecondary education after graduation. Each year about 10 of those FIS graduates are welcomed into South Dakota State University (SDSU), with generous scholarships and with an array of support services designed to ensure their success.

This book, about FIS-SDSU Success Academy, describes critical theory in action. It is written for those who realize that our country's purportedly meritocratic educational system, in fact, reproduces existing social inequalities.

Realization is simple. Solutions are not. A major criticism of critical theory, as explained by one of its most articulate proponents, William G. Tierney (2000:

214), is that "individuals cannot often envision what abstract ideas look like when they are employed."

Consequently, this book is written for those who want to move beyond just understanding inequality in education to actually remedying it. The story is compelling because those of us responsible for the birth of Success Academy were ordinary K–12 educators and state university faculty. Starting without huge resources, we were united by a passion for making higher education accessible to American Indian students.

This book is written for those who, like us, want to use critical theory to design innovative programs. We know that major systemic change—at a high school, a university, or other institution—*is* possible. Our hope in writing this book, covering both our challenges and our successes, is to provide a model to guide others through similar systemic change.

Systemic Change

A Definition

What do we mean by "systemic change" in an educational institution? "Systemic change is just that," write H. O. Kunkel and C. L. Skaggs (2001: 15), "change of the system." Kunkel and Skaggs identify *vision* and *values* as two factors that influence the degree to which higher education systems can change.

Developing a new *vision* is a fundamental first step toward systemic change—and also one of the most difficult aspects of the change process (Kunkel and Skaggs 2001: 16). Vision develops only through honest discussions among all of the stakeholders of the institution. Senior administrators and faculty provide the leadership, working to create a safe environment that brings others in the university into the conversation.

Rethinking the institution's *values* is a second necessary step in bringing about systemic change. Values are "ways of seeing," and change involves "ways of being" (Grinnell 1987). The W. K. Kellogg Foundation argues that "educational reforms should be seen as part of a fundamental transformation of the *values* and *vision* [italics mine] of American society as a whole" (Astin and Astin 2000: vi).

Systemic Change and College Access

Most Americans value the principle of education as "the great equalizer" (Tierney and Hagedorn 2002: 1). The vision held dear by most Americans is that of a quality education being delivered to all, regardless of ethnicity or income. The notion that public education benefits all students equally (and consequently benefits society as a whole) is taken as a central tenet of "the great equalizer" theory.

In its simplest form, theory is a way of thinking through what one observes and then making general statements. There is, however, a major difference between this kind of theory and the kind of theory developed by sociologists. Sociological theory must stand up to continuous scrutiny and testing.

"The great equalizer" theory does not. As the minority population throughout the United States has dramatically increased, college access for students of color has not kept pace. African American, Hispanic, and Native American youth still lag far behind their white and Asian American counterparts in rates of college attendance, retention, and graduation (Tierney and Hagedorn 2002: 1).

The concept of education as "the great equalizer" grows out of structural functional theory. This theory suggests that schools function primarily as mechanisms for meeting the needs of society. Students are presumed to compete on a level playing field, with those who succeed doing so on the basis of ability and effort. Those who prove themselves most qualified in school ultimately get the best jobs in society (Riordan 2004: 25–28).

This book and indeed the entire Flandreau Indian School-South Dakota State University Success Academy program operate from a different theoretical perspective, that is, from the perspective of critical theory. As explained by Barry Kanpol (1999):

> Critical theorists view schools as inherently unequal places of knowledge distribution that in large part serve to divide the United States by race, class and gender. That is, different people divided by race, class and gender receive and/or are privileged to receive certain forms of educational knowledge, skills and curriculum in unequal ways. (2–3)

The theoretical lens through which we, as educators, view schools fundamentally affects the way we serve students. Nowhere is this more true than in the area of access to college for students of color.

The functionalist's way of increasing college access for students of color is through remediation, that is, through attempting to "fix" those presumed to be unprepared for higher learning. The scaffolding upon which Success Academy rests, however, is critical theory. The educators involved in creating Success Academy chose to "fix" their institutions, institutions that were actually discouraging instead of encouraging Indian students from entering college.

Flandreau Indian School-South Dakota State University Success Academy is, first and foremost, about major systemic change. This systemic change came about via a comprehensive school reform plan adopted by the Flandreau Indian School and a K–16 partnership embraced by South Dakota State University. Both of these initiatives, along with the vision and values behind them, will be explained in more detail later in Chapter 1. First it is necessary to provide some background information, specifically on the two institutions that became Success Academy collaborators, and more generally on Indian education during South Dakota's first century.

South Dakota and Indian Education

The Need for Change

South Dakota, with a Native American population of 10.1 percent, ranks fourth highest among all of the states in its proportion of Natives per capita (U.S. Census Bureau 2011). Most of the state's predominantly Native American counties have young populations and high fertility rates (Brooks, McCurry, and Hess 2008: 1).

South Dakota is also home to the three counties with the nation's highest poverty rates: Ziebach County, where the Cheyenne River Sioux Indian Reservation is located; Todd County, where the Rosebud Sioux Indian Reservation is located; and Shannon County, where the Pine Ridge (Oglala Sioux) Indian Reservation is located (Lengerich 2012). According to the U.S. Census (Ogunwole 2006: 12), 38.9 percent of all Sioux people live in poverty, the highest percentage among all American Indian tribal groups.

More than half of South Dakota's Native American children live in poverty (South Dakota Voices for Children 2012). "My grandchild, education is the ladder," said the renowned 19th-century Navajo Chief Manuelito, "Tell our people to take it" (San Juan School District 2003). Today many families, both Indian and non-Indian, see education as the way out of poverty. But the statistics regarding American Indian outcomes do not bode well for South Dakotans.

Only 57.1 percent of all Indian children in the state graduated from high school in 2011, compared to 85.9 percent of all students (Rick 2012). According to the Alliance for Excellent Education (2011), nearly 2,600 students of all races who should have graduated from South Dakota's high schools in 2010 did not do so. Estimates put the lost lifetime earnings of these individuals at about $700 million (Alliance for Excellent Education 2011).

Other observers have studied South Dakota's educational statistics and have also found the state notably lacking. The title of a 2010 report, *The Dropout/Graduation Crisis Among American Indian and Alaska Native Students: Failure to Respond Places the Future of Native Peoples at Risk*, tells much of the story (Faircloth and Tippeconnic III 2010). Of the seven states with the highest percentage of American Indian and

Alaska Native students, South Dakota had the lowest high school graduation rate for Native students (30.4 percent) compared to non-Native students (75.6 percent) during the year studied (2005). This was the widest graduation rate gap (45.2 percentage points) of any state examined (Faircloth and Tippeconnic III 2010: 11).

These figures vary from those given elsewhere due to data collection being done in different years. There is also a wide variation between state reported, federally reported, and independently reported graduation rates. Variation is due to differences in rate calculation, poor definitions, and inconsistent implementation.

That said, there is similar cause for concern at the college level. The state's four tribal colleges and universities are greatly increasing access to higher education for American Indians—but they cannot be expected to shoulder the burden alone. Native American students accounted for only 1.9 percent of all students who enrolled for the fall 2010 semester at the state's six public universities (South Dakota Board of Regents 2011: 12).

Only 41 percent of all new American Indian students in 2002 graduated from South Dakota colleges within six years of entering; this compared to a 47 percent graduation rate for all new students in the 2002–2008 cohort (Alliance for Excellent Education 2011). A 2012 "report card" from the Institute for a Competitive Workforce gave South Dakota's four-year universities a D on "student access and success" (Kohli and Sneve 2012: 1A).

Clearly, an achievement gap exists. It results, in large part, from Native American students as a group not having educational opportunities equal to those enjoyed by other American students. The U.S. Commission on Civil Rights (2003: xi), in a landmark study titled *A Quiet Crisis: Federal Funding and Unmet Needs in Indian Country*, blames "deteriorating school facilities, underpaid teachers, weak curricula, discriminatory treatment, outdated learning tools and cultural isolation" for the persistent achievement gap between Native American students and those from other racial/ethnic groups. In its report to the President and Congress, the Commission (2003) writes:

> This study reveals that federal funding directed to Native Americans…has not been sufficient to address the basic and very urgent needs of indigenous people.…The federal government, through laws, treaties, and policies established over hundreds of years, is obligated to ensure that funding is adequate to meet these needs. (iii)

Land for Education

In 1794 the United States signed the first treaty that included provisions for federal funding of Indian education in exchange for tribal land (American Indian

College Fund 2011). As Karen Gayton Swisher (Standing Rock Sioux), the former president of Haskell Indian Nations University, explains, "In exchange for nearly 1 billion acres of land, certain services…were to be provided in perpetuity" (Szasz 1999: 206). In numerous treaties, Indian tribes ceded land to the United States in exchange for providing education to Native children in perpetuity (National Congress of American Indians/National Indian Education Association n.d.).

In what was to become the state of South Dakota, the Yankton Sioux signed the Treaty of Washington in 1858, ceding most of the land east of the Missouri River to the United States (Thompson 2005: 69). The Fort Laramie Treaty of 1868 designated the half of present-day South Dakota west of the Missouri River as the Great Sioux Reservation. The Lakota Sioux, Yankton Sioux, and the Arapaho Nation, signers of that treaty, were assured by the federal government that outsiders would not be allowed to enter (Thompson 2005: 90). Both of these treaties, like so many others between Native Americans and the United States, included provisions for the education of Native children (Kappler 1904).

"Treaty promises were made in perpetuity, remain the supreme law of the land, and do not have an expiration date," Eugene "Ribs" Whitebird of the Leech Lake Band of Ojibwe says. "These promises have not been kept, and our children suffer because of it" (U.S. Congress 2012). The truth of Whitebird's remarks is borne out by South Dakota's poor record of educating American Indian youth.

The Education of American Indian Children

Nine American Indian reservations lie within or partially within South Dakota's borders, and they occupy almost 20 percent of the state's land mass. Native American children from these reservations attend schools of four kinds (Faircloth and Tippeconnic 2010):

- Public schools: In South Dakota, 12,775 Native children attend public elementary and secondary schools, 10.5 percent of the state's total public school enrollment (DeVoe, Darling-Churchill, and Snyder 2008:160).
- Private schools: Many of these are former missions schools, such as the Red Cloud Indian School on the Pine Ridge (Oglala Sioux) Indian Reservation and the St. Joseph Indian School near the Lower Brule Sioux Indian Reservation and the Crow Creek Sioux Indian Reservation.

- Tribal contract or grant schools: These are run by tribes with operating funds received under a contract or grant from the federal Bureau of Indian Education.
- Federal Bureau of Indian Education (BIE) operated schools: These include elementary, secondary, day, or boarding schools.

BIE Off-Reservation Boarding Schools. Only four federal off-reservation boarding schools (ORBS) remain in the country: Chemawa Indian School in Salem, Oregon; Riverside Indian School in Anadarko, Oklahoma; Sherman Indian High School in Riverside, California; and Flandreau Indian School in Flandreau, South Dakota (Bureau of Indian Education 2009).

The Flandreau Indian School is a partner with South Dakota State University in the Success Academy project. A brief history of FIS follows in the next section.

The Oldest of the ORBS: Flandreau Indian School. In 1869 a group of Santee Sioux tribal members, homesteading along the Big Sioux River in an area that would later become Flandreau, organized a Presbyterian church (Bauske 2003: 2B). In 1873 Presbyterian missionary John P. Williamson wrote to the Secretary of the Interior, asking for these Santee Sioux to "be furnished a teacher, with perhaps a little aid in the way of school books" (Flandreau Indian School Archives 1995: 1).

A government day school for American Indian children living in the Flandreau area was opened in the church building later that year. Soon a second room was added to the Indian school to educate "white children of the community" (Mashek 1988). The noted Indian physician Charles Eastman and his siblings were pupils in the "white man's school room," at the request of their Santee Sioux father (Mashek 1988).

By the 1880s Indian and non-Indian residents of Flandreau "were equally anxious to have a government boarding school built near their town" (Landrum 2002: 37). By then boarding schools had become part of the official U.S. government policy toward American Indians. The intent was to assimilate Indian children into European culture, and attendance was mandatory. In most cases, boarding schools were established far away from reservations so that students would have no contact with their families. The Flandreau Santee Sioux wanted a government boarding school nearer than the distant schools to which they would otherwise have been forced to send their children (Kizer 1940: 16).

South Dakota U.S. Senator Richard F. Pettigrew successfully campaigned for office in 1889, in part on the promise of locating a government boarding school in Flandreau. In 1891 the federal government purchased 160 acres of land one-half mile north of Flandreau, land that, not coincidentally, was owned by Pettigrew.

The old mission school building was moved from near the Big Sioux River to the highest land on the new property. Despite operating out of temporary quarters, 98 pupils were enrolled in classes. By 1893 three buildings had been constructed at the new site with more to follow rapidly. The school was named the Riggs Institute, in honor of Alfred L. Riggs, a missionary to the Santee Sioux.

By 1895 the school could accommodate 300 students (Landrum 2002: 37–40) in grades 1 through 8. In addition to South Dakota, students were drawn from the contiguous states of Minnesota, North Dakota, Montana, Iowa, Nebraska, and Wyoming, and also from more distant states such as Wisconsin, Michigan, and Utah (Child 1998: 111). Early students came to Flandreau by train, and later students by chartered bus. At any one time, these students represented as many as 60 different tribes. The "particularly pan-Indian quality of the boarding schools is not what assimilationists, who were committed to the repression of tribal languages and culture, had in mind when they founded the institutions," writes Ojibwe historian Brenda J. Child (1998: 2).

"The main objective in constructing such institutions was to build a model for assimilation," Cynthia Landrum (2002: 39) says. "The purpose of the school was to provide vocational training and language skills to American Indians."

The study of boarding schools has become one of the richest areas of American Indian scholarship. There is substantial documentation of the tragic consequences of boarding school education on students and tribes. Some recent work by American Indian scholars, however, has portrayed boarding schools as the embodiment of both victimization and agency for Native people. "They served as sites of both cultural loss and cultural persistence," remarks historian Julie Davis (2001).

The experiences of students attending the Flandreau Indian Boarding School and the Haskell Institute have been richly documented in a book by Child (1998). Through a collection of letters, written by Indian parents and children from 1900 to 1940:

> Students described their bouts of homesickness, their regimens of work and study, their instances of rebellion, and often their struggles with serious diseases such as tuberculosis. The letters sent from Indian parents to the schools are just as revealing regarding problems parents confronted: the agony of separation from children, their concerns about health care and diet in the schools, and sometimes their despair when children grew sick or died at school....The boarding school letters, sometimes poignant and always candid, establish a complex history of the Native Americans who were involved with residential school education. In part, it is the history of people who experienced forced assimilation, and who to varying degrees lost control over important aspects of their own lives....At the same time, Native students and their families resisted and frequently triumphed over that bureaucracy, and they used government boarding schools for their own advantage. (7–8)

By 1899, 25 off-reservation boarding schools, like the one at Flandreau, were operating in 15 states (Zephier 2008). They followed a model established by Captain Richard Pratt at the Carlisle (Pennsylvania) Indian School: "Kill the Indian, not the man." This meant attempting to totally assimilate Indian children into European culture. Students were taught that school was a place to become "civilized" by deliberately rejecting their Native cultures. Students wore school uniforms and had their hair cut. They were forbidden to speak their native languages. Their days were filled with manual labor.

An early "bulletin" of the Flandreau Indian Vocational High School (1936?) lists courses "intended to prepare students to earn their living on or off the reservation." These courses were commercial dressmaking, commercial laundering, nursery school, library science, commercial foods, nursing, dormitory administration, Native arts and crafts, and beauty culture for girls. Metal work, woodwork, electricity, engineering, auto mechanics, dairying, barbering, agriculture, painting and decorating, masonry, baking, cooking, and leatherwork were offered for boys.

Besides learning these skills, students employed them to keep the school running. The entire campus became a classroom with the students primarily responsible for building and maintaining it. The Flandreau community also benefited greatly from having a vocational high school in its midst, with services provided by students ranging from a barbershop run by male students to a tearoom run by female students. An "outing program" sent FIS students into surrounding towns to work as domestic servants during summer vacations (Child 1998: 82).

Major changes resulted from the Meriam Report, commissioned by the Secretary of the Interior and published in 1928. The report sharply criticized Indian education in general and boarding schools in particular. Student labor, overcrowded conditions, medical service, food, teachers, curriculum, and discipline—all fell under the scrutiny, and censure, of the investigators. The report concluded that "provisions for the care of the Indian children in boarding schools are grossly inadequate" (Meriam 1928: 11).

Byron Brophy assumed his post as Flandreau Indian School administrator in 1931, shortly after the publication of the Meriam Report. Brophy was a welcome change from his predecessors, who had been career men in what was then called "the Indian Service" before coming to FIS. Unlike them, Brophy was an engineer who had traveled the world and lived abroad for several years. Child (1998: 86) describes him as "not an assimilationist but a cultural pluralist with a high regard for his American Indian students."

During Brophy's nine-year tenure, the school's academic standards were raised, and students' manual labor time was reduced. For the first time, vocational training became firmly linked to academic programs. The institution became an accredited high school, the lower eight grades having been eliminated due to low enrollment. Even the name of the school changed, from the Riggs Institute to the Flandreau Indian Vocational High School. Standards improved to the extent that local non-Indian students petitioned to be admitted, and some were, for a small fee (Child 1998: 86).

Over time, almost 60 buildings were built on the Flandreau Indian School campus, most of them now long gone (Mashek 1988). By 1939, student enrollment had risen to 563 (Child 1998: 109).

Brophy was reassigned to a new post in 1940, leaving behind him "a more humane institution" (Child 1998: 86). But by then, the heyday of government boarding schools had passed (Child 1998: 86).

U.S. government policy had shifted once again, this time in favor of placing American Indian students in local public schools rather than in federal boarding schools.

In the summer of 1947 the Flandreau Indian School, like other federal Indian boarding schools before it, faced the possibility of closure (Landrum 2002: 89). It was uncertain whether the school would reopen in the fall. It did reopen, but grave threats of closure would continue to haunt the school for decades to come.

Moves Toward Change

Fortuitous timing is often a catalyst for change in tribal school–state university collaborations (Nichols and Nichols 2006: 71). Two reform movements, one affecting K–12 education and the other affecting higher education, were sweeping the country starting in the late 1990s. These movements on the national level gave impetus to change on the local level, change that ultimately gave birth to the Flandreau Indian School-South Dakota State University Success Academy.

The Comprehensive Schoolwide Reform (CSR) movement focused on "improvement for entire schools rather than on particular populations of students within schools; and it is not limited to particular subjects, programs, or instructional methods" (Desimone 2002: 434). How the CSR movement affected the Flandreau Indian School will be discussed first. Then another education reform, K–16 partnerships, and its implications for South Dakota State University, will be covered.

Comprehensive Schoolwide Reform at the Flandreau Indian School

Teaching American Indian children in off-reservation boarding schools presents challenges different from those faced by educators in other settings. Staff members at the Flandreau Indian School were not immune to these challenges. By the start of the new millennium, the dropout rate was high, and academic achievement was low. The year 2000 brought a new administrator to FIS. Superintendent Betty Belkham, a Cherokee educator with decades of experience in teaching and administration, came to the school ready to enact change.

At about the same time, the federal government was starting to make funds available to encourage schoolwide change and to improve student success (Epstein 2003: 1). Under the Comprehensive School Reform Demonstration program, FIS and similar institutions were required, in order to receive funding, to examine numerous nationally recognized models for change.

FIS administrators and faculty studied more than 20 school reform models. The one chosen was Talent Development High Schools (TDHS), a school reform model for restructuring large high schools with persistent attendance and discipline problems, poor student achievement, and high dropout rates. The model includes both structural and curriculum reforms. It calls for schools to reorganize into small "learning communities"—including ninth-grade academies for first-year students and career academies for students in upper grades—to reduce student isolation and anonymity. It also emphasizes high academic standards and provides all students with a college-preparatory academic sequence (What Works Clearinghouse 2007). TDHS was developed at the Center for Research on the Education of Students Placed at Risk (CRESPAR) at The Johns Hopkins University during the mid-1990s. Volumes have been written about the Talent Development High School model. (See McPartland, Jordan, Legters, and Balfanz 1997; McPartland, Balfanz, Jordan, and Legters 1998; Jordan, McPartland, Legters, and Balfanz 2000; and Legters, Balfanz, Jordan, and McPartland 2002 for thorough descriptions of the TDHS model, its implementation, and its results.)

In adopting the TDHS model, the Flandreau Indian School joined a group that eventually numbered more than 80 high schools in 20 districts nationwide (Kemple, Herlihy, and Smith 2005: ix). The model was designed primarily to improve the academic achievement of students in large, urban high schools across the country. Only one other Indian institution, Wingate High School in Fort Wingate, New Mexico, was among the original TDHS adopters. Obviously, the national model needed local adaptations to function successfully at the Flandreau Indian School. And it was that need for adaptation that led to the partnership begun in 2000 with South Dakota State University.

The TDHS model starts with a ninth grade "Success Academy," a "school-within-a-school" for incoming freshmen with its own principal, space, and faculty typically organized into interdisciplinary teams of teachers who teach the same group of students in common. At FIS this meant that Success Academy freshmen attended classes on the second floor of the academic building and lived on the second floor of the dormitory. Teams of math, English, science, and social studies teachers worked, day in and day out, with the same small groups of students. "Block scheduling" extended each class period to 90 minutes. Transition Math and Strategic Reading classes supplemented the usual Algebra and English classes taken by freshmen, in essence giving poorly prepared students a double dose of subject matter in problem areas (Koester 2004).

But most relevant to what was to become the Flandreau Indian School-South Dakota State University partnership was a course called Freshman Seminar, introduced into the curriculum to help ninth graders make a smooth transition from middle school to high school. College and careers were among the topics to be addressed in the seminar.

In a typical Talent Development High School, students in grades 10, 11, and 12 move on to "career academies." Some examples are career academies in Arts and Humanities, Business and Finance, Environmental Sciences, Sports Studies and Health Wellness, and Transportation and Manufacturing Technology. Students in each academy take a common core of academic courses as well as their own set of career-focused electives (Learning Forward 1998b). Opportunities that urban Talent Development High Schools have—to work with their surrounding communities, to develop career academies for upperclassmen and to introduce academy-related careers to Success Academy freshmen—simply do not exist in Flandreau. That can best be explained by describing the Flandreau Indian School campus in more detail.

A Closer Look at FIS

The FIS campus covers 170 acres near South Dakota's eastern border. The campus is located in a region called the Coteau des Prairies, which consists of gently rolling land formed by receding glaciers. Some of the acreage lies near the Big Sioux River and the site of the first school. Five original buildings remain. Quarters for staff are occupied and well-maintained. The school received stimulus funds amounting to more than $20 million in 2009 (Keloland 2009), monies used for improvements to infrastructure such as roads, sidewalks, heating, and air conditioning.

The FIS campus has become a highly desirable location for cross-country track meets, at which FIS students have excelled. Land outside the school compound itself has a horse area, pasture land, and hay land, used for the FIS equine project. There are sweat lodges for boys and for girls who wish to practice their traditional cultures.

The nearby Flandreau Santee Sioux Indian Reservation occupies 5,000 acres of land, some of it along the Big Sioux River. The town of Flandreau, situated in the bend of the river and surrounded by fertile farms, has about 2,300 residents. Large businesses and manufacturers are few and far between. To say that the environment of the Flandreau Indian School is different from that of the urban high schools that adopted the TDHS model is an understatement.

But the Flandreau Indian School discovered, just 25 miles to its north, a neighbor that turned out to be an unexpected ally in exposing Success Academy freshmen to college and to the careers open to college graduates.

K–16 Partnership With South Dakota State University

A Success Academy leadership team from the Flandreau Indian School went to The Johns Hopkins University in Baltimore during summer 2000 for training. Team members were given the responsibility of bringing freshman Success Academy to fruition at FIS. The team, led by Success Academy Principal (and SDSU graduate) Sandra Koester, then approached South Dakota State University for help with the freshman seminar class.

SDSU and the Flandreau Indian School had been backyard neighbors in eastern South Dakota for more than a century, but the relationship between the two institutions had remained relatively distant.

The question that compels many universities to engage with troubled high schools is this: "If we didn't help, who would?" (Morse 2001: 48). That question drives the education reforms that have come to be known as "K–16 partnerships," relationships in which colleges work to improve K–12 schools. K–16 partnerships involve education leaders at all levels, from colleges on down, working together "to turn around troubled public schools and substantially increase high-school and college graduation rates" (Schmidt 2006: B6).

In the years just before FIS-SDSU Success Academy began, about 150 freshmen would enroll at the Flandreau Indian School for the first semester. By the start of the second semester, only about 75 of these freshmen would remain. And by the time four years had elapsed, only a handful of these same students would still be at the school and prepared to graduate. In short, the dropout rate at FIS was alarming.

At that same time, South Dakota State University's record of educating American Indians was not much better. Despite being only 25 miles apart on Interstate 29, on average only one student per year graduated from FIS and then attended SDSU. American Indians accounted for about one percent of the student body at SDSU, this in a state with an American Indian population of about 10 percent. The mission of South Dakota State University, as a land-grant institution established under the Morrill Act of 1862, is "to provide access to higher education for all people" (SDSU University Relations 2012: A2). Clearly, at the start of the new millennium, the university had a long way to go toward fulfilling its mission. Both FIS and SDSU had much to gain by partnering to help more American Indian students prepare for and succeed in college.

A *Time* article in 2001, the year after the FIS-SDSU Success Academy was born, called K–16 partnerships "the next big thing in education reform" (Morse 2001: 48). Five years later, a vice chancellor in the Maryland State university system told *The Chronicle of Higher Education* that "K–16…is no longer thought of as anything innovative anymore. It is more the way we do business" (Schmidt 2006: B6).

The need for K–16 partnerships is well documented at the national level. A 2003 Stanford University study, "Betraying the College Dream: How Disconnected K–12 and Postsecondary Education Systems Undermine Student Aspirations" (Venezia, Kirst, and Antonio 2003), is one example. The U.S. Department of Education's report of a serious high school–college "disconnect" (Hoover 2006: A1) is another. At the local level in 2000, the stage was set for a significant K–16 connection to be established between the Flandreau Indian School and South Dakota State University.

FIS-SDSU Collaboration

Memorandum of Understanding

The request for help in implementing the Talent Development High School model, particularly its freshman-year Success Academy component, came through me (MaryJo Benton Lee), a clinical sociologist. I was then the diversity coordinator for South Dakota State University's College of Engineering, a position I held for 10 years. At that time, Engineering was the first of SDSU's colleges to employ someone whose sole job was to focus on issues of access and success for underrepresented students. Obviously, the College of Engineering and its deans were strongly committed to diversity.

The Engineering College had routinely engaged FIS students in a number of its outreach activities, such as Engineering Exploration Days, over the course of several years. FIS hoped that the Engineering diversity coordinator and her dean could successfully carry forward the request for help with Success Academy to both the university administration and to SDSU's other colleges.

Initially, the request was for help in providing a one-semester experience, focusing on college and careers, for all of the freshmen at the Flandreau Indian School. Meeting the TDHS model's standards would require all 100 FIS freshmen to spend six days during spring semester 2001 on the SDSU campus. Activities for these students would need to cover a broad range of academic disciplines. At the most basic level, as explained by FIS administrators, their intent was to expose students to college and to the careers open to college graduates. At a deeper level, these experiences were intended to inspire excellence in academics and stem the tide of dropouts at their school. Before the start of Success Academy, few FIS freshmen had visited a postsecondary institution or considered themselves "college material." The opportunity presented to the SDSU College of Engineering—a chance to host 100 American Indian students for six full-day visits to campus—was perceived, by those who first heard the idea, to be both exciting and overwhelming.

Shared Values. FIS's request to the SDSU College of Engineering did not fall on deaf ears. The late 1990s and the early 2000s were times of great change for the College of Engineering. Between 1999 and 2001, the college had three deans. All were passionate about diversity in engineering, and all were involved in the discussions leading up to the founding of the FIS-SDSU Success Academy.

Duane Sander, who served as SDSU's dean of engineering from 1990 until 1999, was also the cofounder of Daktronics, a worldwide leader in electronic display systems. For many years he has endowed SDSU scholarships for Native American engineering students, on behalf of Daktronics and also on behalf of his family. When approached by FIS about a possible partnership, Dean Sander's question (and that of Dean Virgil Ellerbruch who followed him) was: "If we decide to do this, who at SDSU would help us?"

To answer this question we decided initially to approach only SDSU colleagues who had proven track records of working with American Indian high school students. The College of Agriculture and Biological Sciences and the College of Family and Consumer Sciences for many years had been engaged in a highly successful K–16 partnership project called 2+2+2. It was a collaborative effort between SDSU and the state's tribal colleges, designed to enhance educational opportunities for American Indians (Kayongo-Male, Nichols, and Nichols 2003). The College of Arts and Sciences had an active Native American Journalism Program. The value of introducing American Indian students to careers in areas in which American Indians are seriously underrepresented—agriculture, biology, family sciences, consumer sciences, and journalism, to name but a few—was well-recognized in some quarters of SDSU. With initial firm commitments from the Colleges of Agriculture and Biological Sciences, Family and Consumer Sciences, and Arts and Sciences (and with promises of help from other colleges soon to follow), SDSU's College of Engineering was ready to take the idea of a partnership with FIS to the next level.

Shared Visions. As mentioned earlier, systemic change in education requires shared values and shared visions (Kunkel and Skaggs 2001: 16). The vision that FIS Superintendent Belkham and Success Academy Principal Koester had for their school in 2000 was revolutionary. With the start of Success Academy (and for the first time ever) *all* Flandreau Indian School students were encouraged to pursue postsecondary education. Be that education at a university, tribal college, vocational school, or other institution, FIS promised all of its students they would be academically and socially prepared for higher education by the time they graduated. This was a sea change for a federal Indian boarding school that for decades had emphasized vocational training.

FIS's approach to SDSU came at an opportune time. Garnering administrative support is fundamental when establishing programs that benefit American Indian students. These programs, to take root and thrive, must be recognized campus-wide, from the top down, as legitimate equity endeavors. It takes visionary leaders who value diversity to make this happen.

In 1998 Peggy Gordon Elliott had become South Dakota State University's 18th president (and its first female president). Shortly thereafter she appointed Marcus Dahn as SDSU's director of diversity enhancement and equal opportunity. (After leaving SDSU, Dahn ran for president of Liberia.) Both of these key administrators demonstrated tremendous energy and enthusiasm for access, inclusion, and equity as these issues relate to American Indians.

In October 2000 Dahn drafted a Memorandum of Understanding (MOU), laying the official groundwork for collaboration between SDSU and FIS. The Memorandum of Understanding (South Dakota State University-Flandreau Indian School 2000) read in part:

> South Dakota State University is committed to providing, through its various programs and services, educational opportunities for the students at the Flandreau Indian School. By providing them experiences with campus life at SDSU while they are in high school, South Dakota State University hopes to encourage Flandreau Indian School students to enter higher education. SDSU also commits itself to seeking educational resources, including tutorial and mentoring services for the students. The university will also provide assistance in acquiring scholarship and grant monies for them. In anticipation of the arrival of these students, a new Native American Cultural Center at SDSU has been furnished and equipped by the Office for Diversity Enhancement, and the recently formed SDSU Native American Advisory Council is seeking resources to provide more professional educational

services for Native American students....Both institutions must be committed to the principle of culture based education. Cooperation from the Flandreau Indian School in building and nurturing this partnership will be crucial to narrowing the educational achievement gap that has long existed between major society students and Native American students. (1–2)

In other sections of the MOU, SDSU promised to offer resources to enrich FIS course offerings and to serve as an educational avenue for FIS students going on to higher education. FIS agreed to educate and counsel its students in ways that would prepare them to function in diverse workplaces and communities. The intent of the MOU was to create the scaffolding for a "long-term partnership" between the institutions, one in which the partners would explore "further areas of cooperation and collaboration" (South Dakota State University-Flandreau Indian School 2000). By signing the Memorandum of Understanding (FIS Superintendent Belkham in November 2000 and SDSU President Elliott in December 2000), the leaders agreed in principle to "begin building and nurturing this collaboration between the two institutions" (South Dakota State University-Flandreau Indian School 2000).

Precedents for Partnership

"To promote satisfactory transition from high school to college, state governments and postsecondary institutions need to promote K–16 partnerships with tribal communities to elevate the overall level of precollege academic preparation, postsecondary aspirations, and postsecondary orientation of American Indian students," wrote Skokomish scholar D. Michael Pavel (1999: 248) in 1999, a year before the signing of the FIS-SDSU Memorandum of Understanding. That same year, Lumbee scholar Dean Chavers (1999), then director of the Native American Scholarship Fund, published the third edition of *Exemplary Programs in Indian Education*. *EPIE* established 11 criteria that make a program exemplary. These are: acknowledgment of the problem; setting priorities for problems; vision; planning; commitment; restructuring and retaining; goal setting; experimentation, testing, and evaluation; outreach; expertise; and administrative support. Both Pavel's words and Chavers's examples guided the establishment of the FIS-SDSU Success Academy partnership.

It would be impossible to review all of the K–16 partnerships that focus on college preparation for Native students. We have already mentioned one of them, the 2+2+2 initiative involving South Dakota State University, the state's tribal colleges, and several reservation high schools. What follows is a sampling—one early, one local, and one tribally controlled. (Excluded from the sampling are programs that are discipline specific, for example, college preparatory efforts focused on particular fields such as medicine or journalism.)

School, College and University Partnership Program at Northern Arizona University. The SCUP program, begun in 1988 and funded by a $696,000 U.S. Department of Education grant, led the way for many other K–16 partnerships between Native and non-Native institutions. SCUP involved Northern Arizona University (NAU) together with seven secondary schools educating children from the Navajo Nation and the Hopi Tribe. The three-year project was multifaceted, but a key SCUP initiative was the Nizhoni Academy. The five-week summer program, still running on the NAU campus today, introduces high school students to the rigors of university life while improving academic skills necessary for college success (Gilbert 1992). Nizhoni participants show significant improvement in mathematics and English when tested before and after the Academy. In addition, upon completion of the program, students have "a better knowledge of and a very positive feeling" about careers they are interested in pursuing (Gilbert 2000: 51–52).

Gaining Early Awareness and Readiness for Undergraduate Programs (GEAR UP) at the South Dakota School of Mines & Technology (SDSM&T). In 1992 Stacy Phelps, a graduate of Little Wound High School on the Pine Ridge Reservation and of SDSM&T in Rapid City, started a college preparatory program for American Indian youth in South Dakota. The program has since evolved into SD GEAR UP. GEAR UP is a nationwide U.S. Department of Education effort, supported in South Dakota by a $3.4 million annual grant (South Dakota Office of Indian Education 2012). SD GEAR UP operates in collaboration with the Oceti Sakowin (Seven Council Fires) Education Consortium, 24 middle schools and 14 high schools. With the exception of one partner school, the others have student bodies that are more than 95 percent American Indian. A key component of SD GEAR UP is its "cohort based, summer residential pre-college enrichment program" (South Dakota GEAR UP n.d.). Every alumnus of the summer program has graduated from high school, 87 percent have gone on to postsecondary education, and 65 percent have graduated from college or are still enrolled (South Dakota GEAR UP n.d.).

Circle of Learning Project at Fond du Lac Tribal and Community College. The nation's 37 tribal colleges and universities have become leaders in bridging the gap between themselves and their local schools. The Circle of Learning project, developed in 1995 with funding from the U.S. Department of Education, is a good example. The project's goal is "to form collaborative relationships to bridge the gaps that exist between local agencies, schools, postsecondary institutions and the reservation business community" (Ness 1998: 16). A highlight of the project is a summer experience called Future Bound. This two-week program teaches preparatory skills for life after high school. Students develop an understanding of "their individual learning styles, personal career interests, self-advocacy, problem-solving, study strategies, cultural identity, and necessary work-related behavior" (Ness 1998: 17). Students attending Future Bound classes at Fond du Lac are treated like (and expected to perform like) college students. Each student receives a stipend for successful completion of the course. Also covered are lunches, child care, and transportation. Those who complete the course are awarded one college credit in study skills. In the first two years of the program, 47 students finished the training. Most of the instructors were American Indian.

The most well-known K–16 partnerships, like those discussed so far, are financed by federal grants and operate at public institutions. The writers of *Powerful Partnerships: Independent Colleges Share High-Impact Strategies for Low-Income Students' Success* point out that "some important success stories…take place at small and mid-sized independent institutions" (Ekman, Garth, and Noonan 2004: 2).

Exemplary Multicultural Practices in Rural Education (EMPIRE) at Heritage University is one of these success stories. Heritage University is a small, nonprofit, nondenominational college on the Yakama Nation reservation in central Washington State. Heritage University leads the EMPIRE consortium, which consists of 16 schools, primary schools through high schools. EMPIRE helps these schools maintain healthy learning environments so that students from all backgrounds can succeed. Because of EMPIRE, "students in these schools become aware of Heritage and the possibility of attending college," writes the university's President Kathleen A. Ross (2004: 88).

The College Board (Breneman 2006) weighs in with a definitive last word on K–16 partnerships and systemic change:

> Currently, most collaborations between schools and colleges can be described as voluntary, localized efforts that are dependent upon ad hoc leadership commitments. States that are seeking to improve college readiness and success must move their educational systems beyond localized collaborations by taking action in four key areas of statewide policy: alignment of course work and assessments, state finance, statewide data systems, and accountability. If states are not using their policy levers in at least these four areas to align K–12 and postsecondary education, they cannot expect significant improvements in college readiness and success. (150)

In this section we have been discussing micro-level interventions, that is, K–16 partnerships between schools and universities designed to increase college access for Native Americans. Obviously these interventions occur in larger, macro-structural contexts. Educational policymaking can either help or hinder local initiatives. In Chapter 6 we will revisit larger structural issues and the impact they have had on the Flandreau Indian School-South Dakota State University Success Academy.

Ethnicity Matters

Looking at existing K–16 partnerships, which focused on college preparation for American Indians, was useful. None of these, however, was quite the right model for the collaboration we were establishing between the Flandreau Indian School and South Dakota State University. Developing our vision for an FIS-SDSU Success Academy happened over time with inspiration from many sources.

Enrique (Henry) T. Trueba

In large part, our work was shaped by Enrique (Henry) T. Trueba, who is recognized as "a Latino critical ethnographer for the ages" (Foley 2005). Trueba was the keynote speaker at a conference titled "Ethnicity Matters: Rethinking How Black, Hispanic and Indian Students Prepare for and Succeed in College" held at South Dakota State University in 2002.

Trueba wrote more than 20 books and 85 articles focused on ethnic minorities and education. In the words of his colleagues, "he gave life to what it means for minority students to strive and succeed in the dominant culture" (University of Texas at Austin 2005). His works centered on issues of race, ethnicity and adaptation as these affected Hmong children in California (Trueba, Jacobs, and Kirton 1990), Miao people (the ancestors of the Hmong) in China (Trueba and Zou 1994), and Latino/a immigrants and transnationals in Texas (Trueba 2004).

For Trueba, the educational underachievement of ethnic minorities results from a discontinuity between the culture of the home and the culture of the school (Trueba 1988). Minority children perform poorly in school because schooling promotes middle-class, majority-culture values. Put another way, academic failure is due to culturally incongruent exchanges between minority students and the schools they attend.

Trueba sees a strong ethnic identity as empowering minority students to succeed. Trueba believes there is a positive correlation between ethnic identity and academic performance. In other words, the stronger the ethnic identity, the stronger the academic performance (Lee 2006: 11–12). In short, just as the conference title suggests, "ethnicity matters"—greatly.

Programs in Which Ethnicity Matters

The Ethnicity Matters conference was organized by six SDSU faculty members and student affairs professionals—black, white, and Indian—and sponsored by the university's Office for Diversity Enhancement. As conference organizers, we sought out four model programs from across the United States, programs noted for being highly effective in preparing underrepresented students for college and in supporting these students through baccalaureate degree completion. All four programs were deliberately selected for inclusion because they were built on the understanding that ethnic identity plays an empowering role in educational achievement. The four programs selected departed significantly from most minority college recruitment and retention programs, programs that rest on the assumption that integration into mainstream culture is the route to success for students of color.

In short, the model programs were chosen because their organizers developed ways in which students' identities were "affirmed, honored, and incorporated into the organization's culture" (Tierney 2000: 219). To repeat, students served by these programs were *not* expected to leave their own cultures behind and "fit in" to alien university cultures (Tierney 2000: 219).

The model programs featured at the conference exemplify systemic change undertaken from a critical theory perspective. In the words of critical theorist Tierney (2000: 219–220), "The challenge...is not to develop ways for people to integrate into the system, but instead to change that system by way of programs, activities, events, and curricula that affirm and honor individual identities."

Short descriptions of the model programs in which "ethnicity matters" follow. All represent efforts by universities to rethink what it means to effectively serve students of color.

Neighborhood Academic Initiative (NAI). NAI involves middle school students, primarily African American and Hispanic, from south-central Los Angeles. NAI scholars attend accelerated English and math classes at the University of Southern California (USC), receiving academic credit from their respective home schools. NAI scholars also attend Saturday Academy, a weekly four-hour workshop covering communication, math, science, information technology, and college entrance exam preparation skills. NAI scholars who meet admission requirements receive four-and-one-half-year tuition scholarships to USC (Colyar 2006: 39–56).

First Generation Student Success Program (FGSSP). FGSSP at the University of La Verne in Southern California is a comprehensive program for first-generation college students and their families. The program fosters academic achievement among Latino/a students, who constitute about 35 percent of the university's enrollment. FGSSP encourages students to complete their degrees through the use of mentors, scholarships, and workshops. "Family engagement services," another important component of the program, ensures that family members are key partners in working toward students' success (Vergara and Hightower 2006: 81–98).

Critical Moments. Critical Moments is a retention, awareness, and change project for students of color, for other underrepresented students, and for the institutions they attend. Critical Moments has been implemented at the University of Nebraska–Lincoln and at several colleges throughout Washington State. Critical Moments prepares students, faculty, and administrators to respond proactively to campus events that involve race, gender, class, and other differences. A multicultural team of case writers interviews underrepresented students. Each interview focuses on an experience that caused the student to think about dropping out of college, that is, a "critical moment." These experiences then become the basis of small-group class discussions involving faculty, students of color, and other students. Together they develop critical-thinking skills, problem-solving strategies, and communication tools that foster student success (Gillespie, Malnarich, and Woods 2006: 99–113).

The three programs just described continue to operate at their respective schools a decade after the Ethnicity Matters conference ended.

2+2+2. The 2+2+2 project, mentioned earlier, was a collaborative effort among reservation high schools, tribal colleges, and South Dakota State University to help more American Indians complete baccalaureate degrees in agricultural, biological, family, and consumer sciences. Students who completed 2+2+2 were prepared to work toward solving some of the most pressing challenges facing tribal people—economic development, land and resource management, and family and community well-being (Nichols and Nichols 2006: 57–80).

The 2+2+2 project began in 1996 with a $175,000 Fund for Improvement of Post-Secondary Education (FIPSE) grant from the U.S. Department of Education. Important components of the 2+2+2 project were articulation agreements, faculty development, curriculum revision, student support, distance education, and experiential learning. Much of the 2+2+2 work done in these key areas has lived on well beyond when the FIPSE support ended.

More than any other single factor, the presence of a vibrant and successful 2+2+2 effort on the South Dakota State University campus paved the way for the

Flandreau Indian School-SDSU Success Academy collaboration. There were three main reasons for this.

First, faculty development was taken seriously by the 2+2+2 organizers. They threw a large net across the entire university and brought in colleagues from many disciplines and colleges to work with them in carrying out the 2+2+2 mission. In the process, I and many others learned from them firsthand about working with American Indian communities in respectful ways that honor and affirm identity.

Second, 2+2+2 demonstrated the effectiveness of experiential learning in increasing the college and career awareness of American Indian high school students. The programming delivered during the early years of Success Academy mirrored that developed by 2+2+2 leaders for their annual three-day summer institutes and 10-day research apprenticeships. In many cases, the same hands-on workshops taught by the same university faculty were delivered to Success Academy students, as they had been years earlier to 2+2+2 scholars.

Third, 2+2+2's principal investigators Laurie Stenberg Nichols, formerly dean of the College of Family and Consumer Sciences, and Tim Nichols, formerly assistant dean of the College of Agriculture and Biological Sciences, were wholeheartedly behind the FIS-SDSU Success Academy collaboration from the start. Laurie Nichols later became SDSU's provost and vice president of academic affairs, while Tim Nichols became the dean of the Honors College. As mentioned earlier, garnering administrative support is fundamental when establishing programs that benefit American Indian students. Such programs, to take root and thrive, must be recognized campus-wide, from the top down, as legitimate equity endeavors.

A Model for Understanding How Students of Color Succeed

In 2006, four years after the Ethnicity Matters conference, its organizers published a book by the same title (Lee 2006). The book's purpose was to allow others to learn from the successes and challenges of the programs featured at the conference. Each of the four programs was described in a chapter, including myriad details on creation, planning, implementation, and evaluation. Needed was some generalization, useful to others tackling issues of minority underrepresentation in higher education. A theoretical model was developed. (For a complete presentation of the model, "Understanding How Students of Color Succeed," see Lee 2006: 119–126.)

Like all models, this one is tentative and limited. The model attempts to explain how students of color construct selves that allow them to succeed in school. The model also attempts to explain how programs that help develop a strong ethnic identity in their participants can bolster student success. In short, the model explains the essential mechanisms that make the programs described in *Ethnicity Matters* innovative, effective, and worth emulating (Lee 2006: 117–118).

The *Ethnicity Matters* model did, in fact, inform practice, namely the development of the FIS-SDSU Success Academy program. Key components of the model are discussed briefly below.

Social Construction of Self. The successful student builds a personal identity by comparing his or her own definition of self with that of significant others (Heiss 1981). Significant others include people with whom the student interacts in the family, neighborhood, ethnic group, and school. The successful student of color must be able to overcome "stereotype threat," that is, others' judgments that minority group membership means lowered academic achievement (Steele 1997). Furthermore, it must be remembered that this identity construction process occurs within a larger structural context that often limits the occupational, educational, and economic attainment of minorities (Ogbu 1978, 1985, 1992). Issues of identity construction, as they are addressed collaboratively in the freshman and sophomore years of Success Academy, will be covered in Chapters 2 and 3, respectively.

Community Cultural Wealth. Tara J. Yosso (2005: 77) defines "community cultural wealth" as the accumulated assets and resources derived from the histories and lives of African American, Hispanic American, and American Indian communities. Students of color inherit their "community cultural wealth" from their families, neighborhoods, ethnic groups, and, in some cases, from their local schools. Put another way, "community cultural wealth" is "an array of knowledge, skills, abilities and contacts possessed and utilized by Communities of Color to survive and resist macro and micro-forms of oppression" (Yosso 2005: 77). Chapter 5 will explain how the concept of "community cultural wealth" provides the scaffolding for the senior-year Success Academy program.

Scholar Self. Carolyn R. Hodges and Olga M. Welch (2003: 2) explain that for a student of color to succeed academically, a "scholar self" must evolve over time, as a result of a series of negotiations and reconstructions of personal identity. Developing a "scholar self" means cultivating the ability to see academic achievement as possible, even in a larger structural context strewn with racial and ethnic barriers. Daphna Oyserman, Kathy Harrison, and Deborah Bybee (2001: 379) call this "perceived efficacy" or the ability to believe one has the power to influence one's environment and control one's destiny. A sense of efficacy can bolster adolescent resilience and academic achievement, leading to persistence in school (Oyserman, Harrison, and Bybee 2001: 379). Connectedness to one's ethnic group, ability to see oneself succeeding as an ethnic group member, and awareness of structural limitations imposed by ethnic group membership—all of these are characteristics of "perceived efficacy" (Oyserman, Gant, and Ager 1995; Oyserman, Harrison, and Bybee 2001). Success Academy has been designed to nurture "perceived efficacy" within its participants. How this is done will be explored further in all the remaining chapters of this book.

The Founding of FIS-SDSU Success Academy

By the late 1990s, attacks on affirmative action, which started in California and Texas, were rapidly spreading to other states (Howarth 1999: 12). While overall college enrollment rates have improved, the disparity between the college enrollment rate for American Indians (23 percent) and whites (46 percent) is growing (Kim 2011: 2). This lends strong impetus to innovative efforts aimed at increasing access to higher education for Native Americans.

What makes the Flandreau Indian School-South Dakota State University Success Academy an innovative effort? What sets it apart from many other K–16 college preparatory programs for Native American students? What is the scaffolding that has supported Success Academy through a dozen years? There are three main factors.

- Success Academy is an *early* intervention.
- Success Academy is an *intensive* experience, for individuals at the Flandreau Indian School and at South Dakota State University.
- In Success Academy, ethnicity matters. It not only matters, it has been at the heart of the matter from the start. Success Academy *honors students' identities* in every aspect of its programming.

These three characteristics will be discussed in some detail below.

Early Intervention

"It is well established that the earlier a student develops college aspirations, the more likely it is that the student will attend college," writes Lumbee scholar Bryan McKinley Jones Brayboy and his co-authors (Brayboy et al. 2012: 49). Consequently, early intervention programs that focus on enhancing college awareness at the start of high school have the best chances of success.

Minority students generally begin to underachieve at an age when they start to realize the limitations of their environment and social position. Significant numbers of minority students begin lowering their educational aspirations during early adolescence. This is when students become more aware of the world around them and of their chances for success in it (Lee 2001: 220–221).

Eileen Maynard and Gayla Twiss (1970: 94–99), in interviews with Indian high school students, found them very concerned about their education. All wanted to complete high school, and most desired to continue on to postsecondary education. That said, the students interviewed feared failure and dropping-out, fears that for many were justified. "Most destructive to (academic) motivation are the feelings of inferiority and powerlessness of Indian youth," Maynard and Twiss (1970: 95) write. This results in "underachievement and a lowering of aspirations" (Maynard and Twiss 1970: 95).

To be successful, American Indian students must be able to overcome "stereotype threat," that is, others' judgments that minority group membership means lowered academic achievement (Steele 1997). Put another way, successful Indian students are those who develop personal identities that allow them to persist in a world that often limits the occupational, educational, and economic attainment of minorities (Ogbu 1978, 1985, 1992).

Success Academy deliberately assists with this "identity work" (Snow and Anderson 1987: 1348). Many young American Indian students do not have a clear picture of career opportunities available to college graduates (Nichols and Nichols 2006: 61). Through hands-on learning opportunities, in college classrooms and labs, Success Academy allows students to "try on" different professional American Indian identities, such as "I can be a Native American dietician" or "I can be a Native American journalist" (Lal 1995: 421–441).

Success Academy first engages FIS students in the college preparatory process when they are freshmen in high school, the time when most students are making critical decisions about their life chances and deciding whether postsecondary education is possible. FIS-SDSU Success Academy involves *all* of the freshmen who attend the Flandreau Indian School. No one is allowed to opt out. No one is allowed to decide that he or she is not "college material." The expectation is "success for all." From day one the message is clear: Every FIS freshmen is expected to complete high school and go on to postsecondary education of some kind—technical college, community college, tribal college, four-year college, or university (Lee 2007: 104).

Throughout the subsequent sophomore, junior, and senior years of programming, Success Academy provides numerous structures to ensure that students are able to do just that. While Success Academy acknowledges that barriers exist, it simultaneously teaches students strategies to overcome them (Tierney 2000: 228).

In short, Success Academy is an early intervention that consciously promotes a sense of "efficacy" (Lee 2001: 221). "Efficacy," as it is used here, means the power to influence one's environment and to control one's destiny. In their work with students of color, Oyserman, Harrison, and Bybee (2001: 384) found that efficacy is a motivational force that has a major impact on academic achievement. Individuals who believe they can "make it" are far more likely to actually "make it" than those who do not.

Week after week, in their Success Academy workshops at SDSU, FIS freshmen "try on" the identity of "college student" as well as the identities of "nurse," "journalist," "engineer," "pharmacist," "teacher," and myriad other professionals. By involving Native people in all aspects of the Success Academy project, student participants see role models of other Indians who are successful academically and professionally.

To repeat, all of this starts during the freshman year, at a critical time when students are deciding if attending college is truly an attainable goal. Students convinced of this have a far greater likelihood of staying in school and achieving academically.

Intensive Experience

All 100 freshmen come to South Dakota State University for six full-day visits during their first year at the Flandreau Indian School. The freshmen rotate through hands-on workshops in all six of SDSU's academic colleges: Engineering, Pharmacy, Nursing, Arts and Sciences, Education and Human Sciences, and Agriculture and Biological Sciences.

All 100 FIS sophomores come to SDSU for four full-day visits during their second year of high school. These visits focus on areas identified by the first cohort of Success Academy students as being of particular interest to them and not covered in the freshman year program. The sophomores participate in a Focus on the Arts Day, a Focus on the Military Day, a Focus on American Indian Studies Day, and a Focus on Health and Nutrition Day.

Freshmen and sophomores are accompanied on their Success Academy visits to SDSU by teachers and aides from the Flandreau Indian School. All FIS students, upon entering their junior year of high school, have spent 10 full days on a college campus.

Success Academy juniors participate in a four-day "Preparing for College, Native-Style!" program each spring. The junior-year program gives students access to well-placed adults, such as admissions staff and faculty members, who can provide institutional resources and opportunities. The juniors gain access to the "social capital" (Bourdieu 1977, 1986) they need to progress through the educational system and exercise control over their futures (Mehan et al. 1996: 214). Capital acquisition and "border crossing" (Giroux 1988) activities, as they relate to the junior year of Success Academy, will be discussed in detail in Chapter 4.

FIS seniors come to the SDSU campus once a week to take Success Academy English and Math classes. In addition, the senior year "Countdown to College" program ensures that students complete all the steps necessary to enroll in postsecondary education before graduating from high school.

The groundwork for FIS students enrolling in college is laid by the frequency of SDSU visits and the length of the visits over all four years of high school. As mentioned earlier, each visit to SDSU is a chance for FIS students to picture themselves successfully attending classes and events as college students.

It is important to note that the frequency of campus visits, the length of the visits, and the number of students served have required a large investment of time and effort by faculty and staff at South Dakota State University over many years. (See Appendix.) Beginning in the fall of 2000, about 300 faculty and staff have presented Success Academy workshops, served on planning committees, and otherwise assisted with programming. Most of these individuals have involved SDSU students as co-presenters and co-planners.

"Success Academy is the premier diversity program at SDSU because it directly engages faculty members and students with American Indian people," says Allen Branum, who was the university's director for diversity enhancement during most of the Success Academy years. "No amount of classroom diversity training can compare with personally getting to know American Indian individuals and learning from them their hopes, dreams, issues and rich cultural heritage" (Lee 2007: 105).

Tierney (1993a: 142), writing from a critical theory perspective, says that "prolonged involvement" is the only way to transcend borders and work together to empower students. Certainly in the Flandreau Indian School-South Dakota State University collaboration, there were ample borders to transcend—between Natives and non-Natives, between K–12 and university educators, between students and teachers—to name just a few. The intensive nature of our contact with one another—week after week, year after year—is an example of the "prolonged involvement" Tierney (1993a) describes:

> We come to understand one another not by broad, sweeping actions, but by living and learning on a daily basis. We are not tourists on a week-long excursion with a guidebook in our hands to show us the interesting sites and lives of a people. To the contrary, we cannot understand differences in a momentary fragmentary fashion, and we do not have a Michelin guide to tell us what to do. Instead, we engage people where we are most at risk with questioning our own identities, and we do so through prolonged involvement....By "prolonged involvement," I mean that learning about the Other never stops; we are always in a process of redefinition. (142)

Honoring Identities

FIS-SDSU Success Academy has two goals. The first is to help more Flandreau Indian School students prepare for and succeed in college. The second goal is to make South Dakota State University into the kind of place where that can happen.

Achieving these two goals is a dialectical process. Through its work of helping more American Indian students prepare for college, the university becomes an environment where these students are more likely to succeed. And, as the university is recognized as an environment that honors American Indian identities, then this compels more Native students to prepare for and enroll in college, with high expectations for success.

As mentioned earlier, SDSU moved through much of its first century with Native American student numbers holding steady at about one percent—this in a state with a Native American population of about 10 percent. Both Native American recruitment and retention were challenging. Many early retention efforts, though perhaps well intentioned, involved helping Indian students fit into an existing white educational system. Not nearly enough attention was paid by the university to developing ways to adapt to Native Americans, a group hugely underserved in higher education.

In fact, a study done in the 1990s, of Native American students attending SDSU (Spencer 1994), reports that

> The vast majority made reference to the racism and prejudicial behaviors they encountered in Brookings and specifically SDSU. Several pointed to the ignorance displayed about Native Americans, not only by some white students, but also by some faculty members. This ignorance led to their complaint that the negative stereotypes about them and their culture had hurt them and made them angry. Several of the students felt that racial discrimination was a problem at SDSU....It is evident from these students' statements that SDSU must continue its systematic efforts to create an environment that is welcoming to all people. (3–3)

South Dakota State University has invested a considerable amount of time, money, skill, and effort in its Success Academy partnership with the Flandreau Indian School. In the process SDSU as an institution is learning about structural barriers that prevent Native students from succeeding—and is making strides in eliminating these obstacles to American Indian success.

The FIS-SDSU Success Academy began as a grassroots effort. It started without federal grants or external funding. I, as the Success Academy coordinator, was the only person who received a salary.

To honor the commitments made to FIS in the Memorandum of Understanding, Success Academy required the enthusiastic participation of hundreds of SDSU faculty and staff members. Week by week, over 12 years, these individuals have worked one-on-one with American Indian students. Collectively they have built the capacity of SDSU as a whole to more effectively serve American Indians.

Honoring American Indian Identity Through Systemic Change

What occurred through the birth of Success Academy was a reorientation of the culture of schooling at two institutions. What occurred was systemic change. At the Flandreau Indian School this has meant the adoption of a comprehensive school reform model aimed at preparing all students for postsecondary education. At South Dakota State University this reorientation has involved developing ways in which American Indian identity is affirmed, honored, and incorporated into the institution's culture. The particular mechanisms by which Success Academy has brought about systemic change will be explored in the remaining chapters of this book (with particular emphasis in the concluding Chapter 6 on counterhegemony).

I begin by taking a look at one day in the life of Success Academy. I believe that it illustrates how the university, through Success Academy, is moving toward being more appreciative of and responsive to American Indian culture. I use the words of a Native American teacher/colleague from FIS to help me tell the story.

The day was February 18, 2005, five years after the start of Success Academy. As usual on a "Success Academy Friday," all the sophomores were dismissed from their last-block classes at the Flandreau Indian School. They were off to be college students for a day at South Dakota State University. One sophomore, who stayed behind for "home leave," was overheard saying to relatives, "Friday is the day I usually go to *my* university." This was the second visit of the school year to SDSU for the FIS sophomores.

Two busloads of students made their way north on Interstate 29 to SDSU, about a half-hour trip. Once on campus, they tumbled, laughing and talking, off the buses, in front of DePuy Military Hall. SDSU professors and students from the Aerospace Studies and Military Sciences departments were on hand to welcome the FIS students. Success Academy Focus on the Military Day was about to start.

American Indians have the highest per-capita service in the U.S. military of any ethnic group (LeMay 2012), so many of the FIS students attending had family members in the service or plans for military careers themselves. Interest in this particular Success Academy ran high.

The FIS students divided into three groups, each accompanied by a teacher. Then the hands-on workshops began—a team-building exercise run by Air Force ROTC cadets, a leadership reaction course organized by Army ROTC cadets, and a military information discussion group led by Air Force and Army faculty.

A Native American teacher, who accompanied the FIS sophomores, described the three afternoon classes:

> I had never attended Success Academy before, and that whole experience intrigued me. The first thing I noticed was that the people in those departments were VERY welcoming. They were very flexible about how the students were during their visit. They made sure they felt comfortable there more than following everything the way it should be. For example, some of the students were really shy and somewhat intimidated and sat way in the back. However, the instructors in that department didn't force the students to move, they just went with the flow. If anything, it was the FIS staff that did most of the moving and prodding the students to stay in a certain area. But the SDSU staff and students reached out to them where they were....Being Native American myself, I watched very carefully as the instructors made an effort to help the students feel comfortable....It showed the students that SDSU was coming to them in a good way. The most important observation that I noted was during the time that the instructors were talking about their particular field of Army, Air Force, etc., they took the time to ask questions about people that the students knew who were in the military....They just managed to slowly gain the students' trust by REALLY listening to them about where they came from and what they were proud of about their relatives and community.

At the end of the afternoon the students and faculty, from both FIS and SDSU, gathered on the drill floor. Others from across campus trickled in, one by one, to join the group for dinner—a dean, a department head, the university's diversity director, other faculty, staff, and students. The SDSU Native American Club hosts the Success Academy evening meals. One of the club members offered a blessing for the food, and then the eating began.

The same teacher who accompanied the students to the afternoon workshops recalled certain aspects of the dinner:

> One thing I noticed right away was the atmosphere that MaryJo provided with the students. She came across as positive and made the students feel at home. She offered more food to the students, and then she informed them that someone else would clean up for them. I know that in a small way this made the students feel a little uncomfortable, but they were not used to that kind of treatment. I sensed that by the end of the dinner, many were starting to feel quite at home.

Success Academy focus days usually end with on-campus events to give the high school students a sampling of extracurricular life outside the college classroom. This evening's activity, held in the Lincoln Music Hall, was titled "Three Voices: Speaking From the Past." It was a controversial event to follow this particular focus day because the performance focused on the Wounded Knee massacre of 1890, one of the most tragic encounters between the military and Native Americans in all of U.S. history.

The teacher who was with the sophomores that day later wrote:

> The evening presentation we attended was very interesting. There was a program where three women (one Dakota, one Euro-American and one African-American) had the dialog about the incidents that took place at Wounded Knee. It was kind of a one-act play with scenes depicting women during that timeframe. The presentation itself was amazing. The women who portrayed the characters afterwards really took the time to find out where the students were from and even what they knew about the incident. I noticed that the students seemed to enjoy the presentation. This was so different than what the students are used to hearing from teachers and leaders at home. The play showed these women learning and experiencing and showing emotion in their own cultural ways. I enjoyed this portion of the program the most....By the end of the evening, I was so proud of the students' behavior and how respectful they were. Their good-byes to MaryJo were heartwarming.

This was one day in the life of Success Academy. There have been 275 other days like it during our FIS-SDSU partnership. Perhaps it suggests some small steps toward change at SDSU—in the way university faculty work with Native students, in sharing a meal in a culturally appropriate manner, in a program confronting head-on our painful shared history.

It has been said that change happens when each small moment is lived differently. Still, we cannot minimize the immensity of the work that remains to be done. The racial divide between Indians and non-Indians runs deep. The challenges in Indian education are great.

As 2+2+2 co-founders Nichols and Nichols remind us, it is important to keep the long-term perspective in mind and not expect to see enrollment or retention rates for Native students jump overnight. Persistence is in keeping with Lakota philosophy "which considers not only what is good for today and tomorrow but also what will be good for seven generations into the future" (Nichols and Nichols 1998: 41).

In this spirit, in 2005, my Native American teacher/colleague wrote:

> I just want to say that I think that the programs that are offered through SDSU are a real benefit to our students. I can tell that things are starting to take shape with this relationship. I know that at times it may seem like things are not going well, but I think of how

many students enrolled at SDSU this year compared to last year....It takes Native Americans a long time before they realize that this is a program that is here to stay. Native Americans are used to government grants and programs that last only one or two years, and then it is time to move on to something else. They think this commitment will last only so long, and they will be forgotten about. The main thing I have noticed that works well with Native Americans is consistency. If they know that this is something they can count on, they will pay more attention to it. Many of the students (who enrolled at SDSU) this year got to know some of the students from last year, and it is sticking in their minds that if the former students can do it, maybe they can, too....But the main thing I notice, too, is that the current support system is slowly making progress.

I believe that collaboration with colleagues at the Flandreau Indian School has opened up new ways of seeing and knowing for me and for others at SDSU. We now help American Indian students prepare for and succeed in college in ways we never dreamed of before. And every Success Academy visit—from the first "Freshman Friday at State" to the last "Senior Countdown to College"—provides a new opportunity for learning, growing, and improving. The remainder of this book tells that story.

2

Honoring Ethnic Identity and Freshman "Fridays at State"

Success Academy began as a one-semester program for all 100 freshmen at the Flandreau Indian School, and this chapter explains the first-year activities. All freshmen come to the South Dakota State University campus for six Friday visits throughout the academic year. During the afternoons students rotate through hands-on workshops in all six of SDSU's academic colleges (Engineering, Pharmacy, Nursing, Arts and Sciences, Education and Human Sciences, and Agriculture and Biological Sciences). Success Academy workshops expose students not only to college but also to the careers open to college graduates.

As critical educators, our task is to develop ways in which Native students' identities are affirmed, honored, and incorporated not only into the Success Academy programming but also into the larger university culture. In other words, rather than trying to change the students into people who could presumably succeed in the university, we instead try to change the university into a place where these students can succeed. In this way we strive to open admission and ensure success for those previously excluded from higher education.

Theory, in this case critical theory, must be linked to action to bring about change. Therefore, Chapter 2 focuses on telling how ethnic identity is honored in each and every aspect of Freshman Fridays at State—primarily in workshops, but also in the meals and co-curricular activities that follow. Comments from participants—most of these gathered through written evaluations after campus events—serve as illustration throughout the chapter. Chapter 2 begins with a brief review of literature on ethnic identity and student success, as these relate to Native students moving from high school into college.

Ethnic Identity and Student Success

In High School

Native students are often "vocationally tracked" in high school (Pease-Windy Boy 1995: 406). This means they are encouraged to take vocational skills classes such as welding or cosmetology, while other academically tracked students take more advanced courses such as higher mathematics and foreign languages. As Janine Pease-Windy Boy (1995: 406), a member of the Crow Tribe of Indians of Montana and a past president of Little Big Horn College, explains, "The selection processes in our system of education are powerful and political sifters of human potential. For the American Indian, the educational sifting process has damaged the potentialities of those hundreds of American Indian people who attempted the educational gauntlet."

Universities routinely practice selective systems of admissions, which emphasize academic classes completed and grade point averages. Native students (like other students of color) often fall short of these standards because of tracking (Oakes 2005). Educators who practice "untracking" (Mehan et al. 1996: 10), that is, those who offer an enriched and challenging environment for all, send powerful messages to the students they serve. They allow students of color to construct "scholar self" (Hodges and Welch 2003: 2) identities, identities that make possible academic achievement and college admission.

So in addition to deliberate efforts at "untracking," what other strategies can educators use to nurture and support college-bound Native students? There is an overarching answer, woven throughout the literature of the past 20 years, and it is this: A strong ethnic identity empowers students of color to succeed in school. Many scholars, working from a critical theory perspective, have found this to be true. The previous chapter introduces one of them, critical ethnographer Enrique (Henry) T. Trueba, who significantly influenced the development of the FIS-SDSU Success Academy. Trueba believes there is a positive correlation between ethnic identity and academic performance. In other words, the stronger the ethnic identity, the better the academic performance.

Donna Deyhle (1995), in an ethnographic study of high schools serving Native Americans, finds that

> The more academically successful Navajo students are more likely to be those who are firmly rooted in their Navajo community....School failure is *less* likely for minority youth who are not alienated from their own cultural values and who do not perceive themselves as inferior to the dominant group. Failure rates are *more* likely for youth who feel disenfranchised from their culture and at the same time experience racial conflict. Rather than viewing the Navajo culture as a barrier, as does an assimilation model, "culturally intact" youth are, in fact, more successful students. (419–420)

In research by Mark Lysne and Gary D. Levy (1997), students who attend a predominantly Native American high school have a greater commitment to their ethnic identities and a stronger desire to explore these identities than do students attending a predominantly white high school. This suggests that ethnic identity and its exploration need to be front and center when designing a college preparatory program like Success Academy for students at a federal Indian boarding school.

How ethnic identity influences the college aspirations of Indian, Eskimo, and Aleut high school students is examined by Carole L. Seyfrit, Lawrence C. Hamilton, Cynthia M. Duncan, and Jody Grimes (1998). They find that ethnicity affects expectations indirectly through what they call "cultural tool kit" variables.

Ann Swidler (1986: 273) first developed the metaphor of culture as a tool kit, "a collection of symbols, stories, rituals, and world-views, which people may use in varying configurations to solve different kinds of problems." Seyfrit and her colleagues use this metaphor to explain the responses of the college-bound Native students they surveyed about higher education. "Their tool kit includes an image of themselves as college students," Seyfrit et al. (1998: 360) write. Native parents and grandparents, who encourage college aspirations or provide role models, supply a kind of cultural "permission." For Native youth, support from elders can bestow an important cultural legitimacy on the pursuit of college goals.

In College

Terry E. Huffman, together with his mentors Maurice L. Sill and Martin Brokenleg, has been looking at college achievement among Native students for more than 20 years (Huffman, Sill, and Brokenleg 1986; Huffman 1999). Huffman (2008) notes that

> The most dramatic and promising change that has taken place in American Indian education studies specifically has to do with assumptions surrounding the role that Native her-

itage and identity play in the academic experience....Research is establishing the relationship between the retention of cultural traditionalism, heritage, and personal identity, and academic success....What is ironic is that traditional Native people have long understood that educational success can only truly occur within the proper cultural context of Native traditions. Only now are education professionals catching up to their wisdom. (xxv–xxvi)

Official Encouragement, Institutional Discouragement: Minorities in Academe— the Native American Experience, by William G. Tierney (1992), is the only longterm ethnographic study to examine American Indian experiences beyond 12th grade and into higher education (Deyhle and Swisher 1997: 161). Tierney provides a critical analysis of how cultural issues at the micro level and structural factors at the macro level stymie the attempts of Native students trying to succeed in higher education. Tierney reports that Native college students are frequently told they have problems "adjusting" because of their culture. According to this viewpoint, Native culture is seen as problematic, and school success comes only when roots to one's identity are severed. Institutions too often try to change Indian students into different people, people who presumably could succeed in higher education as it currently operates. Tierney instead recommends that change occur within the institutions themselves. Tierney (1992: 152) concludes his book with a number of "ways for individuals to think about American Indian participation in academe in order to develop solutions on their own campuses." Tierney (1992: 152) reminds readers that change occurs not only in "dramatic reorientations" but also in "more minute developments that an individual may utilize."

FIS-SDSU Success Academy has involved myriad minute developments affecting hundreds of individuals at two schools over the course of a decade. Tierney's recommendations—on how institutions can change *their* cultures to encourage Native students—will guide the discussion of the first year of the Success Academy program that follows.

Shared Values, Shared Visions

Systemic change occurs at schools and universities only when those responsible for the change share common values and visions. Early in Success Academy's history, educators from the Flandreau Indian School and South Dakota State University, Indian and non-Indian, together developed a Vision Statement. It begins:

SDSU-FIS Success Academy *assumes* academic success for all students. If a student is attending the Flandreau Indian School as a freshman, that student *will* participate in the college preparatory program called Success Academy. Throughout the program Success Academy planners and presenters will emphasize the strengths of the students involved. Success Academy students will be called "scholars." FIS teachers and SDSU faculty will consistently let students know that academic success is *expected* of them.

Woven through the Vision Statement is the concept of expectation, which has deep sociological roots. One of the pioneers of American sociology, W. I. Thomas, wrote, "If men define situations as real, they are real in their consequences" (Thomas and Znaniecki 1927). Another sociological giant, Robert K. Merton, 40 years later built the concept of the "self-fulfilling prophecy" on Thomas's original observation. As Merton (1968: 477) explained, "Public definitions of a situation (prophecies or predictions) become an integral part of the situation and thus affect subsequent developments."

Robert Rosenthal and Lenore Jacobson (1968) applied the notion of the "self-fulfilling prophecy" to the sociology of education in what is now considered a classic study. If teachers were told to expect academic "blooming" to occur among certain elementary school students, then, in fact, academic "blooming" did occur among those students relative to others in the classroom, regardless of whether the "bloomers" were more or less gifted academically.

In short, the importance of communicating high expectations to students cannot be overemphasized. This begins at the very start of our Success Academy program.

Catching the Dream Day, January 2008

Catching the Dream Day is the inaugural event of each Success Academy year. On this particular day, in January 2008, the entire student body of the Flandreau Indian School trooped into the auditorium. Students laughed, talked, and jostled as they took their seats. Principal Stuart Zephier, an enrolled member of the Cheyenne River Sioux Tribe, picked up the microphone, called the assembly to order, and explained the day.

This Catching the Dream Day was special. It not only marked the start of the program year for a whole new group of Success Academy scholars, it also celebrated the completion of seven years of Success Academy collaboration between the Flandreau Indian School and South Dakota State University. Seven is a sacred number to the people of the Great Sioux Nation, also known as Oceti Sakowin or the Seven Council Fires.

Introducing the Success Academy program to freshmen and refreshing the memories of sophomores, juniors, and seniors who had participated in previous years were the purposes of Catching the Dream Day. FIS-SDSU Success Academy began during the 2000–2001 academic year as a one-semester college preparatory program for about 100 freshmen attending FIS. Each subsequent academic year saw the program expand to involve another cohort—about 100 sophomores in 2001–2002 and about 50 juniors in 2002–2003. A special Countdown to College initiative for seniors was added in 2003–2004. Over the years Catching the Dream Day had become something of a pep rally, designed to excite students and faculty from FIS and SDSU and to engage them in the activities planned for the subsequent months.

For this Catching the Dream Day, students were divided into small groups. Together with their teachers, the groups rotated through several mini-workshops held throughout the day in various buildings scattered across the FIS campus. One group worked with Craig Howe (Oglala Sioux) in Sequoyah Hall. Dr. Howe, then professor of graduate studies at Oglala Lakota College, talked with the students about the importance of "Education for Life." Another workshop, in what had once been the old tearoom, explained to students exactly what their Success Academy visits to SDSU during the coming months would involve.

From the start, Success Academy organizers wanted the students themselves to set standards for conduct and participation in this college preparatory program. For this to happen, two sessions were planned during Catching the Dream Day, one for males and another for females. Using smaller classrooms in the academic building, Dr. Elden Lawrence (Sisseton Wahpeton Oyate), president emeritus of Sisseton Wahpeton College, led a session called "Being a Man." Stephanie Charging Eagle (Cheyenne River Sioux Tribe), then director of school improvement for the Oceti Sakowin Education Consortium, led a session called "Being a Woman."

At lunchtime everyone—from FIS administrators to school custodians, from the oldest seniors to the newest freshmen, from the distinguished presenters to the SDSU participants—gathered in the school cafeteria. The noon meal of fried chicken with all the trimmings was supplied by those from SDSU who had traveled to FIS to be part of Catching the Dream Day.

The day ended where it began, in the school auditorium, with an honoring ceremony. Ron Goodeagle (Osage/Comanche/Sac-n-Fox), the FIS cultural education teacher, together with the school's drum group, performed an honor song for all the students. The Success Academy scholars sat quietly as they were recognized for their commitment to pursuing higher education, with all the risks and sacrifices that would involve.

Students Catching the Dream

What did students carry away with them from what was for many their first experience with Success Academy? Student evaluations at the conclusion of Catching the Dream Day provided some answers. Some students expressed appreciation for specific Native scholars and their sessions:

> It was pretty cool when the guy in the auditorium, Dr. Howe, was speaking.

> I thought Ms. Charging Eagle's session was very educational. I thought so because she talked about how we, as Native women, should carry ourselves and our general place in society.

> Dr. Lawrence was an outstanding speaker. I enjoyed his lesson a lot.

Other students commented on what they had learned about the FIS-SDSU partnership and the Success Academy program itself:

> I thought it was interesting to find out how much Flandreau Indian School and SDSU stay in touch to get a lot of students out to prepare them for their future accomplishments. Also to see how much SDSU stands behind each student to give them the education of a lifetime.

> I AM going on with my education! I have a BIG DREAM, and I know college will help me accomplish my dream. Education is everything....Catching the Dream Day showed me some career opportunities after high school. The FIS-South Dakota State University Success Academy can help me with the basics for college while still in high school.

Before the start of Success Academy, about 150 freshmen enrolled at FIS in the fall, and by the start of spring semester, only about 75 remained. Similarly, in a graduating class of about 50 students, those who had been at FIS for all four years of high school could often be counted on just one hand. A goal of Success Academy, and one we hoped to communicate through Catching the Dream Day, was convincing students to stay in high school through graduation, so college would be an option. In their evaluations of the day, students reflected:

> What I learned was I'm going to go to school and try my best to stay in school, too.

> This has changed my life, because we all need to stay in school in order to make it through life.

As educators planning a kick-off event for Success Academy, linking the short-term goal of completing high school to the long-term goal of attending college was important. At the end of Catching the Dream Day one student wrote:

> I learned that there are many opportunities here at FIS to help me graduate and get the education I want. Watching all the sessions made me think about what I want to do after school, and it made me think about college really hard.

Another student concluded:

> Catching the Dream Day helped me learn that Natives can make it in the world. After I
> listened to all the speakers, I am wanting to go to college and just can't wait till I go. I guess
> dreams do come true.

A Day in the Life of Freshman Success Academy

Catching the Dream Day has been described in some detail, because it was designed
to communicate up front, to all students, from the start, that they do *not* need to leave
their identities parked outside the university gates in order to attend college. The honoring of ethnic identity is woven throughout the entire tapestry of the freshman-year
Success Academy program—afternoon workshops, evening meals, and co-curricular events. How this is done will be covered in the remainder of the chapter.

Afternoon Workshops

Flandreau Indian School freshmen arrive on the SDSU campus mid-afternoon. For
much of Success Academy's history, South Dakota State University was divided into
six academic colleges (Engineering, Nursing, Pharmacy, Agriculture and Biological
Sciences, Education and Human Sciences, and Arts and Sciences). Similarly, for
much of Success Academy's history, the FIS freshman class was divided into six sections, each with a teacher or teachers assigned to it. Success Academy workshops
run 90 minutes each. Over the course of the spring semester, FIS freshmen come
to SDSU six times, always on Fridays. Week by week, the six FIS freshman classes
rotate through the six SDSU college workshops. FIS classes have remained small,
varying in size from year to year but generally having about 16 students each. FIS
teachers participate with their students in Success Academy activities.

All FIS and SDSU participants—students, teachers, and presenters—wear
printed nametags bearing the Success Academy logo. Wearing nametags and learning others' names has been important from the start. Becoming well-acquainted—
SDSU faculty with FIS students and FIS students with SDSU faculty—has two
purposes.

First and foremost, as Tierney (1992: 161) points out, while faculty have specific kinds of knowledge to impart, they are also learners—in this case, learners
about the past, present, and possible future of Indian people. As one SDSU dean,
who served as a workshop presenter, explains:

> My experience as a Success Academy workshop presenter last year really opened my eyes
> to the challenges facing our Native American youth. I also learned that Flandreau Indian

School has many bright young people who are capable of future careers in engineering, science and technology. I hope we will attract them to SDSU. I learned important cultural lessons about Native Americans, and I'm a better professor, administrator and human being for it. In that sense, Success Academy has been a tremendous success for both SDSU faculty and the students of the Flandreau Indian School.

Second, and also important, by getting to know SDSU faculty, FIS students gain access to the "social capital" (Bourdieu 1977, 1986) they need to progress through the educational system and into college. Over the years, several well-placed SDSU faculty members have become mentors to Success Academy scholars. These faculty members have made available university resources, such as summer camps and lab equipment, to the college-bound students they have gotten to know through Success Academy. At the end of her first year of Success Academy, one FIS student wrote this about SDSU faculty presenters:

> Over the year and the visits to SDSU, I thought the program was a good idea, for both benefit. Our visits were overwhelming and fun. The workshop I thought was interesting was Wokunze: A Life Pathway in Nursing. The best part that interested me in Nursing was Madonna Blue Horse Beard. She has a beautiful way with words, and all the assistants were very good at what they did.

When operating from a critical perspective, "distances between teacher and student will be collapsed" (Tierney 1992: 161). Relationships become cooperative instead of competitive.

Early in Success Academy's history, students were asked to create a logo and a motto for the program. The students' design incorporated the medicine wheel and eagle feathers. The words chosen were "Success Academy: Where All Students Are Honored Students."

Everyone who participates in the weekly Success Academy visits wears T-shirts bearing this symbol and these words. They are a visual reminder of the commitment made to work together for the good of Indian education.

Honoring student identity is central to each freshman Friday workshop. Following are six examples, one from each of SDSU's six academic colleges. These examples are chosen from the hundreds of workshops presented to Success Academy freshmen over 12 years.

Native Americans and Journalism: 21st-Century Storytellers. Tierney (1992: 163) encourages teachers "to think about how culture operates in their classrooms and to learn about the cultures of their Indian students." Native culture is celebrated from the moment the FIS freshmen arrive in Yeager Hall, home of the SDSU Journalism department (part of SDSU's College of Arts and Sciences). Success

Academy scholars gather in the Lakota/Dakota Conference Room. The circular room was added, during a building renovation in 2000, to remind SDSU Journalism students and staff how important Native Americans are to South Dakota. The room has a blue-sky ceiling, Native American art, and a star quilt. A round red table, the color of sacred pipestone, surrounds a four-foot-wide drum, made from a hollowed-out cottonwood trunk.

Students are welcomed by Professor Doris Giago, an enrolled member of the Oglala Sioux Tribe. She explains the significance of the room and the need for more Indian journalists. Then students divide into small groups for hands-on sessions in photojournalism and broadcast. These sessions are led by Journalism faculty, often assisted by Native Journalism students. "I met people from my rez, and that made me feel good," one Success Academy freshman remarks after a Journalism workshop. Some of the students fan out across campus to shoot pictures and then digitally process them in the photo lab. Meanwhile in the new media lab other students do interviews with each other, trying their hands at both news reporting and camera work. All are pleased to view the fruits of their labors, their photos and videos, at the end of the workshop.

Wokunze: Life Pathways in Nursing. Scenes similar to the one in Journalism play out across campus on Friday afternoons. Emphasis throughout Success Academy is on hands-on, interactive activities designed to engage high school students. In Wagner Hall, home to the College of Nursing, faculty and members of the Nursing Student Association work with Success Academy freshmen in the simulation lab. A highlight for FIS students is "SimMan," a computer-operated total body simulator that talks, breathes, and allows students to practice nursing skills in a safe but realistic environment.

FIS students delight in the hands-on approach. As one explains:

> I did have fun. I enjoyed the stuff they taught us about nursing. They taught us how to put stitches in, how to take them out, how to check our ears and how to check our heartbeat. We even bandaged our classmates with real bandages. I had so much fun. I would go to that workshop again if we could.

Every visit to SDSU is an opportunity for FIS students to picture themselves successfully attending classes as college students. Constantly reiterated throughout the program is this message to the high school students: "You can succeed in college, and there are structures in place at FIS and at SDSU to help you do so."

To repeat, Success Academy workshops expose students not only to college but also to careers open to college graduates. "Tribes and communities look at higher education in terms of their own requirements for trained persons to provide skills to solve immediate problems," writes Choctaw/Chippewa scholar Clara Sue Kidwell (1994: 253). Success Academy emphasizes career areas identified by tribal leaders as being of critical need in reservation communities. Nowhere is the need for Native professionals more critical than in nursing.

The Nursing workshop begins with a video or PowerPoint presentation. The focus is on American Indian nurses serving reservation communities. In the presentation, the nurses shown combine their knowledge of Native traditional ways with modern medical practice. The wish to contribute to their home communities is what inspires many Native students to attend college in the first place. Discussing with students this concept of "coming full circle" (Garrod and Larimore 1997: 15) is important, because Native people have in the past associated higher education with acculturation and loss of identity (Kidwell 1994: 254).

Stephanie Bolman, an enrolled member of the Three Affiliated Tribes of New Town, North Dakota, was a Success Academy workshop presenter while studying Nursing at SDSU. She says:

> In whatever capacity I work, I remain a constant advocate for Native American health issues, and I work to help reduce health disparities among Native Americans. I feel it is important for young Native Americans to continue with education, whether it is to explore the world or gain knowledge they may someday bring back to their communities. A famous quote I once heard summarizes best the sentiment I relay to young Native students: "Shoot for the moon. Even if you miss, you will land among the stars." An education is a source of pride for me and something that no one can take away. It allows me to have many opportunities and options for direction in my life. I plan to finish my second bachelor's degree in Nursing and a master's in Health Administration and return home to central South Dakota. I will continue to work towards improving the health care provided to Native Americans and help them to navigate through the health care system in any way I can.

Education: Wiconi Waste ("The Good Life"). The College of Education and Human Sciences consistently has the highest number of SDSU students participating in Success Academy. All 60 teacher education candidates, taking SDSU's required Human Relations class during the spring semester, serve week-by-week as Success Academy workshop presenters. This means that each FIS freshman who attends the Education workshop is paired with an SDSU student. SDSU Teacher Education faculty members are co-presenters, but they clearly allow their students to lead the workshops.

Together, the entire workshop group—FIS students and staff and SDSU students and staff—watch a videotape of Brookings High School teacher Lynn Frederick. From his perspective as a Native educator, he talks about some of the challenges and successes he has experienced.

Next, using a PowerPoint presentation, SDSU students explain to Success Academy freshmen the Theory of Multiple Intelligences (MI) (Gardner 1983). The freshmen take an online MI quiz, and the preservice teachers help them interpret the results. Each freshman identifies his or her particular strength and then produces a quilt square illustrating it. At the end of each school year all of the squares are sewn together into quilts. (Star quilts are considered the best gift of the Lakota, Dakota, and Nakota peoples.) The quilts hang throughout SDSU's Wenona Hall, where the preservice teachers and other students see them every day on their way to class.

Reflecting on an early Success Academy workshop experience, one preservice teacher said, "We need more time to really get to know these students, to learn from them, and to develop our communication skills" (Moeller 2012). Critical theorist Tierney (1992: 153) explains that it is only through "repeated and consistent interaction" with tribal people that non-Indians learn about a culture uniquely different from their own.

Recognizing this, Teacher Education faculty in 2009 established a social networking site called "Wiconi Waste." The site links FIS and SDSU students, who first meet through Success Academy, into a virtual community. Students from both schools post messages to each other as well as share photos and videos for months after the workshops end.

The relationships, started during the Teacher Education workshops and maintained through the Wiconi Waste virtual community, are of benefit to both FIS and SDSU students. As one FIS freshman puts it:

> The workshop was pretty awesome. I loved it a lot. It made me think about what I want to be when I grow up. It also helped me realize who I really am and what kind of "smart" I am. I like coming to SDSU. I met this person named _____, and he's really cool to talk to—pretty cool. He's my SDSU buddy. I love this place so much and can't wait until I come back.

And an SDSU Teacher Education student has this to say:

> I enjoyed the time I was able to spend with the students, and I enjoyed getting to know them…It was interesting to me to experience a different culture. I love learning more about how the differences, no matter how small or big, between cultures can affect our daily interactions and our perspectives. This opportunity has helped me grow as an individual and as a future educator.

Technology and Tradition: New and Old Ways of Viewing Mother Earth. "The manner in which knowledge is constructed and conveyed in an accounting class is as necessary to be culturally appropriate as it is in an English or history class," Tierney (1992: 160) writes. It is important for American Indian students to see their culture reflected in the curriculum across the entire academy (Huffman 1999). It is especially important, in disciplines such as Engineering, that presenters acknowledge the significance of indigenous science knowledge.

This particular College of Engineering workshop, "Technology and Tradition," has evolved over several years. Its purpose is to introduce FIS freshmen to two different geospatial technologies: remote sensing and geographic information systems (GIS). GIS technology is used to support thousands of tribal government initiatives, and there is a critical need for more Native people trained in GIS.

Faculty and student workshop presenters, using a computer lab in SDSU's Crothers Engineering Hall, have experimented with a variety of formats. One group of Success Academy scholars put on 3-D glasses to view imagery of the Grand Canyon. Since a sizeable number of FIS students are Havasupai and live inside the Grand Canyon with their families when not at school, this session was particularly engaging.

Another group looked at U.S. county maps, classified to show the Native American percentage of population. This let students discover that the highest concentrations of Native Americans correlated with the locations of Indian reservations. Students also used satellite imagery to locate their houses, their schools, and other features of their own reservation communities.

The Engineering workshops illustrate a fundamental point made by Tierney (1992: 163): "Linkages need to be developed between what takes place in, and what exists beyond, the classroom," he writes. "The extended family from which American Indian students come offers a wealth of opportunities for the culturally sensitive teacher." One FIS freshman summarizes her Engineering workshop experience this way:

> Today I learned about geographic information systems. I learned that my county only has one African American and ten Asians living in it. I loved the last workshop because I've always wanted to know how many people live in Sioux County. I was so happy to get to see my house again and to see some old buildings that used to be there but now they're gone. The last workshop was awesome.

Medicines: They Can Make You Better. Local definitions of identity are important, Tierney (2000: 229) says. The value of "role models who students recognize as coming from similar backgrounds" (Tierney 2000: 229) cannot be overstated. In planning workshops at South Dakota State University, an overwhelmingly white institution, involving individuals who can be role models is challenging. While SDSU's professional colleges have made significant strides in opening their doors to (and graduating) students of color, finding American Indian students and faculty to serve as workshop presenters remains difficult.

Tasha Standing Soldier, who graduated from SDSU with her Doctor of Pharmacy degree, was an early College of Pharmacy workshop presenter. Later Erica Fleury, a descendant of the Crow Creek Sioux Tribe, worked with Success Academy in her role as SDSU Native American Club president. In remarks addressed to Success Academy scholars before her 2012 graduation, Fleury said:

> I plan to graduate with my PharmD. degree and serve the Native American people. I have been served at the Fort Thompson Indian Health Service facility on the Crow Creek Sioux Reservation my entire life. Seldom did I ever see a health care professional who looked like me. None of the physicians, nurses, dentists, or pharmacists were Native American people. My hope is that the Native American people can come into my pharmacy and know that people, just like them, are getting their education and becoming respected and trusted figures in society.

The Pharmacy workshop, like so many others across campus, allows high school students opportunities to "try on" different professional American Indian identities (Lal 1995), for example, "I can be a Native American pharmacist." These workshops provide students with hands-on learning, designed to motivate them to pursue careers in one of these disciplines (Nichols and Nichols 2006: 61).

In a state-of-the-art lab in the Avera Health and Science Center, small groups of Success Academy students rotate through three different pharmacy stations. Some students test the Ph levels of water and water mixed with hydrochloric acid. Others use mortars and pestles to fill capsules with "medicine" (in this case, talcum powder). A third cluster of students types in prescriptions and watches them being filled by a newly developed robotics machine. Members of Kappa Epsilon, the professional pharmacy fraternity, and a professor from the College of Pharmacy encourage and assist when needed.

"Going to SDSU helped me on making a decision to go to college because of everything the students at SDSU said," explains one FIS freshman, reflecting on the afternoon spent in Pharmacy. "I wasn't going to go to college, but now I think I could do something with my life."

Ethnobotany: Exploring Native Plants. "The faculty member who has learned and continues to learn about the culture of Native Americans will realize that the way the classroom is structured influences how people learn," Tierney (1992: 162–163) writes. "Whenever possible teachers need to acknowledge the culture of Indian students and incorporate such learning into the *content* and *structure* of the class."

An example of such a faculty member is Professor R. Neil Reese of SDSU's Biology and Microbiology department. Reese has presented a number of Success Academy workshops for the College of Agriculture and Biological Sciences. Every

Friday during the Fall 2001 semester (shortly after Success Academy began), Reese taught a three-hour course called Traditional Plants and Herbs at Sisseton-Wahpeton Community College on the Lake Traverse Reservation (Nixon 2002: 6). His co-instructor was Dorothy Gill, a tribal elder.

Reese brings what he learned, that is, *content*, back to his classroom in SDSU's Northern Plains Biostress Lab. Plant species of special significance to indigenous peoples, where to find these plants in their native habitats, and how the plants look when harvested—all of these are topics researched by Reese (2012) and covered in the ethnobotany workshop he does for Success Academy.

Professors like Reese, who regularly visit Indian reservations and collaborate with Natives, also bring back to the SDSU campus an understanding of how better to *structure* classes involving Indian students. Tierney (1992: 163) points out that "cooperative group activities…are more in keeping with American Indian culture than are individualized projects that emphasize competition." Tierney (1992: 160) further recommends that large lecture classes, "where an Indian student sits passively taking notes," be rejected in favor of small classes, "where everyone is encouraged to be involved."

Success Academy students in Reese's workshop respond favorably to this approach—handling Native plants, working in groups, talking with SDSU faculty and students. "It was a lot of fun to learn about plants," one FIS freshman remarks. "The people seemed very helpful and very good to work with. They seemed to know a lot about college. I learned you could learn a lot if you listen. If you really want to go to college, SDSU could be the help you're looking for."

Evening Meals

"One important way to enhance a feeling of belonging at college is to celebrate American Indian ethnicity on campus," Huffman (1999: 174) writes. Sharing food has always been an important part of Native American celebrations. Great emphasis is placed on the Success Academy dinners that follow the afternoon workshops,

Everyone involved in the workshops is encouraged to attend the dinners—and most, in fact, do attend. SDSU faculty and student workshop presenters have found over the years that some of the best interactions with FIS participants occur in Larson Commons over dinner. Eating in Larson Commons with the older university students gives the younger Native students yet another chance to picture themselves as college students and experience a sense of belonging on campus. (Larson Commons is one of SDSU's three dining venues, one that before Success Academy was relatively deserted on Friday evenings when many university students left campus for the weekend.)

As the Success Academy workshops end, SDSU presenters, FIS students, and FIS teachers wend their way across campus to Larson Commons. Tables in the dining room are marked so that SDSU presenters sit with the FIS students and teachers with whom they have worked during the afternoon sessions. Each FIS workshop group has a name—Deer, Eagle, Wolf, Bear, Buffalo, or Turtle. Each FIS student's nametag bears the name of the group to which he or she is assigned. In the dining room, table tents with group names help participants find their seats easily.

As the Success Academy partnership has evolved through the years, one important lesson SDSU has learned is that time is a "cultural construction" (Tierney 1992: 164). Precise starting times and ending times, for events or parts of events, are no longer as important as they once were to the non-Natives.

The dining room fills rapidly. Always first to arrive are the members of the SDSU Native American Club, who serve as hosts for all the Success Academy dinners. Over the years the Club has grown to include Success Academy scholars who have graduated from FIS and who now attend SDSU.

"Giving back" or "reciprocity" is a core value of many American Indian communities, write D. Michael Pavel and Ella Inglebret (2007: 160). Native students indicate that their ability to give back is one of the most significant indicators of their success as students. SDSU Native American Club members take seriously their service to the Success Academy program. They are role models of success for the FIS students who aspire to attend college.

Others file in to join the group already in the dining room—some deans, some department heads, and the university's director of diversity enhancement. As Tierney (1992: 154) explains, "Faculty respond to positive reinforcement that is genuine." SDSU faculty and students, who serve as workshop presenters, know that Success Academy is valued when they see administrators supporting it. A commitment to making SDSU a welcoming place and to fostering a sense of belonging for Natives runs deep. For SDSU and FIS faculty, spending their Friday evenings at Success Academy signifies their serious commitment to Native students' futures.

As the tables fill—a typical Success Academy meal may have as many as 150 attendees—the dining room becomes a sea of black T-shirts. At the start of the semester, all Success Academy participants are given T-shirts bearing the program's logo. Lakota people use the colors black, red, yellow, and white to represent the four directions, so those are the colors of the T-shirts for Success Academy freshmen, sophomores, juniors, and seniors, respectively (and also for the SDSU presenters and FIS teachers who work with those groups).

Guests arrive for the meal at varying times, coming from multiple workshop locations across campus. What could be "excess time" for the earliest arrivals is occupied by filling out evaluation forms on the afternoon workshops. Success Academy practices a form of "continuous improvement assessment" (Vergara and Hightower 2006: 93). The evaluation forms the FIS freshmen complete one week are copied and distributed to the SDSU presenters before the next Friday. This allows for making improvements in workshop content and presentation, to better serve students, as the Success Academy year progresses.

Once the evaluations are completed, a traditional prayer is offered, by either a Native American Club member or one of the club's advisers. Then the meal begins in earnest. Food is abundant with separate "bars" extending across two rooms for pizza, salads, entrees, sides, drinks, desserts, and even cereal. A pasta buffet and a grill crank out made-to-order dishes for those who desire them. Dinners are "all you can eat," with guests encouraged to return for food as many times as they wish.

For students attending boarding school and eating institutional meals each day, Friday Success Academy dinners are a treat. The generosity of the SDSU administration, in granting Success Academy an ample hospitality budget, is appreciated by both FIS and SDSU students and staff. Universities "need to come to terms with which programs are proven successful," and "the institution needs to incorporate them into its budget," Tierney (1992: 157) says. Generosity, one of the core values of the Lakota people (Marshall 2002: 180), needs to be at the heart of programs like Success Academy.

"Give-aways" are practiced in many Native American communities. Success Academy dinners end with a "give-away" table filled with SDSU memorabilia such as lanyards, backpacks, and water bottles. The SDSU Admissions office and the bookstore supply many of these items. Students turn in nametags, some names are drawn, and those chosen select gifts from the table.

Success Academy dinners at South Dakota State University are planned to honor the identities of students from the Flandreau Indian School. These meals are cultural bridges between the college workshops beforehand and the co-curricular events that follow.

Co-curricular Events

"An organizational culture that truly celebrates diverse groups will have myriad activities, symbols, and events that speak to diversity," Tierney (1992: 159) writes. "Indian ways of life and values will be celebrated and affirmed."

Success Academy freshmen and their teachers often stay on campus after Friday dinners and attend co-curricular events. SDSU faculty, staff, and students at the dinners are invited to attend as well.

As a midsized state university with more than 12,500 students, there are many events from which to choose. Whenever possible, for the Success Academy freshmen, we deliberately select campus activities that celebrate Indian identity. These have included the following:

- A hoop dancing performance by Jackie Bird, an enrolled Sisseton-Wahpeton Sioux tribal member. Bird, a graduate of the Flandreau Indian School, has sung and danced around the world, including at the opening ceremony of the Olympics in Salt Lake City.
- A special exhibition of works by Lakota artist Arthur Amiotte. Amiotte's paintings, collages, and prints were displayed in the South Dakota Art Museum on campus.
- SDSU's wacipi, held in the Frost Arena. The two-day pow wow each year draws hundreds of dancers as well as drum groups from throughout the Midwest.

In addition to these events, over 12 years, Success Academy freshmen have sampled almost every other kind of co-curricular activity that South Dakota State University has to offer—from plays, concerts, and rodeos to poetry readings, wrestling matches, and basketball games.

Every visit to SDSU is an opportunity for FIS freshmen to picture themselves attending college classes. Every visit is also an opportunity for the freshmen to picture themselves extending their learning beyond the walls of the academic buildings, just as we hope they will do as college students.

All freshman year Success Academy programs—afternoon workshops, evening meals, and co-curricular events—are designed to encourage Native students to consider higher education. Having "fun" is a strong motivator, as participant comments show. For this reason, Success Academy deliberately includes a variety of experiences, in and outside the classroom, chosen to appeal to a diverse group of students with a wide range of interests. Success Academy freshmen say:

It was fun. I liked it very much because we weren't in a classroom all the time.

Well, I thought it was fun because they made it seem like college wasn't all work. You can have fun and do work at the same time.

I never thought I would go to college, but now that I went there, I feel that I want to. It seems really fun.

Commencement: One Year Ends, Another Begins

By the end of Spring 2001, Flandreau Indian School freshmen and their teachers had come to South Dakota State University for six Success Academy visits. By then Success Academy was deemed a "success" by most of those involved, and it was decided that the program would continue for another year. As educators, we felt we could not, in good conscience, excite 100 FIS freshmen about college without making plans to nurture and support them on their educational journey. SDSU also was experiencing many benefits, unimagined when Success Academy began.

A Success Academy commencement, marking the end of our first year, was held in April 2001. Success Academy commencement subsequently became an annual event.

"We call ceremonies like this 'commencement,'" I said to those gathered that first year. "'Commence' means to begin. You, as students, are not so much ending the academic year that has just passed, but rather you are preparing to commence or to begin the next phase of your life ahead." Just as we were encouraging our students to look ahead, so, too, were we, as program organizers, already planning for the future.

As the years passed, the commencement ceremonies grew in many ways. That first year 100 Success Academy scholars, and the staff who worked with them, gathered in a tiny dining room in a residence hall. By 2005, about 300 people—students and faculty, from FIS and SDSU—were regularly attending Success Academy commencements held in the Peterson Recital Hall of the Lincoln Music Center on the SDSU campus.

We end our school year much as we begin, with a ceremony honoring our students and their cultures, and communicating to them our expectations for their success. The president or the provost of South Dakota State University welcomes the administrators, faculty, staff, and students from the Flandreau Indian School and thanks them for the gift of their presence on campus, week after week. The superintendent of the Flandreau Indian School responds. Next an honor song is performed for all the Success Academy students.

Commencement honors the commitment of the Success Academy participants to complete high school, attend college, and stay connected to their cultures. Our students often face difficult challenges on their educational journeys, and it is important that we acknowledge that as well.

The commencement speech is always delivered by a prominent Native American leader. Students need to hear firsthand from Native people about "maintaining hopes and dreams for the future, even in the face of real and perceived barriers" (Yosso 2005: 77). Our commencement speakers have included State Senator Ron Volesky, Miss South Dakota Vanessa Short Bull, and *Indian Country Today* founder Tim Giago. Nanabah Allison-Brewer, the first female Native American head coach at an NCAA Division I school, and Keith Moore, who soon after speaking became director of the federal Bureau of Indian Education, have also given commencement addresses.

The presentation of plaques to the Success Academy scholars is the highlight of the ceremony. To begin, I read these words:

> These plaques are presented in recognition of your enthusiastic participation in one full year of Success Academy activities. Just as importantly, these plaques are presented in expectation of your continued success in your academic pursuits. We find you truly worthy. This is an expression of our faith in you to continue to achieve to the best of your ability. You may become an engineer, an artist, a nurse or a journalist. Whatever career you choose, we hope that you will live your life in such a way that the world will be a better place because you have lived here.

Each plaque is engraved with "FIS-SDSU Success Academy," the year, and the scholar's name. The plaques are the colors of the four directions— black for freshmen, red for sophomores, yellow for juniors, and white for seniors.

The university's vice president, provost, and most of its deans present the plaques. Their presence signifies that this is an important day for SDSU as an institution as well as for the FIS students as individuals. Each student crosses the stage as his or her name is read. The student receives the plaque and a handshake from each platform party member. Applause and cheers follow.

Many of the FIS freshmen have never before received an award or a trophy or, for that matter, any recognition for academic achievement. High fives and hugs are often exchanged as the scholars leave the stage and return to their seats.

A final way we honor our students on commencement day is with a noon meal on the campus green under gigantic tents. The university's catering staff calls this "the president's lunch" because it is the same menu the president serves faculty members at her home each fall.

Summing Up and Looking Ahead

To repeat an important idea from Tierney (2000: 219–220): "The challenge…is not to develop ways for people to integrate into the system, but instead to *change that system* by way of programs, activities, events, and curricula that affirm and *honor individual identities*." Chapter 1 discusses aspects of Success Academy that exemplify *systemic change.* Chapter 2 describes how the freshman year of Success Academy *honors the identities* of the students served through programming such as workshops, meals, and events. Two signature events—Catching the Dream Day at the start of the program year and Success Academy Commencement at the end—communicate our expectations that the students served will succeed in higher education without abandoning their identities.

Honoring Ethnic Identity in a College Preparatory Program: What Works?

In reflecting on Success Academy's freshman "Fridays at State," six key points bear repeating. The points will be framed as directives to those planning to use critical theory to design innovative programs.

Structure Opportunities for Learning So They Are Two-Way. Throughout Success Academy's history, hundreds of non-Native SDSU faculty have worked with hundreds of Native FIS students, delivering academic workshops and encouraging college attendance. Many faculty report that the content and the structure of the classes they offer for their SDSU students have been enriched because of their Success Academy experiences. Native American perspectives have been integrated into course offerings where they did not exist previously. In addition, SDSU professors have increased their cultural competency in working with Native American students. Department chairs, academic deans, and other administrators have come to realize that Success Academy is a legitimate equity endeavor *and* to reward faculty for their participation in it.

Allow American Indian Students to See Their Cultures Reflected Throughout the Curriculum. Links must be consciously developed between what takes place in and what exists beyond the classroom. Native students' ethnic identity is strengthened by culturally relevant and substantive classroom experiences, such as viewing one's reservation community via remotely sensed data or hearing a Native American teacher discuss his work.

    What is taught, that is, *content,* must acknowledge American Indian histories and cultures. *How it is taught,* that is, *pedagogy,* is equally important. Consequently…

Stress Experiential Learning, Done in Small Groups. "Cooperative group activities…are more in keeping with American Indian culture than are individualized projects that emphasize competition" (Tierney 1992: 163). Hands-on activities, such as monitoring blood pressure in the Wokunze workshop or identifying Native plants in the

Ethnobotany workshop, give students the opportunity to picture themselves working in college classrooms and labs. In this way students begin to construct "scholar identities" (Hodges and Welch 2003: 5–6). "Scholar identities" can serve as a counterbalance to messages of intellectual inferiority that students of color often receive through processes like tracking.

Emphasize Career Areas of Critical Need in Tribal Communities. In other words, show students that higher education can provide "tools to ensure Native American cultural survival" (Garrod and Larimore 1997: 16). The best workshops are those that allow students to "try on" different professional American Indian identities, such as "I can be a Native American journalist" or "I can be a Native American pharmacist." Journalism Professor Doris Giago, co-founder of the *Lakota Times,* discusses the importance of having more Native journalists in the Indian and non-Indian press. Former Pharmacy student (now Dr.) Erica Fleury tells of growing up on the Crow Creek Indian Reservation and never being served by a Native health care professional. "Coming full circle" (Garrod and Larimore 1997: 15) refers to the hope of many Native American students to attend college and to gain knowledge that will benefit their home communities after graduation. This should be acknowledged by professors and others whose job it is to help these students prepare for higher education.

Introduce Role Models, Recognized by Students as Coming From Similar Backgrounds as Themselves. At every juncture, positive Native role models, from throughout the university and from the larger community, present Success Academy programming. The participation of these individuals speaks to Success Academy students about the importance of a college education. Especially significant are the SDSU Native American Club members who host the weekly Success Academy dinners. Many of the club members are Flandreau Indian School graduates and Success Academy scholars. "Being a role model is a two-way street," the club's adviser explains. "You can't be a role model for a high school student if you are not a successful college student yourself."

Constantly Develop New Ways to Affirm and Honor Ethnic Identity. Incorporating Native culture into programming such as workshops, meals, and events is obvious. More subtle, however, are the many other aspects of our work that celebrate culture, such as where we meet (in the Lakota/Dakota Conference Room), what we wear (student-designed shirts bearing the medicine wheel symbol), and what we are called (Deer, Eagle, Wolf, Bear, Buffalo, and Turtle groups). These myriad details are part of an overarching mindset, which is to change "the entire campus environment so that Native Americans can be successful" (Nichols and Nichols 2006: 75).

Moving From Minute Developments Toward Dramatic Reorientations

Tierney explains that systemic change is a multifaceted, complex process. Exactly how systemic change occurs ranges across a spectrum from "minute developments" to "dramatic reorientations" (Tierney 1992: 152).

Chapter 2 starts at the "minute developments" end of the spectrum. I have described how we, as Indian and non-Indian educators, began developing culturally responsive strategies designed ultimately to increase college access for Native students.

Chapter 3 is titled "Power Relations and Sophomore 'Focus Days.'" This chapter moves a bit farther along the spectrum of change by discussing how the "culture of power" (Tierney 1992: 152), at SDSU and at FIS, was influenced by the continuing development of Success Academy. Chapter 3 covers some of the structural underpinnings of Success Academy. Matters such as budget and leadership needed to be addressed by the end of our first year. At the same time, the day-to-day business of developing programming for a new sophomore cohort had to proceed. Chapter 3 describes both the macro and the micro issues faced by us, as Success Academy collaborators, starting in our second year.

3

Power Relations and
Sophomore "Focus Days"

"The doing of critical theory has been called in the educational literature critical pedagogy," Barry Kanpol (1999: 27) writes. This book has promised to illustrate the "doing of critical theory" by describing in some detail the Flandreau Indian School-South Dakota State University Success Academy.

Critical pedagogy confronts both educators and students with questions of power and how it plays a role in teaching and learning. At issue is the fact that power in schools favors some and not others (Pozo 2003). As William G. Tierney (1993b) explains:

> The emphasis of a critical analysis shifts away from what strategies those in power can develop to help those not in power, to analyzing how power exists in the organization, and given how power operates, to developing strategies that seek to transform those relations. All organizational participants will be encouraged to come to terms with how they may reconstruct and transform the organization's culture. (323)

Chapter 3 begins by addressing power issues in Success Academy from a macro-structural perspective. Specifically, how is the "culture of power" (Tierney 1992: 152) being reformulated through the Success Academy partnership in strategic ways, such as the structuring of planning committees and the development of organizational budgets?

Chapter 3 then moves on to power issues at a more micro-interactionist level. That is, how are individual students empowered through their participation in Success Academy "such that each is more affirmed in his or her identity" (Cummins 1997: 424)? The focus here is on Success Academy programming, as it developed in the second year, to serve sophomores through a series of "focus days."

In this chapter the voices of Success Academy planners, presenters, and participants will continue to be heard, through their comments shared in program evaluations and other written documents.

Reformulating the Culture of Power Through Success Academy

A university truly engaged with its communities is one that demonstrates a respect for partners, says the Kellogg Commission on the Future of State and Land-Grant Universities (1999: 11). "Such partnerships are likely to be characterized by problems defined together, goals and agendas that are shared in common, definitions of success that are meaningful to both university and community," the commission (1999: 11) explains.

It is important to note that the original idea for the FIS-SDSU partnership was developed by administrators, teachers, and staff at the Flandreau Indian School. It was the Flandreau Indian School that first envisioned a Success Academy program as a way to stem its alarming tide of school dropouts and academic underachievement. It was the Flandreau Indian School that invited South Dakota State University to develop a partnership that would allow more Native students to graduate from high school and move on to college, all of this in a state where American Indians were and still are seriously underrepresented in higher education.

"As opposed to a rhetoric of what mainstream organizations will *do* for minorities—a top-down managerial approach—the struggle for critical theorists is to develop strategies and policies that emerge from a vision of working *with* minorities toward a participatory goal of emancipation and empowerment," Tierney (1992: 41–42) writes. South Dakota State University's partnership with the Flandreau Indian School is an example of a mainstream institution working *with* a tribal school to empower American Indian students—and to do this by increasing access to higher education.

"What might an educator do who seeks to create a classroom, organization, or system where empowerment is viewed as the scaffolding for the program?" Tierney (1992: 150) asks in his book on Native Americans in academe. He offers five strate-

gies: organizational adaptation, organizational voice, organizational bridges, organizational effectiveness, and organizational culture (Tierney 1992: 152–160). How
these five strategies are being used to reformulate the "culture of power" (Tierney
1992: 152) through the FIS-SDSU Success Academy will be explained in the following sections.

Organizational Adaptation

Repeated and consistent contact with tribal people lets Anglo faculty and staff learn
about a culture very different from their own and teaches them how to best interact with Indian students, Tierney (1992: 153) writes. Starting in its second year
Success Academy expanded to include all 100 sophomores attending FIS, in addition to the 100 new freshmen entering the school. SDSU's College of Arts and
Sciences stepped forward to assume much of the responsibility for the added programming. This meant that 14 academic departments, which had not been involved
with Success Academy previously, began presenting Friday afternoon workshops for
sophomores. The number of SDSU faculty and staff involved with Success
Academy more than doubled overnight, all of these individuals benefitting from
their increased contact with American Indian students.

As one SDSU professor, who has presented many Success Academy workshops,
explains:

> I think SDSU gains a great deal from partnering with a minority high school. We gain
> insight into how American Indian students function in an academic setting and perhaps
> clues to help us be more welcoming and inclusive. As an SDSU teacher I gain insight into
> better ways of teaching scientific material. Outreach is an important part of the role of a
> land grant university, and the partnership with the Flandreau Indian School is an impor-
> tant outreach activity.

"Faculty respond to positive reinforcement that is genuine," Tierney (1992:
154) says. SDSU faculty who present afternoon workshops have always been
encouraged to accompany FIS students and teachers to the evening meals. A huge
incentive to do so, particularly in the early years of the sophomore program, was
knowing that the dean of Arts and Sciences would be in attendance at the meals
as well.

SDSU faculty and staff have been extraordinarily generous with their time and
talents throughout all of Success Academy's history. Material rewards, in a grassroots effort like Success Academy, are few and far between, so it has been important to "give" as we are able. Faculty have been appreciative of small gestures such

as receiving Success Academy T-shirts just like the students and being able to bring family to Friday meals.

Success Academy has been well-served by having a photographer who attends every Friday session. He creates sets of photos for presenters of workshops. Each Friday morning, as program coordinator, I walk across campus delivering what has become known as the week's "Success Academy survival kit." The kits contains photos and evaluations from the previous week's workshops and T-shirts, nametags, and schedules for the current week's workshops. Expressing appreciation for faculty service and getting feedback on program operation, face to face, have been important in ensuring that Success Academy continues to run smoothly with enthusiastic support.

It is also important to note that photos taken of Success Academy workshops frequently appear in SDSU departmental publications and on the university website. This generates positive feedback for both the academic departments and the faculty involved.

At the end of the school year, I write a letter to each SDSU workshop presenter, with a carbon copy sent to that individual's dean. (I write similar letters to all the FIS faculty and staff involved with Success Academy as well.) In the letter, I offer my thanks to the faculty or staff member, and I review our program's accomplishments for the past school year. At SDSU, recognition by one's dean for commitment to diversity efforts is significant. Faculty who are Success Academy presenters or planners list this service activity on their yearly professional staff evaluations.

A final "positive reinforcement" (Tierney 1992: 154) for faculty involvement in Success Academy bears mentioning. SDSU is accredited by the Higher Learning Commission of the North Central Association of Colleges and Schools. In addition, about 20 of the university's colleges and departments are accredited as individual units (SDSU Catalog 2012). Accrediting boards have standards for diversity and inclusion that must be met. FIS-SDSU Success Academy is cited extensively in reports filed by SDSU for reaccreditation. Having a Success Academy coordinator trained in evaluation research, as well as a part-time secretary who assists with data collection, has meant that detailed records have been maintained on all program activities. Shared regularly with faculty leaders in colleges and departments throughout the university, these records have proved immensely useful for accreditation purposes.

Organizational Voice

"If an organization's participants are actively concerned with enacting a critical perspective, what is necessary will be quite different from most current organizational efforts," Tierney (1992: 158) explains. "Instead of administrators trying to symbolically include Indian voice on a committee by adding one Native American, the committee needs to reconsider how it might constitute itself so that Indian people are fully represented and participate."

Schools tend to perpetuate power relationships that exist in the broader society (Apple 1982, 1986). From the start Success Academy has deliberately tried to disrupt such power relationships, by rejecting the notion that formal education and multiple degrees constitute the only legitimate sources of knowledge. Ample opportunities have emerged for sharing power across educational borders, for example, between high school and college faculty, between Indians and non-Indians, and between students and teachers.

As the FIS-SDSU Success Academy has evolved—from a one-semester experience for only freshmen to a four-year program for all students attending FIS—it has become apparent that such a massive undertaking would only be possible through respectful collaboration. A Success Academy steering committee was formed with balanced numbers of Indian school and state university faculty and of Indians and non-Indians.

Decision-making has proceeded with the recognition that teachers, elders, families, and others who work daily with Native American students have great wisdom in motivating these young people to achieve academically. Success Academy was blessed by having on its steering committee for many years three committed educators who spent most of their careers working with and for Indian children—FIS Superintendent Betty Belkham (Cherokee), FIS Principal Stuart Zephier (Cheyenne River Sioux Tribe), and FIS Assistant Principal Sandra Koester.

An assistant dean at SDSU, who also serves on the Success Academy steering committee, describes the benefits of partnering with FIS this way:

> SDSU gains legitimate access to a relationship with a tribal school—its students, faculty and staff. We get to be a part of the creation of an exciting, informative school reform movement that appears to really be making a difference. SDSU gains the opportunity to learn about how to most effectively *work with* and *learn from* the teachers at the Flandreau Indian School.

Organizational Bridges

"University personnel…need to go out to the reservation and learn more about tribal life if they are to be better acquainted with the lives of their students," Tierney (1992: 156) writes. "Rather than students simply visiting an institution to learn about an alien culture, such an activity ought to be developed within a cultural context that highlights how both groups are going to learn about, and with, one another."

Steering Committee Meetings at FIS and SDSU. Our Success Academy steering committee generally meets twice a year and tries to alternate its meetings between Flandreau where FIS is located and Brookings where SDSU is located. The meetings always begin with the sharing of food and ample time for conversation. This follows the suggestion of Lakota scholar Cheryl Crazy Bull (1997: 17) that non-Native collaborators establish close, personal, and enduring relationships among tribal people.

In keeping with Lakota and Dakota tradition, decision-making at meetings is by consensus, with all members contributing input until collective accord is reached (North Dakota Studies Project 2011). This process of achieving consensus ensures that all have a say.

There is an instrumental, as well as a cultural, reason for "collaborative decision-making" (Wagner 1998: 77). In schools, when individuals have input into designing programs they become stakeholders committed to making those programs work.

Other Visits to Flandreau. In addition to hosting meetings, the FIS administration has provided many other opportunities for SDSU personnel to get better acquainted with the Flandreau Indian School and its students, teachers, and staff. FIS has arranged tours of its campus and chances to observe classes for SDSU workshop presenters and planners. One year the FIS administration invited all of SDSU's freshman and sophomore workshop presenters to attend its day-long fall orientation for employees, held on the Flandreau Santee Sioux Reservation.

Freshman and sophomore Success Academy programming, described thus far, has involved what is called the "academic affairs" side of SDSU. As Success Academy has grown to serve FIS juniors and seniors, the "student affairs" side of SDSU has also been drawn in. Individuals from the SDSU offices of Native Student Advising, Admissions, and Financial Aid, to mention only a few, regularly travel to FIS with me to work with juniors and seniors transitioning to college. SDSU's Financial Aid Director Jay Larsen and I are invited each spring to participate in FIS's commencement ceremonies and present scholarships to graduating seniors.

In May 2002 a special invitation was extended by the FIS faculty to the SDSU staff working with freshman and sophomore Success Academy. The invitation was to have lunch with students in the FIS dining room and then attend a pow wow in the FIS gym. At the pow wow an honor song was performed by the FIS drum group for the SDSU staff members to recognize their work during the first two years of Success Academy.

Making a Difference. In a state with a historic reputation for racial disharmony, Success Academy collaborators at FIS and at SDSU have consciously tried to model a different kind of behavior. This story, told by a Flandreau Indian School administrator, serves as illustration:

> It is so wonderful for our students to become aware of post-secondary offerings at SDSU and to learn that college is not beyond the realm of possibility for them. While at the National Indian Education Association conference in Albuquerque, New Mexico, in November 2002, Valerian Three Irons had an information and recruitment booth for SDSU at the exhibit fair. [At that time Three Irons was a diversity associate for SDSU and a frequent Success Academy workshop presenter.] One woman came up to the booth, and Mr. Three Irons began to tell her about SDSU and its programs. She said, "I know about your school. I have a daughter going to the Flandreau Indian School. She is part of Success Academy and has visited your campus several times." The mother said her daughter talked positively about SDSU and Success Academy at FIS, and that her daughter was now planning to go on to college after high school. Our message *is* getting out, not only to the residents of South Dakota, but across the nation. Our students come from over 20 different states, so the message about education and programs at SDSU, in Brookings, South Dakota, has a far-reaching effect.

Organizational Effectiveness

"When programs are proven successful, the institution needs to incorporate them into its *budget* so that the project administrators have the leeway to plan over a longer period of *time* instead of constantly searching for funds," Tierney (1992: 157) writes. "Far too often one part of an institution develops a program in isolation from the rest of the university or college, so that any sense of *coordination* is absent" (Tierney 1992: 157).

Success Academy began during the 2000–2001 academic year under an unusual set of circumstances, both at FIS and at SDSU. These circumstances created the perfect crucible in which Success Academy could be created and are important enough to be examined in some detail under the headings, suggested by Tierney, of budget, time, and coordination. The overarching concept is this: Organizers of effective programs must be keenly aware of when conditions are ripe for systemic change to occur (Lee 2006: 140). It is important to be conscious of the political climate at one's institution and to take advantage of opportune moments when they arise.

Budgeting at FIS. Shortly before approaching SDSU about Success Academy, the Flandreau Indian School received a demonstration grant from the U.S. Department of Education. The $300,000 grant was for implementing the Talent Development High School model (described in Chapter 1), of which Success Academy is a part.

Over the years, FIS has estimated the cost of participating in the Success Academy partnership with SDSU to be about $83,000 annually. This amount primarily covers overtime pay for FIS staff and bus transportation for FIS students.

Budgeting at SDSU. The Higher Learning Commission (HLC) of the North Central Association of Colleges and Schools completed a visit to SDSU in April 2000, during the academic year just before Success Academy began. The HLC, which reaccredits universities every 10 years, gathers data through what it calls "comprehensive site visits." During the HLC site visit to SDSU, the university was found lacking in the area of diversity. SDSU was given three years to file a written report addressing the HLC's concerns. Timing was fortuitous for a bold new diversity initiative.

At that time a University Diversity Council (UDC) existed, comprising about 50 faculty and staff members and reporting to SDSU's Director for Diversity Enhancement. The council had six subcommittees—staff/faculty recruitment, staff/faculty retention, student recruitment, student retention, international recruitment/retention, and educational programs. I, as diversity coordinator for the College of Engineering, co-chaired the student recruitment subcommittee together with a department head from the College of Nursing.

A budget of about $53,000 was allotted to the six UDC subcommittees for the 2000–2001 academic year. Subcommittee chairs were to submit requests for funding.

Two points about the UDC budget are significant. First, having $53,000 to spend at its discretion for diversity was considered "pretty heady stuff," to use the words of one faculty member serving on the UDC at the time. Second, by making this funding available, SDSU's administration was indicating seriousness about seeing significant diversity programming established before the interim HLC report was due in 2003.

Among the UDC subcommittees, the largest budget requests were from the student retention subcommittee (about $10,000 to start a minority peer mentoring program) and from the student recruitment subcommittee (about $14,000 to fund the first year of Success Academy). Both of these programs received the funds requested. This strong financial support from the university administration continued throughout subsequent years. Both of these programs can be counted among SDSU's most enduring and effective diversity initiatives.

During the next 10 years, the SDSU central administration's support for Success Academy grew to about $20,000 per year. This was during an era of fiscal shortfalls, experienced by most universities nationwide. To repeat, institutions demonstrate their commitment to diversity projects by incorporating them into their permanent budgets.

Time. "Time and staying power" (Tierney 1991: 39) are fundamental to reorienting a university and making it more welcoming to Native students. "Native American recruitment and retention is a generational issue," Tierney (1992: 157) writes. "The question needs to be asked how well equipped the specific institution is to deal with Indian students today, but also with American Indian students who are now in the first grade."

At the time of this writing, FIS-SDSU Success Academy has existed for 12 years. It is important to note that the Flandreau Indian School students who just completed their fourth year of Success Academy are now transitioning into their first year at university. They were in the first grade when our college-prep program began.

Coordination. "Far too often, one part of an institution develops a program in isolation from the rest of the university, resulting in the absence of any sense of coordination," Tierney (1991: 39) writes. From Success Academy's start, all of the academic colleges throughout the university were involved in presenting hands-on workshops to FIS students.

At SDSU, Success Academy was born and came of age in the College of Engineering. The Engineering college covered my salary and benefits (about $25,000) to serve as the part-time Success Academy coordinator. Engineering also paid all of the program's administrative costs (estimated to be about $25,000). Being "home" to Success Academy was considered by the College of Engineering to be an important contribution to SDSU's overall diversity efforts.

Since 2000, Success Academy has grown to involve about 250 students in grades 9 through 12 attending the Flandreau Indian School. This expansion would not have been possible without coordinated effort by all of SDSU's academic colleges and backing by the central administration. SDSU's provost asked all the academic deans to contribute financially to growing the Success Academy program, and they all willingly agreed. The amount of the deans' contributions has varied from year to year, with the College of Arts and Sciences taking the lead in giving (after the College of Engineering). By Success Academy's 10th year, the deans' annual contributions stood collectively at about $15,000. By then SDSU's total annual dollar cost for Success Academy was about $85,000.

Serving a huge number of students with a relatively small amount of money (and being able to sustain a coordinated effort like this over many years) was possible for two reasons.

First, Success Academy started as a grassroots effort. The program began small and slowly built on its successes. Since 2000 about 300 SDSU faculty and staff have served as planners and presenters for freshman-, sophomore-, and junior-year Success Academy. None of these individuals, with the exception of myself as program coordinator, has received payment for service. The cost of in-kind contributions by these individuals to Success Academy, if calculated in dollar terms, would be staggering.

Second, Success Academy began without huge external grants, from either the government or corporate funders. (External grants, to fund college classes for Success Academy seniors, began during the 2003–2004 academic year and will be explained in Chapter 5.) Many programs serving students of color begin with funding from external grants, funding that universities are then expected to assume, but often cannot, once the grants expire. Success Academy from the start had the support, financial and otherwise, of those who controlled a significant share of SDSU's resources. Those people were willing to direct resources toward a program that was proving to benefit Indians students and the university.

Organizational Culture

Universities must be reoriented so that Native American culture is celebrated and affirmed (Tierney 1992: 159). This point has been reiterated time and time again throughout the book.

To repeat, as FIS-SDSU Success Academy moved from its first to its second year, the program expanded to serve all sophomores attending the Flandreau Indian School. Four "focus days" were added to the program, engaging 14 new academic departments that had not been involved with Success Academy previously. (Most of these were College of Arts and Sciences departments.) Following in the footsteps of the freshman workshop planners, the new faculty participants tried to make American Indian culture central to their Friday presentations.

Empowering Students Through Success Academy

Thus far, Chapter 3 has discussed how Success Academy, as an organization, has redefined roles—of high school and college faculty, of Indians and non-Indians—so that power is more evenly shared in collaborative ways. This is in keeping with advice by

Cummins (1993: 101): "Educators and policymakers…must redefine their roles within the classroom, the community, and the broader society so that these role definitions result in interactions that empower rather than disable students."

Student empowerment is a key aspect of Success Academy; thus, students have always had a voice in deciding how the program evolves. In Fall 2001 Success Academy organizers asked the previous year's participants what they would like to learn in a sophomore college preparatory program that they had not covered as freshmen. Based on the students' answers, Success Academy added four "focus days" for the 100 sophomores at the Flandreau Indian School. All FIS sophomores, accompanied by teachers, attend a Focus on the Arts Day, a Focus on Health and Nutrition Day, a Focus on American Indian Studies Day, and a Focus on the Military Day.

The format of the sophomore year "focus days" is similar to that of the freshman year "Fridays at State"—hands-on workshops in the afternoons, presented by SDSU faculty and students, followed by evening dinners and co-curricular activities. The four sophomore "focus days" are deliberately structured in ways that empower students.

So what exactly does the "empowerment" of students mean in the context of Success Academy programming? We turn to two prominent scholars of critical pedagogy for answers.

Paulo Freire (1990, 1994), considered to be the father of critical pedagogy, says that the first step toward empowerment is "conscientization." "Conscientization" is the process through which oppressed people realize that their cultural values are legitimate and worth maintaining. Clearly, "focus day" presenters prepare workshops that introduce their academic disciplines (for example, Music or History) to FIS students. That said, the presenters also make sure that the American Indian students attending see *their* cultures and *their* values reflected in what is taught, perhaps by hearing an indigenous musician or discussing tribal treaty rights.

Peter McLaren, regarded as one of the leading architects of critical pedagogy of the 21st century, offers another useful definition of "empowerment." McLaren (1989: 186) says "empowerment" is "the process by which students learn to question and selectively appropriate those aspects of the dominant culture that will provide them with the basis for defining and transforming, rather than merely serving, the wider social order." "Focus day" presenters, many of them Native American, try to show how the intellectual and vocational skills acquired at a mainstream university can be applied by Native scholars to transform Native communities.

Detailed descriptions of the "focus days" and how they contribute to student empowerment follow in the remainder of this chapter.

Focus on the Arts Day

How does one "teach in a manner that empowers" (hooks 1994: 15)? Make every student "an active participant, not a passive consumer," bell hooks (1994: 14) advises in her classic critical pedagogy text, *Teaching to Transgress*. "Education can only be liberatory when everyone claims knowledge as a field in which we all labor."

Active participation certainly characterizes the Focus on the Arts Day workshops presented by the Visual Arts, Communications Studies and Theatre, and Music departments. The sophomore workshop presenters differ from the freshman workshop presenters described in Chapter 2 in that they are responsible for only one Success Academy visit per academic year, not for weekly visits.

FIS sophomores attend Focus on the Arts Day on one Friday afternoon and evening each spring semester. The sophomores, just like the freshmen, come to campus wearing Success Academy T-shirts and color-coded nametags, dividing them into three groups. During the afternoon, these groups rotate through three hour-long sessions presented by the Visual Arts, Theatre, and Music departments. FIS sophomores get a feel for the SDSU campus as each of these departments is located some distance from the other. Sophomore "focus days" differ from freshman Friday visits in that students during a single campus visit will sample several academic disciplines (in this case, Visual Arts, Theatre, and Music) instead of just one.

Visual Arts Workshops. In Grove Commons, home to SDSU's Visual Arts department, FIS sophomores split their time between three activities—seeing student artwork in the Ritz Gallery, creating computer-generated imagery in the animation lab, and sketching living models in the drawing studio.

Lessons learned during Success Academy's first year influenced preparations for the second. Student evaluations, not all of them positive, informed our planning. The importance of having small work groups, multiple hands-on activities, and sufficient physical movement within an hour-long session for high school students cannot be overemphasized. Student comments reflect this:

> I had a whole bunch of fun doing everything here at SDSU, especially in the pixilation room. I wouldn't mind doing that when I grow up.

> I learned a different way to draw. It was fun. I learned that this could be a possible college in my future to attend. I enjoyed it here. I hope to learn more next time, and maybe they can help me to prepare myself better.

Theatre Workshops. Theatre faculty and students host their workshops in SDSU's world-class Performing Arts Center. From start to finish activities are hands-on, interactive, learning by doing. In one afternoon, Success Academy students get a taste of what it would be like to study Theatre at SDSU. Different sessions have been added and dropped throughout the years as new SDSU faculty and students have become involved.

In the stagecraft area, FIS students try their hands at some theatrical pyrotechnics. In the costume shop, sophomores first see how hundreds of garments from past productions are stored before creating some designs of their own. Favorite make-up techniques include applying cuts and bruises to show to one's friends upon returning to FIS.

As Focus on the Arts Day has evolved, sessions on acting and dancing have also been added. Students remark on their experiences:

> I thought Theatre was enjoyable. It was fun and all new. It showed me a little…oh, all right, most of the things, about the outfits and make-up of an actor or actress. I'm so glad I have learned and went to this event. My older sister is enrolling in Theatre. She is going to a college on the Coast. I'm proud of her because it's been her dream to be an actress. I envy her a lot, and she has inspired me to follow my dreams.

> Something new I learned about in Theatre was how to make scrapes, burns and bruises. I even got stitches. I thought it was awesome! It was actually something I enjoyed. I've made my mind up. I'm going to SDSU when I graduate. I just think it's the best!

Throughout the years Theatre and Music department faculty have involved large numbers of their students in presenting Success Academy workshops. In fact, during many Focus on the Arts days, the SDSU students outnumber the FIS students.

Music Workshops. Like Theatre, Music has tried a variety of approaches to engage Success Academy sophomores since it began presenting workshops in 2002. Early workshops had FIS students in the keyboard lab, composing music under the direction of an SDSU faculty member. SDSU student ensembles, such as the jazz band and the drum line, have performed for FIS sophomores. There have been sound and light booth demonstrations in the Performing Arts Center and talks on Native American music.

One of the most compelling Focus on the Arts Days featured a harpist who performed the indigenous music of South America. Student comments reflect excitement about getting to know both the musician and his work:

> I highly enjoyed Alfredo Rolando Ortiz. It showed me that the harp is native to Venezuela. He also showed me that if you find something you love to do, you can make a successful career out of it.

> I learned that if you're interested in something you should go for it because you never know what's going to happen. Sometimes a little leap of faith will take you far. Music is a great way to express yourself. You can do whatever you set your mind to.

Evening Meals. Workshops are followed by dinners, attended by all Success Academy sophomores, their teachers, and SDSU presenters. These meals are hosted by the SDSU Native American Club, just as they are for the freshmen. Tierney (1992: 145), when talking about Native Americans and power relations, emphasizes how important it is "to reduce the status hierarchy between teacher and student." Success Academy dinners are an opportunity to do this.

Co-curricular Activities. Campus events follow sophomore dinners in Larson Commons, again just as they do for freshmen. After almost all of the evening arts activities, FIS students have opportunities to interact with the performers and discuss their work. These events have included a reading by David Allan Evans, South Dakota's Poet Laureate, and a performance of *Equus* by the State University Theatre.

Many of the evening arts activities attended by Success Academy sophomores center around cultures, Native and other. A step-dancing show draws African American fraternities and sororities from across the Midwest to SDSU each year to perform to packed houses. The Little Bird Band, which has been called the only garage band in which no one is old enough to drive a car (Keloland 2008), features six American Indian cousins from the Bushnell, South Dakota, area, all of them at the time under the age of 13. Bringing to campus young artists who are students of color—and giving FIS students a chance to visit with them—is another way that the university and Success Academy try to honor ethnic identity and, by so doing, empower Native scholars.

Focus on Health and Nutrition Day

This "focus day" is organized by the Health and Nutritional Sciences Department, which is part of SDSU's College of Education and Human Sciences. Focus on Health and Nutrition Day has a clear vocational emphasis. A sense of vocation relates closely to what Tierney (1992: 50) calls "rituals of empowerment."

In discussing rituals of empowerment, Tierney (1992: 50) points out that "all students need to be equipped with the intellectual and vocational skills necessary to function in a postmodern world." But as Richard Pottinger (1989: 3) explains, this may create a dilemma for Native students: "While recognizing the importance of cultural traditions, few individuals wish to be handicapped by inadequate preparation for the 'real world,' a real world which demands skills relevant to the latest advances in technology. How does one achieve this competence without losing touch with one's heritage?"

Across South Dakota, tribal leaders indicate that one of their greatest educational needs is for more Native professionals trained in health and nutrition

(Nichols and Nichols 1998). "Education, the acquisition of knowledge, status and academic skills, is the main door to the empowerment" of minorities, Henry T. Trueba and Yali Zou (1994: 133) write. It follows, then, that in South Dakota, an important path to empowerment for both Native students and Native communities is through the pursuit of careers in the health and nutritional sciences. This is exactly what Focus on Health and Nutrition Day attempts to illustrate.

Four of the day's workshops are held in SDSU's Frost Arena, using the basketball court, the upstairs track, and the wrestling room. Each of these workshops, led by SDSU faculty and students, focuses on what it would be like to study a particular health major and then to pursue a career in that field.

Park and Recreation Management Workshop. This workshop involves SDSU students leading FIS sophomores through a series of sports activities. These range from relays with hula hoops to students working themselves out of a human knot.

Physical Education Teacher Education (PETE) Workshop. This workshop covers the steps necessary to become a PE teacher or a high school coach. SDSU students, preparing to be teachers, lead FIS sophomores in some physical education activities they might do in a school setting.

Health Promotion Workshop. This is one of the most interactive workshops, with students checking blood pressure, testing hand-grip strength, and measuring vertical jump. Students run a lap on the track, calculating their pulse before and after their sprints.

Athletic Training Workshop. This workshop centers around rehabilitation exercises, using elastic bands, balance boards, and giant balls.

To repeat, there is a critical need for more Native professionals, trained in the fields of public recreation, teacher education, and community health, to serve both on and off reservations. The workshops described here address this need. In their post-workshop evaluations, Success Academy sophomores offer these thoughts:

> I learned that being in the health area is a full-time strenuous job. You are always caring for someone, making sure they are doing exercises right, making sure they don't get hurt, but in the end I guess it pays with money and the thought that you helped somebody walk or throw or dance. Definitely a job I might go into.

> I had a really good time talking to the coaches and students. It helped me learn about what my future career might be.

FIS students move to Wagner Hall, where the Nutrition and Food Science labs are located, for their final two workshops of the day. Both of these workshops place

FIS students in laboratory settings, doing science, with the encouragement of SDSU students and faculty. Two SDSU faculty members who organize these workshops are Native American and serve as strong positive role models for the visiting FIS students.

Empowerment has been called by Concha Delgado-Gaitan and Henry Trueba (1995: 141) a "socialization process whereby individuals internalize high self-esteem, ability to function effectively, confidence to work well, and the creation of opportunities to find access to information and resources enhancing individual or collective goals." The hands-on experiences the FIS sophomores receive in the labs, together with the opportunities provided to picture themselves as Native American scientists, are designed to increase students' feelings of self-esteem and confidence.

Nutrition and Food Science Workshop. This features a number of "learning by doing" activities, once again performed under the guidance of SDSU faculty and students. FIS sophomores work their way around stations in the Nutrition lab. At one station, they make jam to bottle and carry home. At another they compute the nutritional value of various foods displayed on plates before them.

Dietetics Workshop. Like the Nutrition workshop just described, the Dietetics workshop has changed subject matter as well as faculty presenters many times over the 11 years since it began. Presentations have included one on food that astronauts carry into space with them. Students actually taste test some of the offerings, such as freeze-dried ice cream. At another station in the lab, FIS and SDSU students together figure out how much sugar is in pop and other foods they regularly consume. Dietetics faculty talk about the wide variety of jobs that are available to their graduates in places such as hospitals, schools, and the military. FIS attendees share these thoughts on the sessions:

> I loved this workshop. It was enjoyable for me. I think I want to be a nutritionist when I get older. I loved it!

> I thought about how it would be when we go to college or even if people go to college. I think nutrition would be a fun thing to do for college.

Health and Nutrition Day ends, as do other "focus days," with meals and co-curricular activities, attended by all FIS and SDSU workshop participants. Meals have sometimes been in the Larson Commons dining room. Co-curricular activities have included attendance at basketball games, wrestling matches, and even collegiate rodeo.

But the best meals and co-curricular events so far have been those involving SDSU's student-athletes (and their coaches). As many as 60 student-athletes, representing almost all of SDSU's sports teams, come to the Frost Arena at the end of the afternoon Success Academy workshops. Garbed in Success Academy T-shirts, SDSU athletes and FIS students alike have their picture taken with South Dakota State's mascot, the Jackrabbit.

Next the entire group spreads out across the arena's seats and shares a "sack lunch" supper. The SDSU student-athletes deliberately break into small groups to better engage the Success Academy sophomores in conversation.

At the end of the meal there is a short talk on what it means to be a student-athlete at a school like SDSU, where the emphasis is on scholarship. (For many years SDSU, an NCAA Division I school, has led all divisions of women's college basketball in team grade point average.) Featured speakers include Jackrabbit volleyball coach Nanabah Allison-Brewer, the first female Native American head coach at an NCAA Division I school, and SDSU basketball star Mackenzie Casey, an enrolled member of the Oglala Sioux Tribe.

Then FIS students divide up into small groups and attend "clinics," all run by the SDSU student-athletes and their coaches. On the arena floor, FIS students are coached in basketball and volleyball skills. Upstairs on the track, other students run relays and leap hurdles. In the weight room, SDSU wrestlers lead FIS sophomores through strengthening exercises, while in the studio Jackrabbit dance team members teach routines. The action extends outside the building as well, with more activities happening on the soccer field, on the softball diamond, and at the equestrian stables.

The importance of athletics to students attending tribal schools like FIS cannot be overstated. While the collegiate sports represented at Focus on Health and Nutrition Day change from year to year, as do the student-athletes themselves, the response of the FIS students to this event has been consistently enthusiastic:

> I really liked playing volleyball and listening to that woman talk about how you could be one of the Native coaches.

> The Equestrian Center was fun. To be there and to see the horses was great. I hope I get to go again. The people there were great and had great demonstrations. Really, I had a good time here today.

> What I learned was that to be a college basketball player you have to work hard and do good in school.

> The people were very supportive. I like how they can show respect to us.

Focus on American Indian Studies Day

"Empowerment is gained from knowledge and social relations that dignify one's own history, language, and cultural traditions," McLaren (1989: 186) writes.

Native American history, language, and culture are central to the sophomore Success Academy's Focus on American Indian Studies Day.

The format of this "focus day" follows that of the other days already described—afternoon workshops, evening meals, and co-curricular events. SDSU has an American Indian Studies (AIS) minor, which includes courses in English, Lakota, Anthropology, History, Geography, Political Science, and Sociology. Faculty members from these departments, all of them part of the College of Arts and Sciences, present the "focus day" workshops with the help of SDSU students.

Each Focus on American Indian Studies Day has three workshops, and the FIS students attending rotate through all of them. Groups are small, and activities are hands-on. Faculty from the various departments that teach AIS courses take turns organizing "focus day" workshops, year by year, with the most consistent presentations coming from the English department, under the direction of Distinguished Professor Charles L. Woodard.

Writing Workshop. The workshop rotation each year organized by the English department features a Native American writer who often reads some of his or her work and then helps FIS students tell their own stories through poetry or prose. Many of these workshop presenters (such as Karen Lone Hill, Lanniko Lee, and Elden Lawrence) are members of the Oak Lake Writers' Society, a statewide group of tribal writers dedicated to strengthening Dakota, Lakota, and Nakota cultures (Oak Lake Writers 2012). FIS students comment:

> I was heavily influenced by the workshop on Native American poetry. As a writer, I found the workshop to be interesting. I enjoy poetry, especially Native American poetry.

> I liked the poetry workshop. I liked it because I like poetry, and it's very enjoyable....I actually like going to SDSU. It's very educational and fun at times.

Art Workshop. A second consistent contributor of "focus day" workshops, year after year, is the South Dakota Art Museum, located on the SDSU campus. The museum has a comprehensive collection of 20th-century Plains Indian art. The museum's director and its docents have been stalwart supporters of Success Academy, passionate about sharing the Native American collection with Native American students.

One of the best workshops in the museum was done with History Professor Joseph Brewer (Cherokee Nation of Oklahoma and affiliate of the Oglala Sioux Tribe), then AIS program coordinator. Brewer used a special exhibit, "The Art of the Basket," to explain to FIS students how many Native American nations relied on baskets not only as useful tools but also as works of art. After his talk, students did a pencil-and-paper treasure hunt, matching museum items, such as a Navajo wedding basket, with printed descriptions, such as "We can celebrate a long, successful marriage by the look and color of this basket." Students reflected:

> I learned how ancestors made baskets and how they used them for different things and in different ways....This made me think about college and opportunities I can do in my life.

> It made me think more seriously about my future. I'm thinking of being an artist and becoming a voice for my tribe. I thought that the teachers and staff were nice, kind and easy to get along with, interesting people to meet if I decide to attend SDSU. It would be a lot easier because of the kindness and respect they have for Native Americans.

Clearly, in both the Native American art and writing workshops, activities are hands-on, culture-based, and Native-led. "A ritual of empowerment is one where the educational process enables students to unearth their subjugated histories and voices," Tierney (1992: 149) says, "not so that they can assimilate into the system, but so that they will be able to challenge and change it." It is important for Native students, like those from FIS who visit SDSU, to see their histories, languages, and cultures reflected in the university's libraries, museums, and curricula. Focus on American Indian Studies Day tries to do just that.

Other Workshops. Numerous other departments and many Native scholars contribute workshops to Focus on American Indian Studies Day. For example:

- AIS Professor Valerian Three Irons (Mandan, Hidatsa, and Arikara) gives an overview of Indigenous Studies as a discipline, focusing particularly on how it is taught at SDSU.
- Sociology doctoral student Lenora Hudson (Oglala Sioux Tribe) teaches students how to do the rabbit dance, an important social dance for Native American tribes of the Northern Plains.
- History Professor Joseph Brewer talks with the sophomores about South Dakota reservations and tribal sovereignty, using maps and PowerPoint presentations.
- The SDSU Native American Club (NAC) also assists with Focus on AIS Day workshops. NAC member and Gates Millennium Scholar Valeriah Vasek (Yankton Sioux Tribe) teaches hand games to one group of FIS sophomores, while NAC adviser Ron McKinney (Choctaw Nation) gives another group a tour of SDSU's American Indian Education and Cultural Center.

Following are a few more comments from FIS sophomores, compiled from their post–AIS Day workshop evaluations:

> Today at the Success Academy was very inspirational to me because I found the true meaning of "Indigenous."…I learned a lot from this workshop today. I would like to have the opportunity to learn more about Indigenous Studies.

> Me and my classmates learned how to rabbit dance. That showed us that they really were interested in teaching us some customs we didn't know. We enjoyed that.

> It make me think about my tribe and its background and how I would like to know a lot more about my tribe and its history.

> It was cool…I liked it. It made me think about how I can improve in areas and keep my culture alive by educating myself.

Evening Meals. The NAC also hosts most of the sophomore "focus day" meals, just as it does the freshman "Fridays at State" dinners. These usually occur in the Larson Commons dining room. Like many of the workshop presenters, NAC members speak to FIS students about the importance of a college education. One of the NAC's advisers says the club's participation encourages members to be "role models" for the younger students. And another faculty member, who presents workshops and regularly attends Success Academy dinners, adds:

> One thing I've noticed is the sense of pride in the members of the SDSU Native American Club. It's obvious that they are aware of the unique role that they have in this program and appreciate what they can add to the FIS students' experience.

The importance of role models, who high school students recognize as coming from similar backgrounds as themselves, cannot be overstated (Tierney 2000: 229). For this reason, at the insistence of the Success Academy coordinator (me), the Native American Club receives an annual honorarium of about $2,700 for its service to the program. For the club, this eliminates the need for endless, noncultural fundraising projects, such as bake sales, and allows members to concentrate their efforts on what they do well, that is, getting to know high school students and encouraging them, by example, to consider higher education. This is a truly unique gift that the Native American Club generously gives to the FIS-SDSU Success Academy and one that is genuinely irreplaceable.

Co-curricular Activities. "The manner in which we empower students is based on a cultural understanding of their local contexts and how such understandings might be incorporated into the basic fabric of the institution," Tierney (2000: 221) writes. It is important for institutions such as SDSU to bring to campus performers and exhibits that reveal social practices that have constrained Native people from realizing their empowerment (Tierney 1992: 148). FIS students attend such programs regularly as part of Success Academy.

For example, Jerome Kills Small (Oglala Sioux) portrays Dr. Charles Eastman, a 19th-century Dakota physician who grappled throughout his lifetime with issues of biculturalism. Eastman, one of the earliest students to attend what was to become the Flandreau Indian School, "was keenly aware that his academic success depended on his acceptance of American civilization and the rejection of his own traditional culture" (Wright and Tierney 1991: 14).

An exhibit at the South Dakota Art Museum combines several of Yanktonai Sioux artist Oscar Howe's paintings of tribal people playing traditional games with artifacts of game pieces from the early 1900s. Howe is now recognized as a major Indian artist, yet in 1958 he was rejected from a show of Native American art at the prestigious Philbrook Museum on the grounds that his work was not "traditional Indian painting" (South Dakota Art Museum 2012). Contemporary artist Mike Marshall (Rosebud Sioux Tribe) not only talks about Howe with the FIS students; he also brings to the museum courtyard Lakota games for the FIS students to play with him. Again, the "local contexts" (Tierney 2000: 221) of this particular program are clear—and hopefully empowering—to many of the FIS students, because they themselves are Yanktonai Sioux and Rosebud Sioux. Students respond by saying:

> I had a lot of fun learning about my culture and past, about where we came from.

> This workshop has been by far the most wonderful workshop I have attended this year.

Focus on the Military Day

The fourth sophomore "focus day" relates to the military and is hosted by the Aerospace Studies (Air Force ROTC) department and the Military Science (Army ROTC) department, both under SDSU's College of Arts and Sciences. This "focus day" is organized in much the same way as the other three and was described in detail in Chapter 1.

Summing Up and Looking Ahead

This chapter addressed the issue of power, a central concern of critical theory, as it operates throughout the FIS-SDSU Success Academy program. First we looked at the "culture of power" (Tierney 1992: 152) from a macro-structural perspective.

We considered how relations of power were reformulated to be more collaborative through the development of the Success Academy partnership. Specifically we looked at relationships among Success Academy presenters and planners, that is, those responsible for organizing the program and delivering it to students. We used Tierney's framework to better understand issues of organizational adaptation, organizational voice, organizational bridges, organizational effectiveness, and organizational culture. Cummins (1993: 101) wrote that we must redefine our own roles as educators first before we attempt to empower the students we serve.

Next, Chapter 3 moved on to power issues at a more micro-interactionist level. We addressed ways that Success Academy students are empowered through their participation in four sophomore "focus days." Works on empowerment by critical theorists ranging from Freire, McLaren, and hooks to Tierney, Trueba, and Cummins guided our discussion.

Collaborative Relations of Power in a College Preparatory Program: What Works?

In reflecting on Success Academy's development during its second year, eight key points bear repeating. These points will be framed as advice to those planning to use critical theory to design innovative programs.

The first two points address power issues from a micro-interactionist perspective. In other words, what kinds of programs empower individual students of color, and by doing so, increase college access?

"Early and "Intensive" Describe the Best Programs. Success Academy begins preparing all the students at the Flandreau Indian School for college when they are in the ninth grade. By the end of their junior year, these students have spent 14 days on a university campus. Success Academy seniors come to SDSU once each week for classes. Students of color, like those in Success Academy, are heirs to a centuries-long legacy of racial discrimination and unequal access. Modest interventions and quick "fixes" do not begin to level the playing field for such students. Only through sustained and intensive effort can they be empowered to succeed in higher education. Nothing less will bring about significant gains in educational attainment for underrepresented students.

Persistence Is the Key. Similarly, when trying to design a "best in class" college preparatory program for students of color, it is important to keep the long-term perspective in mind. It took five years for the first freshman who participated in a

Success Academy workshop to begin college. It took five more years for the first Success Academy scholar who began college to graduate. It is important to recognize that the Flandreau Indian School students, who are now transitioning into their first year at university, were in the first grade when Success Academy began 12 years ago. To repeat a key idea: Persistence is in keeping with Lakota philosophy "which considers not only what is good for today and tomorrow but also what will be good for seven generations into the future" (Nichols and Nichols 1998: 41). This point needs to be effectively communicated to those who have the power to sustain or discontinue programs that benefit underrepresented students. Success Academy organizers have struggled with this issue, and it will be discussed in greater detail in the final chapter.

The next six points address power issues in college preparatory programs from a more macro-structural perspective. These points all relate to overall program design. They suggest how college access initiatives can be organized so that the "culture of power" (Tierney 1992: 152) is reformulated.

Consider Crisis an Opportunity to Do Things You Could Not Do Before. "You never want a serious crisis to go to waste," former White House Chief of Staff Rahm Emanuel once said (Seib 2008). The organizers of effective programs are keenly aware of when the timing is right for systemic change. At the time Success Academy began, the Flandreau Indian School was undergoing a much-needed comprehensive school reform, financed by a substantial federal grant. At the same time, South Dakota State University was responding to a regional directive, from the North Central Association's Higher Learning Commission, to improve its diversity efforts. Federal and regional structures at the macro level converged in ways that produced systemic change at a more micro level: Success Academy was born. Would-be collaborators should be keenly aware of shifts in political climates surrounding their institutions. It is important to recognize when a convergence of interests occurs, and capitalize on it.

Be Willing to Take Your Show on the Road. Especially if that road leads to someone else's turf. Geography is of the essence. Face-to-face contact is crucial. Collaborators need to move easily back and forth often between each others' institutions. While most of the college preparatory efforts for Success Academy students actually occur on the university campus, SDSU faculty and staff avail themselves of every invitation offered to travel to FIS and engage with students there. The Success Academy steering committee, made up of administrators, faculty, and staff from both FIS and SDSU, meets alternately in Brookings and in Flandreau. The committee has met in well-equipped Student Union rooms with Aramark-catered meals, but it has also met in FIS classrooms with sack lunches. Programs like Success Academy must challenge locations of power. University educators generally have more flexible timetables and larger travel budgets. They must be willing to literally "go the extra mile" to meet on the campuses of the K–12 faculty and students with whom they work.

It Pays to Have (or Cultivate) Friends in High Places. The importance of having people in power backing programs that benefit students of color cannot be overestimated. Success Academy began in SDSU's College of Engineering with supportive deans willing to invest heavily in the fledgling program. The program grew slowly, year by year, eventually serving all 250 Flandreau Indian School students and involving all six South Dakota State University colleges. The deans of those six colleges became believers in the program, supporting it not only with their faculties' time but also with substantial budget contributions. As the program continued to grow, SDSU's central administration covered an increasingly larger share of the expenses. To repeat, garnering administrative support for diversity initiatives is fundamental. Programs that benefit students of color and the institutions they attend must be recognized as legitimate equity endeavors. This happens only when support comes from those with power.

Collaboration Works. A willingness to share power—between individuals, among institutions, and, most importantly, across races—benefits both the more powerful and the less powerful. It is important to note that, in the case of FIS-SDSU Success Academy, the initial request for collaboration came from a federal Indian boarding school to a predominantly white university. Soon afterward a Success Academy steering committee was formed with balanced numbers of Indian school and state university faculty and of Indians and non-Indians. Steering committee decisions have always been made by consensus. The Success Academy experience has shown that when individuals have input into designing a program, they become stakeholders committed to making that program work (Wagner 1998: 77).

Money Matters. Most programs serving students of color begin with funding from external grants, funding that universities are expected to assume once the grants expire. Those few programs that do survive beyond the expiration of their initial grants are those that have the backing of powerful people (for examples, see Colyar 2006; Vergara and Hightower 2006). Powerful people are those who control a significant share of the resources at their institutions and can, when they choose, direct those resources toward programs that benefit underrepresented students. Success

Academy started small and built slowly. Over time, funding for Success Academy became incorporated into various university budgets—those of the College of Engineering, of other colleges, and of the central administration. A university's commitment to diversity can be judged by the willingness of its leaders to invest in the education of students of color.

Committed Educators Matter, Too. FIS-SDSU Success Academy is a relatively low-budget effort when the number of American Indian students served and the intensity of its college preparatory efforts are taken into consideration. Success Academy began as a grassroots undertaking and in a decade grew into a coordinated, university-wide effort involving all of the academic colleges and most of the student affairs offices at SDSU. About 300 administrators, faculty, and staff from throughout the university have donated their time, effort, and skills, year after year, to sustain and grow Success Academy. Many of these individuals were already committed to Native American outreach before the start of Success Academy. Others became passionate through their engagement with the program. Teaching styles were transformed and research agendas reshaped because of individuals' experiences with Success Academy. The power of social networking, or "bridging capital" as Putnam (2000: 22) calls it, should not be underestimated. As one professor notes, because of Success Academy, "I now recognize an infrastructure within the university supportive of diversity, especially as it relates to Native American students and issues."

My most important work, as Success Academy coordinator, is two-fold. First, it is to ensure that my colleagues' experiences with our program are both rewarding and rewarded. Second, it is to express my personal gratitude, and that of the university, to them for their generous service.

Tierney (1993a: 23) says, and I agree, that universities should be communities of brotherly love and service to humanity, based on the principle of "agape" or "selfless love." It is incumbent upon those who lead equity endeavors like Success Academy to work toward this goal.

Martin Luther King Jr. (1958: 105) writes that "agape" is "love in action. Agape is love seeking to preserve and create community. It is insistence on community even when one seeks to break it. Agape is a willingness to sacrifice in the interest of mutuality."

Mutuality of need by two academic communities, SDSU and FIS, is truly the scaffolding upon which the Success Academy program rests. Betty Belkham, superintendent at the Flandreau Indian School, says that FIS students, because they go to an all–American Indian high school, would not be truly prepared to enter the diverse world that awaits them after graduation without a program like Success Academy. The same holds true for South Dakota State University students, who attend an overwhelmingly white university, an environment far different from the one in which most will work as college graduates.

Clearly there is a mutuality of need, shared by the Flandreau Indian School and South Dakota State University, that unites them in the Success Academy partnership. This mutuality of need leads to what critical theorist Henry A. Giroux (1988) calls "border crossings." "Border crossings," together with the junior-year Success Academy program, will be explained in detail in Chapter 4.

4

Border Crossing and Juniors "Preparing for College, Native-Style!"

The concept of "border crossing" is best explained by critical theorist Henry A. Giroux (1988: 166):

> A student must engage knowledge as a border-crosser, as a person moving in and out of borders constructed around coordinates of difference and *power*. These are not only physical borders, they are cultural borders historically constructed and socially organized within maps of rules and regulations that limit and enable particular *identities*, individual capacities, and social forms. In this case, students cross over into borders of meaning, maps of knowledge, social relations, and values that are increasingly being negotiated and rewritten as the codes and regulations which organize them become *destabilized and reshaped*.

In Giroux's words we find all three issues addressed in the first three chapters of this book—power, identity, and systemic change. When Giroux uses words such as "destabilized" and "reshaped" to describe organizations, he is talking about systemic change.

Certainly the Flandreau Indian School students who participate in Success Academy at South Dakota State University are border-crossers. Every time they visit SDSU, they bravely cross borders from a small, all-Indian, closed-campus high school into a large, overwhelmingly white, mainstream university.

In discussing border crossing by students, Giroux means much more than that students should be able to understand their own cultures and also exist in others. Instead he is suggesting, just like William G. Tierney (1992: 41), that "organizations need to be constructed where minority students' lives are celebrated and affirmed throughout the culture of the institution." In that sense border crossing becomes a two-way street, a transformative activity engaged in by myriad individuals throughout the university.

In the context of Success Academy, this means that SDSU administrators, faculty, and staff (for the most part non-Native) are also called on to be border-crossers. In crossing borders, these non-Native adults who work with Native students have routinely encountered "numerous circumstances, experiences and perspectives that deviated from their own expectations and assumptions" (King 2004: 134). And, in many cases, this has resulted in Success Academy planners and presenters doing as Giroux (1988: 177) suggests and critically examining "the historically and socially constructed forms by which they live." Crossing ethnic and economic borders and forming caring relationships across those borders ultimately change one's perspective in fundamental ways. Again, in the context of Success Academy, this increases the capacity of SDSU to better educate both its Native and its non-Native students.

This chapter will discuss the junior year of Success Academy from the perspective of four key players, people who, in fact, routinely cross borders, week after week and year after year, to make the program work. They are:

- Native professionals (who come to campus as presenters),
- "Academic parents,"
- Student affairs staff, and
- Faculty members.

To repeat, all of these individuals, together with the students they serve, are border-crossers in the junior-year Success Academy program. How this border crossing occurs and the changes that result from it—at both the micro level (that of the individual) and at the macro level (that of the institution)—will be explained in this chapter.

We begin, however, with two brief overview sections. The first is on the actual operation of the junior-year FIS-SDSU Success Academy. This might be thought of as the "praxis" overview. The second is on the concepts of borderlands and border crossing. This might be thought of as the "theoretical" overview.

Praxis Overview: Success Academy's Junior Year

The junior Success Academy program began during the 2002–2003 academic year. It began just like the freshman- and sophomore-year Success Academies. We had another cohort of students, in this case, rising sophomores, who were already engaged in preparing for college. We needed to grow our Success Academy program to help them do that.

During the 2002–2003 and 2003–2004 academic years all the juniors at the Flandreau Indian School (about 75) participated in the program. After that, at the request of FIS administrators, the program began serving only those students who considered themselves bound for postsecondary education of some kind (tribal college, technical school, university, etc.). Juniors apply for admission to Success Academy, and FIS counselors select participants based on grade point average, class rank, and enrollment in advanced science and math classes. These criteria are considered by the counselors to be indications of students' seriousness about higher education.

About 25 FIS juniors come to SDSU on four Wednesdays during the spring semester. The school's two counselors, both Native, accompany the students. Most of the junior Success Academy sessions are conducted in rooms scattered throughout the University Student Union, one of the campus's newest and glitziest venues.

The junior-year program is titled "Preparing for College, Native-Style!" Developing the curriculum that first year, we relied heavily on materials produced by the American Indian College Fund (1999). The themes for the four sessions are Making the Decision to Attend College, Paying for a College Education, Choosing Your Path, and So What's Next? In keeping with "lessons learned" from freshman- and sophomore-year Success Academy, every Wednesday workshop is hands-on and culture-based.

Freshman and sophomore Success Academies create interest in and excitement about college by exposing students to a wide range of academic disciplines. Junior Success Academy channels that interest and excitement into action. American Indian professionals from across the country and student affairs staff from SDSU work with the FIS juniors. Week by week, students learn how to turn their college dreams into realities, without abandoning their Native cultures.

The true strength of junior Success Academy is in the new partners who engaged with those of us already involved in the program during its first two years. These individuals, and their interactions with students, that is, border crossing, are the focus of this chapter.

Theoretical Overview: Borderlands and Border Crossing

Anthropologist Renato Rosaldo (1989) explains that an individual's life is constantly crisscrossing with the lives of people from various gender, age, class, and ethnic backgrounds. Because in a multicultural society ethnic groups are inextricably interconnected with each other, everyday life is lived out in what Rosaldo (1989: 207–208) calls "borderlands." Schools, such as FIS and SDSU, can easily be seen as "borderlands" because they are sites where people of diverse gender, age, class, and ethnic backgrounds come together and influence each other (Montecinos 1995: 294).

A compelling description of borderlands and border crossing is provided by poet and novelist Gloria Anzaldúa (1987):

> Borders are set up to define the places that are safe and unsafe, to distinguish *us* from *them*. A border is a dividing line, a narrow strip along a steep edge. A borderland is a vague and undetermined place created by the emotional residue of an unnatural boundary. It is in a constant state of transition. The prohibited and forbidden are its inhabitants. (3)

At one level Anzaldúa is talking about her life spent navigating the physical borders between Texas and Mexico. For American Indians, this experience might be similar to moving onto and off of a reservation. At a more important level, though, Anzaldúa is talking about her experience growing up between two cultures. She points out that crossing borders, where cultural beliefs conflict, leads to "mental and emotional states of perplexity" (Anzaldúa 1987: 78). Crossing borders forces one to reshape one's mental borders and to adopt new thought processes. Crossing borders requires moving away from set patterns and toward more holistic perspectives that include rather than exclude.

Critical theorists in education, like Giroux (1992: 168), have adopted Anzaldúa's border-crossing metaphor in the following way. We know that schools, both K–12 and postsecondary as they currently exist, support unequal systems of power. Schools do this by privileging certain forms of knowledge over others. This happens, for example, when only Eurocentric histories are taught or when little boys are called on more than little girls (Wink 2000: 55). The process of crossing borders of knowledge—borders established around the axes of race, class, and gender—requires us to question our existing patterns of thought. When we do, we enter into borderlands. "Borderlands should be seen as sites for both critical analysis and as a potential source of experimentation, creativity, and possibility," Giroux (1992: 34) explains.

Border-Crossers and Junior-Year Success Academy

As useful as the concept of border crossing is, concrete descriptions of it in the educational literature are limited (Hayes and Cuban 1997). Yet as we look at Success Academy, we see that our program, particularly in its junior year, offers numerous examples of border crossing—by Native professionals, by "academic parents," by student affairs staff, and by faculty members. These will be explained in some detail in the remainder of the chapter.

Native Professionals as Border-Crossers

The junior-year Success Academy program is called "Preparing for College, Native-Style!" and as the name suggests, the four-week program is led by American Indian professionals and scholars from across the country.

Week One: Making the Decision to Attend College. The following individuals have been among the presenters of first-week programs for Success Academy juniors: Molly Springer (Cherokee Nation of Oklahoma), then coordinator of American Indian Student Support Services at The Ohio State University; Charlotte E. Davidson (Navajo, Mandan, Hidatsa, and Arikara), then a doctoral student at the University of Illinois; and Ashley Tsosie-Mahieu (Navajo), a doctoral student at the University of Arizona. Topics addressed during the "Making the Decision to Attend College" session include the following:

- A sampling of college programs nationwide, designed to foster Native student success,
- A one-year plan for Native American students applying for college, and
- Thinking about college from the viewpoint of a Native student.

One of the Native presenters reflects on her experience with Success Academy students:

> The way I started my presentation was to make very clear about who I was in relation to them. What that meant for me was to introduce myself in my language, identifying the clans that I come from. Growing up primarily on the _____ reservation, that is how I've become accustomed to introducing myself, so when I introduce myself to students I would say that is how we would establish kinship ties. That is how we break down this hierarchy that often exists between students and teachers or students and adults. I wanted to let them know I am coming to them not necessarily as a scholar, but as a person who sat in those very same seats they were sitting in.

Clearly, instances of border crossing are woven throughout the speaker's remarks. It is apparent that she works hard to cross the borders that exist between herself and the students, borders created by difference in age and in education. She continues:

> I tell them what I am offering here is based on what I learned from my own shortcomings, my own mistakes made as a student going through the college experience. Here is what I have to offer to you in regard to navigating new campus environments, environments of higher learning that are often not indigenous....These programs like Success Academy are important. They give Native students exposure to what it is like to be a student, taking college classes. Listening to presenters talk about what helped them survive, orating a survival guide....I would like my children to be part of a program like this. It would help them learn a new language, a new way of being.

This Native American scholar calls her own experience with higher education "a very muddy journey." Her work with the Success Academy juniors, in large part, is done to "facilitate border crossing" (Brandt 2008: 825) that the students have yet to experience. As Carol B. Brandt (2008: 841) explains, for indigenous students attending non-indigenous universities, border crossing is not without "risks and dangers to (one's) identity as an American Indian."

Affirming one's identity while preparing for college is emphasized throughout the first day of junior Success Academy, just as it is through the remainder of the program. During the final afternoon session, students hear a presentation on "Preparing Your College Admission Essay, Native-Style." Sample essays, like one that starts this way, are distributed as illustrations:

> "Kaya poyoh kiskiskinohnamakosi." I still hear my grandmother's words to my mother and now my mother repeats those words to me. In Cree they translate to "don't quit, finish your learning and continue to teach by modeling." My grandmother is gone now, but her voice and her message still ring in my ears. This essay will focus on the effect of those words, which continue to have a profound effect on my personal development as a young native Cree woman.

Essay writing, Native-style, is one strategy that American Indian students can employ to negotiate the borders between family and school cultures. "It appears that, in our culture, many adolescents are left to navigate transitions without direct assistance from persons in any of their contexts (family, peer or school)," write Patricia Phelan, Ann Locke Davidson, and Hanh Thanh Cao (1991: 224). Success Academy tries to address this need. As one of Success Academy's Native American presenters remarks:

> I wanted to give examples of how the students can be tribal architects of their personal statements. The infusion of their culture can only add to these personal statements....I want to

let them know that when you forefront that, that is not something to be ashamed of, but that is something that is going to get the readers' attention, to let them know who you are, where you come from, what you stand for, how this educational pathway is going to advance what you know and what you are going to be able to bring back to your community.

Success Academy students try their hands at writing personal statements. These essays are read later by the FIS counselors and other Success Academy staff, in part to determine which students will be formally accepted into the junior-year program during week two.

Academic Parents as Border-Crossers

Individuals who we call "academic parents" enter the junior-year Success Academy program during week two. Academic parents are retired SDSU faculty (and some current faculty and community volunteers), each individual paired with one FIS junior. Academic parents have lunch with the juniors week by week and discuss with them their plans for higher education. Academic parents, as older individuals, play a critical role for FIS juniors, all of them attending boarding school and all of them geographically far removed from their families for months at a time.

Youth need opportunities to interact with elders. This is particularly important for American Indian youth. In American Indian culture elders are men or women, older than others in the family and community, who are widely recognized and highly respected for their wisdom and spiritual leadership. As Simon Looking Elk of the Pine Ridge Reservation explains (Clark and Sherman 2011):

> Elders are often known for being the kind of people who have paid attention, gaining knowledge and wisdom from life—during their childhood they watched and listened carefully to ceremonies and traditions, and as youth, they paid attention to the ways the elders in their communities behaved. For it is by the way they live that elders teach younger tribe members about the tribe's culture and traditional ways of life. (14)

The best academic parents in the Success Academy program are those who have throughout their careers "paid attention" to the culture of the academy and, to borrow from Tierney (1992), are willing to demystify this culture for indigenous students. This happens during Success Academy when older academics cross borders to meet younger scholars—and when lasting relationships are formed. As one academic parent says:

> I had taught on college campuses for 30 years, so I knew the ins and outs of campus life. I had advised so many freshmen students over the years that I knew what worked well and what didn't. I saw my role as answering questions, smoothing things along for these young

people and at the same time making sure I constantly encouraged them to go to college....Success Academy gives students an idea of what a college professor is. They take a look at us and see that we are okay, that we are not mean, and we don't talk down to them. They see us as human beings so they get an idea of what it's like to work with a college professor.

SDSU academic parents meet FIS juniors for the first time at a formal awards luncheon, arranged in the students' honor, during week two. A luncheon address is given each year by a prominent Native American leader, such as Lisa Lone Fight (Mandan, Hidatsa, and Arikara Nation), the director of the Wind River (Wyoming) Native Science Field Center. After the speech, each academic parent presents his or her student with a framed certificate, recognizing acceptance into the junior-year program.

As mentioned earlier, Success Academy juniors write admissions essays during week one that describe why they want to participate in the program. While selection is not extremely competitive (with most applicants chosen to participate), the process gives students a sense of accomplishment, along with the experience of writing culture-based college essays.

The relationships academic parents establish with junior students begin at the awards luncheon, but they extend throughout the school year, into the next, and sometimes beyond that. As one academic parent reflects:

> Academic parents can do so much for the young people, as much as the students want. When we go around to departments [students visit the academic departments in which they intend to major during week four], when the student is being told what it takes to major in such and such, sometimes the student is so intimidated by a fast-talking professor, operating in kind of a public relations mode. So the kid is just overwhelmed and doesn't get any questions asked. One of the roles we play is to make sure all the information gets to the student. The fact that we know our way around the university, we can bring that to the student. Also if the student decides to come to SDSU, we're there if they have any questions or problems. Since we're retired, we have more time. All those things help the student feel more comfortable with the university.

Giroux (in Torres 1998: 149) says, "Intellectuals have got to make some kind of connection outside the university. Intellectuals need to cross borders in order to live and learn with others, to get a sense of what the struggles are that we teach about." Clearly, faculty members who serve as academic parents do cross "borders of identity" (Hayes and Cuban 1997: 76) through the Success Academy program. Academic parents learn from—as well as teach to—their Native students. As one academic parent, who has been retired since 2004, explains:

Success Academy brought me back in touch with Native students on an even more personal level than when I was teaching. Then the FIS students would talk to you about their lives, their parents. They had a lot of assumptions about themselves because of the things they were told about themselves. At one time FIS had a reputation for being a place where they sent the bad kids.…Kids would say things like, "I had to come here because I was getting out of hand and my parents couldn't handle me anymore." They just said it matter-of-factly, "That's just who I am." When I came back to work with FIS and Success Academy I didn't know if anything had changed. But now I hear them saying, "I'm going to college and I don't care what happens. I know what I want to do. Even if my parents don't support it, I'm going to college."

Besides meeting their academic parents during week two of Success Academy, the juniors continue on with the "Preparing for College, Native-Style!" curriculum begun during week one. Week two's topic is "Paying for a College Education."

Week Two: Paying for a College Education. The largest misconceptions that FIS students bring into the Success Academy program concern questions of paying for a college education. Almost universally, Success Academy juniors overestimate the cost of college and underestimate the amount of financial aid available. With these beliefs, higher education seems unattainable, and college preparation seems unnecessary.

Consequently, addressing the issue of paying for a college education by necessity comes early in the junior-year program. Michelle Pasena (San Felipe/Hopi), formerly the coordinator of outreach services at the American Indian Graduate Center, has tackled this topic for Success Academy for a number of years. Her organization, the AIGC, since its founding in 1969, has provided more than 15,000 graduate fellowships for American Indians (American Indian Graduate Center 2011). The AIGC also helps administer the Gates Millennium Scholars program, which generously funds undergraduate education for high-achieving minority students, including American Indians.

Pasena's presentation focuses on the steps students need to take during high school that will allow them to submit competitive scholarship applications for college. She talks about the importance, first and foremost, of preparing academically. She then addresses the need to develop leadership skills, both at home and at school. She points out that those who read scholarship essays think activities such as helping with childcare or participating in ceremonies are just as important as—or more important than—leading the cheer squad or winning debate awards.

Mentioning summer camps, work experiences, and internships can also positively influence judges who award scholarships. Pasena says these are opportunities that juniors can seek out while still in high school.

Finally Pasena emphasizes what she calls "community connections—finding the road back home." This means being able to explain how the pursuit of post-secondary education will benefit one's tribe or American Indians generally.

Student Affairs Staff as Border-Crossers

When the junior Success Academy began during the 2002–2003 academic year, we added another cohort of FIS students, students who had already been engaged with our college preparatory program for the past two years and who had vastly different needs than our freshmen and sophomores. Consequently, we, as organizers, had to reach out to university colleagues from the student affairs side of SDSU for assistance with programming. Their response was quick and enthusiastic. Professional staff from offices ranging from Native American Student Advising to Financial Aid and from Admissions to Multicultural Affairs became engaged in Success Academy as planners and presenters. They began having border-crossing experiences similar to those that others of us had undergone during the previous two years.

Critical educator Maxine Greene (1995) describes well what we sometimes experience as SDSU staff when we work with FIS students:

> In the presence of a work from the border, let us say, from a place outside the reach of my experience until I came in contact with the work, I am plunged into all kinds of reconceiving and revisualizing. I find myself moving from discovery to discovery; I find myself revising, and now and then renewing, the terms of my life. (4–5)

Student affairs professionals are key resources for students moving from high school into college. Personally knowing individuals in university offices such as Financial Aid and Admissions helps students smoothly cross "institutional borders" (Hayes and Cuban 1997: 76).

But to work most effectively with tribal people, student affairs staff and others "need to come to grips with how the cultures of individuals frame their understandings of the world" (Tierney 1992: 164). Success Academy provides opportunities to better understand the cultures of individuals different from ourselves. As one student affairs staffer, who became a regular Success Academy presenter, explains:

> Thinking back to my first year, when I was asked to do Success Academy, I was really nervous. Just growing up in South Dakota, I didn't have that much experience specifically with having any Native students in my classes, or Native friends, or really even knowing anybody Native. I wasn't exposed to different populations. Of course, I knew it was a really

important part of South Dakota heritage and culture. You learn that in school. But you don't know really what it's all about until you meet some of the people.

This individual went on to present many Success Academy programs after her first year. She continues on with her story:

As things went along I was really happy I could attend all the Success Academy sessions, regardless as to whether I was a presenter or not. Just because that way I got to hear all sorts of perspectives. I think that the Native speakers we had come in were the ones that really helped me understand this population a little more....And after hearing all the trials and tribulations the students had gone through, I was amazed at how well they were doing. I got excited about that. As the years went on, I got less and less nervous and more and more comfortable.

The student affairs staff member recalls the many students she has worked with during the past five years, students who she first knew as Success Academy juniors and later as SDSU freshmen:

We had a lot of fun in the program. We joked around a lot. That was pretty cool....And there were a lot of different students that I thought, that student is really going to do some-thing....[She names one particular student.] He ended up on campus, and he always comes up and says "hi." He remembers me, and I remember him. That is so fun. He'll say, "Hi, _____, how's it going?"

Knowing key people in university offices is beneficial to incoming college fresh-men. And, to repeat, it is essential that Anglo staffers know how to interact with Indian students. Many important lessons have been learned from SDSU staff par-ticipation in junior-year Success Academy, and not all of them have been easy.

One student affairs staff member, who was a Success Academy presenter, reflects on a presentation by educator Marin Webster Denning (Oneida Tribe of Wisconsin Indians). Denning showed a video about a vicious treaty rights dispute that pitted white fishermen against American Indians. The SDSU staff member recalls:

The things he was saying and the way he was presenting, it was hard for me to take. I didn't know how to come back from that. I didn't know how to react to that while I was in the room with the students. There were some hard things like that that culturally just kind of shocked you. That was his experience he was sharing, his perceptions. Things like that were hard.

Tierney (1993a: 10–11) reminds us that "our struggle is constantly to cross these borders and exist in tolerable discomfort with one another as we confront

94 | Success Academy

difference." Border crossing in junior-year Success Academy is sometimes difficult but also rewarding for those willing to persist beyond their initial discomfort. As a student affairs staffer who has worked with junior Success Academy for a number of years concludes:

> I learned more from the students than I've ever taught them. We have a lot here on campus. We know a lot, and we need to share that. I think that is a responsibility for people like me on campus. I have learned a lot from Success Academy.

Week Three: Choosing Your Path. Over the years, the organization of junior Success Academy has changed, with certain topics moving from one week to another as we searched for the best fit. What follows are some of the "Choosing Your Path" sessions, led mainly by student affairs staff and usually occurring during week three.

- Staff from the First Year Advising Center meet with juniors in a university computer lab and introduce them to "Choices Planner" software (Bridges Transitions 2011). Students explore their interests, values, and skills and how these might influence their choice of a college major. Also discussed during this session are the differences between "majors" and "careers."
- The minority recruiter distributes SDSU catalogs and teaches students how to use them. Students select one major and, following a set of structured questions, learn all they can about it.
- Admissions counselors talk about what the juniors should look for when choosing colleges and majors—and what schools will be looking for in them. Admissions criteria such as ACT scores, class rankings, and grade point averages are covered. At the end of the day a "College Bowl" competition, with two teams going head to head, tests the students' knowledge of the application process.
- The financial aid director addresses topics related to paying for a college education—the Free Application for Federal Student Aid (FAFSA), work study, tribal assistance, grants, and loans.
- SDSU student ambassadors take FIS juniors on tours of the campus. Important stops are the university's American Indian Education and Cultural Center and the adjacent Tiospaye Lodge. The tour groups also visit residence hall rooms, always of great interest to students who themselves live in dormitories at FIS.

Success Academy lunches for the juniors and their academic parents are planned to further familiarize students with the SDSU campus and its eating venues. During week one students get university meal cards and go through the line in the Union Marketplace. They then bring their trays into a meeting room for a "working lunch" with the Native American student adviser.

During week two, FIS students and academic parents lunch in the university's Campanile Room, one of the campus's more formal dining rooms. Week three features a hotdog and hamburger cookout in the city's Hillcrest Park. During week four pizza and pop are served in the Tompkins Alumni Center.

Each Success Academy session is organized so that juniors experience a day in the life of a college student—in classrooms and dormitories, on campus and off, with professionals and academics, having fun and working hard. The juniors carry with them notebooks, personalized with their names and stocked with pens and paper. Presenters' handouts and students' notes are collected in the notebooks week by week. The notebooks then become permanent "toolkits" for the students to use as they move from high school to postsecondary education.

Faculty Members as Border-Crossers

Much has already been said in earlier chapters about border crossing by SDSU faculty. The border-crossing experiences of the freshman and sophomore presenters are similar to those of faculty members who interact with the Success Academy juniors.

In working with Native students, Success Academy faculty encounter "cultural borders" (Hayes and Cuban 1997: 76), giving them opportunities to develop new perspectives on their own values and practices. Similarly students who participate in Success Academy also run into numerous circumstances that deviate from their own expectations and assumptions. John T. King (2004: 134) calls this kind of border crossing—by faculty, by students, and by others—"a process of defamiliarization." By developing relationships with others different from ourselves we make the familiar strange, and the strange familiar. Put another way, we find ourselves "reconceiving," "revisualizing," and "revising" what we once thought we knew (Greene 1995: 4–5). In the process we learn how to respect ethnic identities and honor cultural differences (Trueba and Zou 1994: 5). How border crossing by SDSU faculty (and FIS juniors) occurs during week four of the program will be further explained in the next section.

Week Four: So What's Next? Weeks one, two, and three of the junior-year program all prepare students for week four, when they visit academic departments of interest to them. Based on their earlier work with the "Choices Planner" software, students selected departments in which they might choose to major. Admissions staffers taught the students how to use the SDSU catalog to research their potential majors. A handout titled "Questions to Ask in Your College Search" was distributed. For homework the juniors developed lists of questions about the academic disciplines of interest to them and about the careers open to students majoring in these areas. In the meantime, Admissions counselors were scheduling one-on-one departmental visits for the students.

Week four begins with a role-playing session involving an Admissions staffer and a faculty member. Together they enact for the juniors, first the way not to conduct oneself during a departmental visit. The Admissions staffer "plays" the prospective student—checking his cell phone, wearing earbuds, asking how many members of the opposite sex are studying in the faculty member's department. Usually this draws lots of laughs. Next the pair demonstrates a better way for the departmental visit to proceed. After each performance, the juniors are asked to identify behaviors that either facilitate or hamper the interview.

Next the juniors and their academic parents team up. They receive their "assignments," that is, they are given cards identifying the professors with whom they will be visiting and the locations of their offices. Students and parents fan out across campus, collectively visiting many different departments and exploring numerous college majors. Most often the meetings arranged for the FIS juniors involve SDSU department heads or senior faculty. In the early years, many of these individuals had little previous contact with Success Academy students.

"Pay attention. Be astonished. Tell about it." These "instructions for living a life," by poet Mary Oliver (2008: 37), capture the spirit of our final day with the Success Academy juniors. As we send them off across campus, we know they will be meeting faculty who, in some cases, will mentor them through their last year of high school, their first year of college, and beyond. Week four of junior Success Academy, occurring as it usually does in April, is one remaining opportunity for border crossing.

Juniors do "pay attention" during their departmental visits. These visits are arranged for our Success Academy students just as they are for all prospective students and their parents, for the purpose of gathering information on majors and careers. Far more than that, however, is generally shared during visits, including information about the departments themselves and about the faculty who teach there.

FIS students are sometimes "astonished" by what SDSU faculty members share with them. FIS students readily see themselves as border-crossers, attending an all-Indian boarding school and coming, week after week, to an overwhelmingly white university. But FIS juniors are often surprised to learn that the SDSU faculty with whom they meet have had border-crossing experiences, too.

For example, in the Health and Nutritional Sciences department, Professor Padmanaban Krishnan tells about being one of 20 SDSU faculty members participating in a collaborative research project with the Flandreau Santee Sioux tribe. The project's goal is to enhance the role of bison in local economic development and to increase the consumption of bison meat among tribal members. In Krishnan's lab, FIS students and cooks learn about bison meat preparation. "Bison, after all, is a symbolic animal," Krishnan says. "It's more than just food, it's also a part of spirituality" (Johnson 2012: 11).

In the Journalism department, Professor Richard Lee talks about his advanced reporting, editing, and photography students making trips to South Dakota's Indian reservations each spring. Journalism students and faculty, both Indian and non-Indian, then produce a tabloid newspaper exploring an issue of importance to the state's Native peoples. "We started reporting on reservations 20 years ago, before the FIS students were born," he says with a smile. "In our department we have physically taken hundreds of students across borders in order for them to better understand and report on those on the other side."

In the Music department, the junior visiting with Professor David Reynolds learns about his long and deep interest in Native American music. While studying at the University of Kansas, Reynolds took a class on Native American music at the nearby Haskell Indian Nations University. He then went on to teach Native American music at Fort Peck Community College and at Salish Kootenai College, both tribal colleges in Montana. Reynolds has been involved with Success Academy for many years, regularly organizing sophomore workshops on Native music and other topics related to his department. "Often both non-Native and Native people are not aware of how broad and diverse the musical traditions of Native peoples across North America are," Reynolds says. "It's exciting for me to work with someone who, for example, knows the Sioux grass dances, and then introduce them to the music of the Iroquois or the Navajo."

When the departmental visits are finished, the FIS juniors, together with their academic parents, return to the Tompkins Alumni Center for a pizza and pop lunch. Time is devoted to "telling about it," "it" being information gathered over the course of the morning. As these students report:

I learned a lot. What I thought I wanted to major in was not what I hoped for. Just knowing that, I'll be ready for what there is out there. I have a lot to think about.

I learned that you don't have to have your decision on majors right after you graduate. I also learned that you could change your major whenever you want, until you find one that is suitable for you. This really helped me because I was very unsure and worried about what major I was truly interested in.

While at the sessions I was able to find exactly what I am going to major in. The actual visit to see a professor was very exciting. It helped me to see what I should be prepared for. Every time I come back to FIS from SDSU I feel I have achieved something.

After lunch, juniors complete end-of-year evaluations. Then they hear about what lies ahead for them in the senior-year Success Academy program.

The day ends with a postcard exchange between the juniors and their academic parents. Each person addresses a blank, pre-stamped card and then exchanges it with his or her partner. This allows juniors and parents to keep in touch during the summer months. A Success Academy reunion dinner the following fall gives everyone a chance to reconnect once school is back in session.

Summing Up and Looking Ahead

Chapter 4 examined the phenomenon of border crossing, explained most thoroughly in the critical education literature by Henry A. Giroux (1992). Giroux (1988: 166) says that borders delineate not just regions on a map but also "particular identities, individual capacities, and social forms." When individuals cross borders, they encounter experiences that deviate from their expectations. They are forced to confront the limits of their own perspectives.

Border crossers involved with K–12 and higher education are compelled to think about the structure of schooling and their own roles in structures that allow inequalities to exist. Sometimes, through deliberate efforts such as Success Academy, these reflections on difference and power in schools can lead to social change.

Border Crossing in a College Preparatory Program: What Works?

The border-crossing metaphor is a powerful tool for rethinking ways to open access to higher education for those previously excluded. The border-crossing metaphor allows us to identify boundaries that may both constrain and enable students of color as they prepare for college. As critical ethnographer Enrique (Henry) T. Trueba (1999) reminds us:

> Entering someone else's culture is somewhat comparable to the immigration experience without the risks and the mourning that immigrants have to suffer....Educators who are serious about their praxis and committed to a pedagogy of hope must be prepared to take a long and hazardous psychological trip into lands and minds unknown before. (160–161)

Creating opportunities for border crossing in college preparatory programs is essential. The organizers of junior-year Success Academy, based on their experiences, would recommend that this be accomplished in the following four ways.

Involve Native Professionals as Border-Crossers. These individuals are the most experienced border-crossers engaged in our program. Being able to involve presenters like these in programming, week after week and year after year, is a gift to an overwhelmingly white university like ours. Without them, we would not have many people willing to share with Native students their personal experiences, experiences of being border-crossers, and, in the words of one presenter, experiences of "surviving." Native professionals facilitate border crossing, as it relates to higher education, for Native students who have not yet experienced it. How to negotiate borders without leaving one's identity on the other side is a critical part of the message.

It is important to note that all of the young Native professionals who worked with the Success Academy juniors over the years are now nationally recognized leaders in American Indian education. We hope their involvement with Success Academy played at least a small part in their empowerment as Native educators. As one of the presenters explains:

> After my first experience of being invited here I thought, wow, how far I have come. I'm not the type of individual who pats myself on the back, but it really made me re-see myself as a bicultural being. I'm a Native person, the ways I bring are based on my own tribal epistemologies. I have used that to survive the institutional experience. I now see these are the very things we have used culturally to survive as well.

To repeat, the Native professionals who graciously come to our university and help with Success Academy fulfill a gigantic need that would otherwise go unmet. They bring their own experiences with border crossing to our Native students who, in turn, learn from them. As one FIS student says, "It's different when you listen to a Native person." And as one Native presenter, reflecting on her Success Academy involvement, adds, "It gives students something to aspire toward, that this can be done, that people like me can do this."

Involve Academic Parents as Border-Crossers. The retired faculty and other older individuals who serve as academic parents also bring to our program an element that would otherwise be missing. For Native students attending boarding school, academic parents in part fill the role of elders with whom the juniors would otherwise be interacting in their own tribal communities. The best relationships that develop are lasting ones, so activities such as postcard exchanges and reunion dinners are important in sustaining the partnerships forged during junior Success Academy.

The function of the academic parents is like that of the Native professionals. Both are called on to assist students with the border crossing necessary to successfully navigate through alien university environments. But the academic parents do this in a different way. Having been long involved with higher education, the academic parents are "insiders." If undertaking college is a journey, then the academic parents hold the guidebook. In the words of one academic parent, "We know our way around." Mehan et al. (1996: 214) call people such as academic parents "institutionally well placed adults who either directly or indirectly provide institutional resources and opportunities." Academic parents provide "social capital" (Bourdieu 1986) to students who might not otherwise have access to it.

The academic parents would not continue to be involved with the program year after year without finding their own experiences with border crossing rewarding. Through their years of involvement, academic parents learn valuable lessons about the daily lives of the students they mentor. Most of the academic parents are SDSU emeriti faculty. Their learning—and its influence on overall university culture—is significant.

Involve Faculty Members as Border-Crossers. Institutions like SDSU can improve their ability to serve diverse students by encouraging more mainstream faculty members to cross borders and connect with individuals different from themselves. This happens at many different times and in many different places throughout the Success Academy program, including the junior year.

Living in a state with huge racial divisions, FIS students are sometimes pleasantly surprised when they are introduced to SDSU faculty members who have long been engaged in research, outreach, and teaching projects with Native collaborators. "It suggests a willingness to cross a border out of your own culture and into theirs," says one such Anglo faculty member. "It doesn't mean I understand everything in their world, but it says to students that I have made an effort."

Involve Student Affairs Staff as Border-Crossers. A gigantic step for our program in its third year was expanding from the "academic affairs" into the "student affairs" side of the university. This was a major leap for the institution in building its capacity to serve Native students, not only through Success Academy but also far beyond.

As Tierney (1992: 153) says, repeated and consistent interaction with tribal students offers opportunities for Anglo staff to learn about a culture uniquely different from their own. For the past 10 years, interaction between FIS juniors and SDSU staff has been repeated and consistent. A willingness to cross borders, particularly when the process was uncomfortable, has taught Anglo staff members how to better work with American Indian students. For example, matters that were once perceived to be "simple," such as requiring a student to pay a $20 admissions fee or to show up for New Student Orientation, are now viewed differently by student affairs staff who have worked closely with Success Academy students. Coming up with the funds to cover myriad student fees or travelling hundreds of miles to campus from western South Dakota can be far more problematic for American Indian people than for the mainstream population. Because of Success Academy, individuals throughout the university have increased their awareness of difference and have found alternative ways of operating that are comfortable for both Natives and non-Natives.

Getting to know key student affairs staffers, in offices such as Admissions and Financial Aid, also gives Native students who decide to attend college an automatic "in." At SDSU these people have been especially helpful to FIS students navigating the somewhat tricky transition from high school to college. This help is a form of "social capital" (Bourdieu 1986) that students can accrue through programs like Success Academy.

Social, cultural, and economic capital—all of these concepts, addressed by French sociologist Pierre Bourdieu (1977, 1986), are important to understanding educational access. They will be discussed, in the context of the senior-year Success Academy program, in Chapter 5.

5

Rethinking Cultural Capital and Seniors "Countdown to College"

This chapter addresses the role that "cultural capital" (Bourdieu 1986: 243) plays in college access programs such as the Flandreau Indian School-South Dakota State University Success Academy. French sociologist Pierre Bourdieu developed the concept of cultural capital to explain how social class influences educational success. We begin with an example.

Bourdieu's Cultural Capital

I am the oldest of nine children, and I am the first to go to college. The day I left my father said, "I never thought I'd see the day one of my kids would go to college." My father didn't graduate from high school. He dropped out and started to work to support his family. He is very proud of what I'm doing and pushes me to do better in the world.

Students like the Success Academy scholar who wrote these words come to college with different cultural capital than students who were raised in affluent suburbs or attended elite private schools. Cultural capital, as defined by Bourdieu (1977), is the informal interpersonal skills and abilities that legitimate the maintenance of status and power. Cultural capital is a resource inherited by children of high-status families and passed on via the system of formal schooling. In Bourdieu's view society is divided between the educational "haves" and the educational "have-nots." Those fortunate enough to have been born into power and privilege use those resources to sustain their positions, to the detriment of those less fortunate.

Patricia McDonough (1997: 9) offers a more succinct but very understandable definition of cultural capital when she writes, "Cultural capital is precisely the knowledge that elites value yet schools do not teach." And Edward P. St. John, Shouping Hu, and Amy S. Fisher (2011) give this concrete example of cultural capital in operation:

> Parental support usually starts with reading to children in early childhood and continues with parents encouraging their children to complete advanced preparatory courses in high school, to apply to a range of colleges based on their interests, and to see what types of scholarships are offered. But this type of cross-generation support—academic capital transmitted across generations—is not available to most children whose parents did not attend college, a replicating pattern in many low-income families. (1)

Bourdieu's notions of cultural capital constitute a fundamentally pessimistic and fatalistic view of society and education. And, despite some challenges (Kingston 2001), Bourdieu's ideas have held sway for more than a quarter of a century. In short, Bourdieu maintains that the dominant classes are able to reproduce and perpetuate their culture to ensure their continued dominance.

As a group, Success Academy students are overwhelmingly from low-income families with few members who have attended college. Consequently a program like Success Academy *must* challenge Bourdieu's notions of cultural capital. The senior year of Success Academy does this in two ways, outlined briefly below and then explored in greater detail in the remainder of the chapter.

Success Academy's first challenge to Bourdieu is informed by the work of Tara J. Yosso (2005: 77) and her theory of "community cultural wealth." Yosso takes Bourdieu's idea of students' resources and refocuses on students *as* resources. Yosso defines community cultural wealth as the accumulated assets and resources derived from the histories and lives of African American, Hispanic American, and American Indian communities. The six forms of capital that constitute community cultural wealth for Yosso (2005: 77–81) are aspirational, linguistic, familial, social, navigational, and resistant. Community cultural wealth is at the foundation of the Success Academy program and of the college classes students take during their senior year of high school. The senior-year classes follow the "cultural integrity" model (Deyhle 1995: 437), which has been described this way: Teachers who truly want to promote Native academic success do everything in their power to affirm the cultures and languages the students bring with them into the classroom.

Success Academy's second challenge to Bourdieu is informed by the work of Hugh Mehan and colleagues (Mehan et al. 1996: 213). Mehan points out that Bourdieu's original idea of cultural capital involved the transmission of cultural knowledge by the *families* of each social class. That is, children of upper-class families inherit fundamentally different norms, skills, and manners than children of lower-class families. Schools then create curricula that reward the cultural capital of upper-class families and devalue that of lower-class families. For Bourdieu, families are at the heart of the reproduction of inequality. Mehan argues that students who do not have access to cultural capital through their families can, in fact, get it from a "state-sponsored source" (Mehan et al. 1996: 216). The FIS-SDSU Success Academy (particularly its senior-year Countdown to College component) is the kind of "state-sponsored source" of cultural capital to which Mehan refers. Success Academy generates cultural capital for its students through activities ranging from providing ACT prep courses to organizing campus visits, activities that may be routinely available to children of college-educated, upper-income parents.

The remainder of this chapter will focus on the two ways that Success Academy challenges Bourdieu's notions of cultural capital through the operation of the senior-year Success Academy program. Before moving on, however, it is important to note that Bourdieu (1986: 243) describes two other forms of capital (besides cultural capital) that also affect student success:

- *Economic capital* is money and material objects used to produce goods and services (Turner 1991: 512). Economic capital is the easiest type to understand because it aligns most closely with the commonsense understanding of what capital is. Examples from Success Academy might include the grant money that funds SDSU classes for FIS seniors and the reduction in college tuition granted to Indian school graduates. These are now taken-for-granted aspects of Success Academy, but their acquisition was hard fought and involved considerable systemic change. Although economic capital was not a central concern for Bourdieu, acquiring grant money and reducing tuition costs have clearly made higher education more accessible for the students we serve. For this reason, these economic aspects of senior-year Success Academy will be discussed briefly at the end of Chapter 5.

- *Social capital* is positions and relations in social networks (Turner 1991: 512). Several examples of social capital were presented in Chapter 4. Through FIS-SDSU Success Academy, juniors get acquainted with staff members in offices such as Admissions and Financial Aid. The senior-year Countdown to College program involves these same staffers who further facilitate the students' acceptance into college. How this is done will also be touched on in Chapter 5.

To repeat, the form of capital most relevant to Bourdieu, to critical theory (Gartman 2013), and to Success Academy is cultural capital. Thus Chapter 5 begins here with a focus on the ways senior-year Success Academy challenges Bourdieu's notions of cultural capital.

First Challenge to Bourdieu: Community Cultural Wealth

The Origin and Definition of Community Cultural Wealth

Community cultural wealth is "a critical race theory challenge to traditional interpretations of cultural capital and shifts the lens from *a deficit view* of communities of color, instead focusing on sources of *strength and resiliency*" (Brayboy et al. 2012: 81). While critical theory is composed generally of criticisms of various aspects of social and intellectual life (Ritzer 1992: 281), critical race theory focuses expressly on racism. Critical race theorists see racism as endemic throughout society and as the root of all oppression. Critical race theory began as a way to examine the black/white racial divide from a legal perspective, but it has splintered into many other variations. These include Asian critical race theory, Latino/a critical race theory, and tribal critical race theory.

There is a small but growing group of tribal critical race theorists studying American Indian education (Huffman 2010: 217). One of these theorists, Bryan McKinley Jones Brayboy (Lumbee Nation), explains that "the primary tenet of TribalCrit is the notion that colonization is endemic to society....European American thought, knowledge, and power structures dominate present-day society in the United States" (Brayboy 2005: 430). Tribal critical race theorists often present stories (called "counternarratives") to explain how Native students successfully combine traditional wisdom and Western knowledge. For example, Lorinda Lindley (2009) uses community cultural wealth theory to study 16 Northern Arapaho women completing degrees at the University of Wyoming. She finds that the women draw upon four of the six forms of capital outlined by Yosso—aspirational capital, familial capital, navigational capital, and resistant capital—to persevere at a predominantly white institution.

While these forms of capital will be discussed in more detail later, Yosso's definition of "community cultural wealth" bears repeating here. Community cultural wealth is the accumulated assets and resources derived from the histories and lives of African American, Hispanic American, and American Indian communities (Yosso 2005: 77). Students of color inherit their community cultural wealth from their families, neighborhoods, and ethnic groups. Put another way, community cultural wealth is "an array of knowledge, skills, abilities and contacts possessed and utilized by Communities of Color to survive and resist macro and micro-forms of oppression" (Yosso 2005: 77).

Why Community Cultural Wealth Matters to Success Academy

Recognizing the "community cultural wealth" (Yosso 2005: 78) that Native students bring with them to school, rather than focusing on the traditional "cultural capital" (Bourdieu 1986: 243) they do not have, calls for systemic change. Changing the university to honor the cultures Native students bring to it is the scaffolding upon which Success Academy rests. Community cultural wealth theory provides a guide for achieving this. Systemic change, from a community cultural wealth perspective, means departing from "the traditional deficit-driven model of education and...creating an aggressive assets-based approach" (Guajardo and Guajardo 2002: 286).

Studying Yosso's theory of community cultural wealth has been transformative for many individuals involved in the Success Academy program. Teacher Education Professor Mary Moeller uses community cultural wealth theory to help her students prepare for the Wiconi Waste workshops they present to the FIS freshmen (Moeller, Anderson, and Grosz 2012; Moeller and Nagy 2013). English Professor Darla Bielfeldt's work with the senior-year Success Academy students (to be discussed later in this chapter) has also been heavily influenced by community cultural wealth theory (Moeller and Bielfeldt 2011).

For me, as Success Academy coordinator, Yosso's concept of community cultural wealth is a theory that both "fits" and "works" (Glaser and Strauss 1967: 3). Yosso's theory well describes the cultural richness that students bring with them into our program. There is a common misperception that Native students attending boarding schools are separated from their cultures. This could not be further from the truth. Over the course of 12 years we have worked with students who participate in Sun Dance, who quarry pipestone, who sweat, sing, drum, and pray. The FIS-SDSU Success Academy and those who participate in it have been enriched by our students' community cultural wealth.

The four forms of community cultural capital found by Lindley (2009) to be most important to individual Native student success—aspirational capital, familial capital, navigational capital, and resistant capital—will be discussed next. They will be discussed in the context of Success Academy programming, specifically the SDSU classes offered to FIS seniors. First, however, some needed background on these classes will be presented.

College Classes for Success Academy Seniors

With external funding from the Citi Foundation and the South Dakota Space Grant Consortium, 10 FIS seniors are able to take two courses at SDSU during their last year of high school. One course is offered during the fall semester, the other during the spring semester. The three-credit courses meet twice a week, once at SDSU and once at FIS.

The 10 seniors are enrolled as concurrent high school/SDSU students. They are the only students enrolled in that particular section of the course. All plan to attend SDSU, as true freshmen, the following year. Because of limited funding, which will be discussed in greater detail later, students apply for acceptance into the senior-year program. FIS counselors, in consultation with SDSU staff, decide who will participate.

Community Cultural Capital and Senior-Year Classes

Classes began in Fall 2003, when the first cohort of Success Academy freshmen became high school seniors. While the academic subjects have changed over the years, the selection of both the classes and the professors has remained very deliberate. An appreciation of students' community cultural wealth underlies the design of senior-year Success Academy. Consequently, the classes offered and community cultural capital will be discussed hand-in-hand in the following sections.

Aspirational Capital.

> I am writing to let you know that I liked going to the freshman workshops. It was a lot of fun. These field trips we have taken were a very educational experience for me to see what college life is like and how the classes look. The tour was fun. I learned things about the campus I did not know. The one I liked most was the Engineering workshop. I think I will be an engineer.

Three years later the Flandreau Indian School student who wrote these words was enrolled at South Dakota State University, taking a Descriptive Astronomy course in the College of Engineering. He was part of the first cohort of Success Academy seniors to take classes at SDSU. The following year he enrolled full-time at SDSU as an Engineering major, with a substantial National Science Foundation scholarship to support his aspirations.

Aspirational capital is "the ability to maintain hopes and dreams for the future even in the face of barriers" (Yosso 2006: 41). The phrase "to hope against all hope" has been used by critical ethnographer Enrique (Henry) T. Trueba (1999: xxxix) to describe the personal resilience of border-crossers who survive oppressive situations and learn to function effectively in two cultures. Joseph M. Marshal III (Sicangu Lakota) explains this phenomenon well when he writes, "I remind myself that darkness, despair, pain, and the absence of hope are what perseverance thrives on" (Marshall 2002: 35).

Drawing on the aspirational capital of its Native students, Success Academy tries to nurture "a culture of possibility" (Gandara 1995: 112). Most of the Success Academy seniors who enroll for classes at SDSU are the first in their families to attend college. The cost of taking a single, three-credit college class at SDSU is about $600, making the experience unattainable for all but a few high school students in the state. Because of Success Academy, a group of students, who would not otherwise get to try out college, do. Aspirations become realities. Programs such as Success Academy can "break the links between the parents' current occupational status and their children's future academic attainment" (Gandara 1995: 55).

DESCRIPTIVE ASTRONOMY. In Fall 2003 the first cohort of Success Academy seniors (including the one whose words began this section) took Descriptive Astronomy. Professor Larry Browning was an ideal teacher for that first course because he began many of the collaborative efforts between SDSU scientists and tribal educators that still operate throughout the state today.

Certainly the course, as Browning taught it, drew on the community cultural wealth of the students. For example, Browning incorporated traditional Lakota star knowledge into the curriculum. During "star parties" Browning and the students viewed and discussed constellations associated with sites sacred to the Lakota, such as Bear Butte and the Black Hills.

The course also generated aspirational capital among its participants. Experiential learning can motivate students to continue their pursuit of higher education and of professional careers. In Descriptive Astronomy, students engaged enthusiastically in projects such as building their own telescopes. Together students and professor observed from atop the roof of Crothers Engineering Hall.

One class trip took the group to the university's Oak Lake Field Station. The field station, nestled along the shoreline of a lake about 20 miles from campus, occupies the site of a former tribal village. There the group made and launched rockets.

Another class trip found students and professor touring the Earth Resources Observation and Science (EROS) Center, near Sioux Falls, South Dakota. EROS is the national archive for remotely sensed images of the Earth. The tour was conducted by Michelle Buffalo Knuppe, a Native student who graduated in Physics from SDSU and went on to work at EROS.

These hands-on approaches to learning, practiced in Descriptive Astronomy, allowed the FIS students to "try on" the professional identity of "American Indian scientist" in many different settings.

In the long term, classes like this foster career awareness in culturally relevant contexts. In the short term, students get a chance to "picture" themselves in university classrooms, successfully undertaking college-level work. Success Academy acknowledges the difficult challenges its students will face en route to higher education. That said, the weekly experience of coming to campus and taking classes for credit affirms the aspirations of the students Success Academy serves. As one student put it, "What I learned at SDSU was that college isn't as hard as it probably looks. I bet that there are some hard classes there, but nothing I can't handle."

Familial Capital.

> About a month ago, I spoke by phone with one of the Success Academy seniors who could not be here for graduation this week. I was in my home in Brookings, South Dakota, and she was in _____, preparing for the birth of her baby. She called me to talk about her future and about going to college. She told me that a college education was even more important to her now than before because soon she would have a child to care for, a new human being who would depend on her for a good life. She said she knows that the best future she can create for herself, for her family and for her community will rest on continuing on with a college education.
> —From Flandreau Indian School Baccalaureate Address

Familial capital is "cultural knowledges nurtured among kin that carry a sense of community history, memory, and cultural intuition" (Yosso 2006: 48). Familial capital involves a sense of obligation and responsibility to one's kinship group, clearly expressed by this student as she reflected on her plans for the future.

"Kin" is defined broadly in American Indian communities to include nuclear and extended family members—siblings, parents, aunts, uncles, and grandparents. For many FIS students "kin" may also include legal guardians, people to whom they may or may not be related by blood. Since Native students often move in and out of higher education at various stages in the life cycle, spouses and children are also key members of their kinship systems.

"Family is the backbone, the foundation of our culture," Marshall (2002: 210) writes in *The Lakota Way*. "We are given substance, nurtured, and sustained by family. Kinship goes beyond family and is the connection we feel to the world at large and everything in it."

Many Native students emphasize the fundamental role their families play in supporting their education (Brayboy et al. 2012: 80–82). Sometimes this support is instrumental as in caring for young children while their parents attend classes. At other times this support is emotional, as it is for one Success Academy senior who wrote, "I am the first person from my family to attend a university right out of high school. My father is very proud of what I have achieved."

Incorporating the familial capital of our students into the design of our program has been challenging. The 2004 FIS graduating class had students from 14 states, many of them distant—Arizona, Colorado, Iowa, Kansas, Michigan, Minnesota, Montana, Nebraska, North Carolina, North Dakota, South Dakota, Utah, Wisconsin, and Wyoming. Relatives of FIS students are generally supportive of their children preparing for college. A shortcoming of Success Academy, however, has been finding meaningful ways to involve family members in this process.

That said, Success Academy tries to acknowledge the importance of familial capital in subtle ways. For example, when FIS students are accepted into the senior-year program, they are expected to complete both the fall and the spring courses offered by SDSU. In fact, seldom in the history of the program has the exact same cohort of 10 students enrolled for both the fall and spring courses. Students "stop out" (Tierney 1992: 163) on a fairly regular basis, leaving school and returning home often to be nearer family. Sometimes these students return to FIS to graduate. Sometimes they transfer to their local high schools.

One example mentioned earlier is the student who was pregnant. Because she had enough credits, FIS allowed her to graduate mid-year in January. By then she had already been accepted for admission to SDSU the following fall. Success Academy staff kept in touch with the student. We assured her that she (and the baby) would be welcomed back onto the SDSU campus whenever she decided to start college. We also assured her that help with settling into family student housing and finding affordable child care would be available when she needed it. She has not yet returned to college at SDSU.

INTRODUCTION TO GEOGRAPHY. In Spring 2004 the same cohort of Success Academy seniors that took the first Descriptive Astronomy course was ready for a second exposure to college classes. The course chosen for them was Introduction to Geography, taught by Distinguished Professor Charles "Fritz" Gritzner. Gritzner, a cultural geographer, has written more than 30 books covering people and societies across the United States and the world.

Gritzner expected the Success Academy students to complete projects on their home reservations or communities. Students drew heavily on their "familial capital" as they gathered needed information, sometimes from relatives and elders in their tribes.

David Flammond (Sisseton-Wahpeton Oyate), an SDSU Geography graduate student and an FIS Geography teacher, was Gritzner's teaching assistant. Gritzner and Flammond loaded the students up in a university van and took a finals week field trip to cultural sites in eastern South Dakota and western Minnesota. Stops included the Pipestone National Monument, where for generations American Indian families have quarried pipestone and carved it into pipes for prayer.

Resistant Capital.

All my life I have grown up around math. My father is an electrician. He said that math deals with every aspect of life. He has had math in his life ever since I can remember. Because he is in my life and it was a subject he could help me with, I grew to love math and adapt well to it. During these four years at FIS, I have tried to take every math class possible. During the second semester of my sophomore year, I begged the counselor to get an Algebra II class. He told me that if I could get enough people who would take the class, he would get a teacher. The school worked something out, and I got the class. At the beginning of my junior year, the same situation arose. No one capable of teaching the class and no class was available. The only way I could get another math class is if I took a twilight class, and I would have to find at least three people who would take that class, too. I got just enough, but the class only lasted until semester break. Everyone graduated besides me or didn't have enough math classes to continue on with me. I tried this year, when they got new teachers, to see if I could take another twilight class in trigonometry, hopefully. They said they would sign me up and see what they could do. Finally, the only thing they said they could do was to teach Algebra II. So since I had an opening in my schedule, I just took Algebra II over again, to refresh my memory for college prepping.

Resistant capital is "knowledges and skills cultivated through behavior that challenges inequality" (Yosso 2006: 49). The Success Academy senior who wrote the words that begin this section is well aware that Native American students do not share the same educational opportunities as other American students. Her personal narrative tells how she challenged several discriminatory school-based structures. The lack of academically demanding courses and the shortage of qualified teachers she mentions are endemic in schools with predominantly Indian populations. While the federal government has sole responsibility for providing education to students at schools like FIS, this obligation consistently goes unmet (U.S. Commission on Civil Rights 2003: xi). Without adequate funding for quality education, college access is not truly open for American Indian students. This became strikingly clear to us as Success Academy leaders by the start of the 2005–2006 academic year.

BASIC ALGEBRA. By then two cohorts of Success Academy seniors had graduated from FIS and enrolled at SDSU as true freshmen. Based on their ACT scores, an increasing number of these students were starting college labeled deficient in English and mathematics. As a result, the students were required to take Basic Writing and Basic Algebra, both remedial courses, during their first semester on campus—a necessary, but not really an exciting, start to their college careers. (More information on remedial courses and college success will be presented in Chapter 6.)

Consequently the Success Academy steering committee decided to forgo offering Astronomy and Geography to the Success Academy seniors. The Basic Writing and Basic Algebra courses would be taught instead to the FIS students during their senior year of high school. The result would be a chance for the students to enter college on a more equal footing with other freshmen.

We began with the Basic Algebra course, and from the start were fortunate to involve Professor Christine Larson. Larson teaches Mathematics Education courses, so is particularly skilled in working with high school students. With the Success Academy students she used "manipulatives," a "Connected Mathematics" teaching technique employed in a number of reservation schools throughout the state (Connected Mathematics Project 2009; Reimer 2000: 3).

It is important to note that, through all the changes in senior-year course offerings over the years, student identity continued to be honored through culturally relevant curriculum and instructional techniques. The Success Academy program as a whole and the individual SDSU professors involved in it grew as we learned from each others' experiences working with American Indian students. This was particularly true when Basic Writing was introduced into the senior program also during the 2005–2006 academic year.

Navigational Capital.

My name is _____, and I am a (tribal member). I am a senior in high school this year, and I want to tell you how I changed my life to get this far. When I was a freshman attending _____ High School I was very good until one day this girl came up to me and unexpectedly started hitting me. I did what anyone else would do, which was fought back. But I broke her nose and made a whole big scene. Then I was the one who got expelled for assault. The bad thing was that I got expelled just one-and-a-half months before school was out. I was devastated. I didn't know what to expect. My life was going so bad that summer, but I found a solution. I could go to boarding school for one year and catch up. Then I would go back to my school. So I started searching but I didn't want to go to a school where there were a lot of (tribal members). Then I came across Flandreau Indian School in South Dakota. It was far, (tribal member)-less and seemed pretty easy to me. So I applied, got accepted, then packed and was off to South Dakota. At first I was homesick, but then I got used to it. My first year I fought a lot and got in trouble for almost everything. And then I got kicked out at the last week, but didn't care. So I went and got drunk with some of my friends. The bad thing was I got caught, but I didn't care because I was going home anyway. The next year came around, and I wanted to go back because I didn't want to go back to my old school. So I made calls to all kinds of people, and they didn't want me back, but I begged, and surprisingly I got accepted. So I came back and decided to show them I could be nice, smart and intelligent. I came back my junior year and didn't get in trouble at all. I joined Student Council, Prom Committee and made Honor Roll throughout the whole year. They were surprised and didn't think I could do it. Now it's my senior year, and I'm still the nice, intelligent, smart girl.

Navigational capital "refers to skills of maneuvering through social institutions" not created with people of color in mind (Yosso 2006: 44). The Success Academy student who told this story employed multiple strategies to painstakingly traverse the academic bureaucracy and eventually graduate from high school. The following year, after writing this narrative, she became a freshman at South Dakota State University.

Skokomish scholar D. Michael Pavel and his coauthor Ella Inglebret (Pavel and Inglebret 2007: 1) describe the movement of Native students through education as "a journey to success…with unique opportunities and challenges for each individual." Students who successfully encounter and overcome obstacles along the way are said to develop "academic invulnerability" (Alva 1991: 18). Academically invulnerable students "sustain high levels of achievement motivation and performance, despite the presence of stressful events and conditions that place them at risk of doing poorly in school" (Alva 1991: 19).

Since Native Americans constitute about 10 percent of South Dakota's population, Native American students in South Dakota have vast experience navigating through institutions not created with them in mind. Through such navigational experiences, students often learn skills that allow them not only to survive but also to thrive academically. "Accommodation without assimilation" is how the late African American scholar John Ogbu (1992: 12) describes the navigational skills of successful students of color. "When in Rome, do as the Roman do, without becoming Romans," Ogbu suggests.

For Native American students, using navigational capital sometimes means engaging in activities that conflict with cultural values (Lindley 2009: 159). For example, the young woman in the narrative above describes approaching people unknown to her for help finding a school that would accept her. She had to speak out for herself to get the assistance she needed to stay in school and eventually graduate. These actions contrast sharply with the values of quietness and observation that are important in many Native cultures.

The term "transculturation" captures the notion of "an individual who is fully capable of interaction with two different cultures without cultural loss" (Huffman 1999: 170). Scholars such as Rosemary White Shield (2004–2005) have used transculturation theory to explain the success of Native students in college. "It is the 'Indianness' within Native college students which gives rise to inner strength and security, and thus, enables them to retain their Indigenous identities, values, and ways of being in the world as American Indians without assimilating into the majority culture as they complete their higher education experiences," White Shield (2004–2005: 120) writes.

BASIC WRITING. The text that began the last section on navigational capital was originally titled "New Start." It was a short, creative nonfiction text written by a Success Academy senior taking SDSU's Basic Writing class. The essay was later recorded and shared with about 75 SDSU Teacher Education students enrolled in EDFN 475 (Human Relations).

How did writing like this come out of a class like that, "that" being Basic Writing? The Basic Writing class covers grammar, usage, punctuation, and paragraph development for students who come to college lacking these skills. Making Basic Writing culturally relevant and engaging proved to be a particular challenge for the professors who taught it to the Success Academy students.

In Fall 2010 Professor Darla Bielfeldt took over the course from Professor Amy Thompson, who left SDSU to attend law school. Thompson was raised and taught in Flandreau, so had close ties with the tribal community there. Native American speakers and readings were foundational to how she taught the course. Bielfeldt, a recognized poet, brought to Success Academy an excitement for teaching and learning, but less familiarity with American Indian literature.

As Basic Writing transitioned from one professor to the next, an opportunity arose to create a "best in class" class, one that would allow Native American students to master basic grammar skills in a culturally relevant context. A small, one-time grant from the Citi Foundation made this possible.

Bielfeldt was mentored through this process by noted American Indian Studies scholar and Distinguished Professor of English Charles L. Woodard. Woodard first arranged for Bielfeldt to work with Elden Lawrence (Sisseton Wahpeton Oyate) and Lanniko L. Lee (Cheyenne River Sioux Tribe), both members of the Oak Lake Writers' Society, to become more familiar with Native American literature. Bielfeldt began incorporating works by Native Americans into the Basic Writing course syllabus. She introduced the texts *I Tell You Now* (Swann and Krupat 2005) and *Touching Home: Stories and Poems by Tribal College Students* (Tribal College Journal 2010) as supplements to the standard grammar handbook the students continued to use.

Next Bielfeldt turned her attention to mastering a particularly culturally relevant instructional technique, that is, digital storytelling. She enrolled in a three-day educators workshop at the Center for Digital Storytelling in Berkeley, California.

A digital story is a short film that combines a narrated piece of personal writing with photographic images and a musical soundtrack. With only a bare minimum of equipment and training, individuals can produce works that tell stories using "moving" images and sound.

"Storytelling is at the core of Native cultures," explains Evelina Zuni Lucero (Isleta/Ohkay Owingeh Pueblo) of the Institute of American Indian Arts. "So much has been written about Indians by non-Indians…much of it erroneous, so it is important that Native people have a voice to tell their own story" (Sorenson 2012: 16–17).

The Basic Writing course, as it is taught by Bielfeldt, gives voice to Native students' experiences. It allows students to easily draw on the community cultural wealth they bring with them into the classroom. Topics have ranged from first love and best friends to track meets and drug use. Personal essays, like the one that began this section, are written, edited, and perfected through numerous drafts. Then using digital cameras and voice recorders, students add images and sound to their "stories." A screening at the end of the semester allows students to view each others' work and showcase it before a larger university audience.

So, whose culture has capital (Yosso 2005: 69)? And how should capital, as a factor influencing educational success, be defined? This section has addressed those questions. By acknowledging students' community cultural wealth and incorporating it into senior-year Success Academy classes, we challenge Bourdieu's original conception of cultural capital.

Trueba (2004) offers an important insight into a new kind of cultural capital, an insight that is a fitting conclusion to this section. His views offer promise for students of color navigating their way through the educational system and ultimately into the workplace:

> As the demographics change drastically from "minority groups" (people of color being marked and indeed fewer than mainstream) to the predominant population in the country (by the mid-twenty-first century), those individuals who can best function in a diverse society will have a large cultural capital and greater ability to function effectively. The mastery

of different languages, the ability to cross racial and ethnic boundaries, and a general resilience associated with the ability to endure hardships and overcome obstacles will clearly be recognized as a new cultural capital, not a handicap. (118–119)

Second Challenge to Bourdieu: Cultural Capital from a State-Sponsored Source

Bourdieu's views on cultural capital represent a "darkly pessimistic view of the possibility of social change" (Mehan et al. 1996: 215). For students to progress through the educational system, they need access to cultural (and social) capital that Bourdieu says they must acquire from their "habitus" (Bourdieu and Passeron 1990). In the context of college preparation, "habitus" means family and community habits that can either enhance or undermine one's chances of enrolling in higher education. Mehan et al. (1996) give this example:

> Lower-class children grow up in an environment where success is rare; they rarely see their brothers and sisters, friends and neighbors secure good jobs. The experiences and attitudes of those close to lower-class children infiltrate their systems of belief. Responding to the attitudes and experiences of those around them, lower-income children lose interest in school and resign themselves to low-level jobs, thereby contributing to the reproduction of existing status relations. (215)

Some educational literature now challenges Bourdieu. It suggests that students like those just described may be able to acquire cultural capital from a "nonhabitus source" (Mehan et al. 1996), that is, from a state-sponsored source. Consequently the definition of cultural capital needs to be expanded beyond the realm of what is *inherited* by elite students from their families. Students not born into elite families can participate in programs that *teach* them the skills, manners, and norms that are part of a college-going ethos.

Acquiring Cultural Capital from State-Sponsored Sources: Three Examples

Students can acquire cultural capital through pre-college interventions like Success Academy. Three examples, prominent in the literature, are the AVID Untracking Program that began in San Diego, Indiana's Twenty-First Century Scholars Program, and the Washington State Achievers Program. These three programs will be described briefly below. Then aspects of Success Academy that involve cultural capital formation, namely the senior-year Countdown to College initiative, will be discussed.

AVID Untracking Program. AVID stands for Advancement Via Individual Determination. It comes from the Latin *avidus*, which means "eager for knowledge" (Swanson, Mehan, and Hubbard 1995: 54). AVID puts previously underachieving students (primarily low-income and ethnic minority youth) into the same college preparation programs as high-achieving students (primarily upper-/middle-income and white). Since 1980, more than 90 percent of AVID's 10,000 high school graduates have attended college (Learning Forward 1998a). AVID was begun in San Diego at Clairemont High School by English department chair Mary Catherine Swanson. AVID now operates in more than 4,800 schools across the United States and the world (AVID 2013).

AVID uses writing, inquiry, and collaboration as methods to accelerate student learning (Swanson, Mehan, and Hubbard 1995). The purpose of AVID is to create a "college-going culture" at the schools that have adopted it, a learning environment where *all* students are expected to graduate ready for higher education (AVID 2013). AVID was introduced to address the serious achievement gap between "majority" and underrepresented students (Swanson, Mehan, and Hubbard 1995: 57).

Mehan et al. (1996: 216) explain that AVID provides an excellent example of students gaining cultural capital from a nonhabitus source. Through AVID, participants acquire skills essential to academic success, for example, test-taking, essay-writing, and note-taking strategies. The students also learn how to talk to teachers and challenge questionable grades, policies, and decisions.

Examples of cultural capital acquisition like those above are difficult to untangle from examples of social capital acquisition. Social capital refers to *who* you know, that is, networks that individuals can use to advance their positions in society (McNamee and Miller 2004: 71). Cultural capital refers to *what* you know, that is, knowledge of the skills, manners, and norms of the groups to which one belongs. Since who you know clearly affects what you are able to know, cultural and social capital are strongly intertwined.

Mehan et al. (1996) point out that AVID coordinators, because of the privileged positions they occupy in productive social networks, are able to "lead their students through the murky maze of the college application and financial aid process…advocating on their behalf with admissions officers or financial aid officers" (Mehan et al. 1996: 216–217). Just as the AVID students gain cultural capital from a nonhabitus source, so, too, do they gain social capital from the same nonhabitus source, that is, the college preparatory program itself.

Twenty-First Century Scholars Program. Indiana's Twenty-First Century Scholars Program asks low-income eighth graders to sign a pledge to take the necessary steps to prepare for college (and to remain drug free). In exchange the state of Indiana provides college preparatory support services to the students and their parents, including workshops, mentoring, and campus visits. The state also ensures that students receive financial aid sufficient to afford in-state tuition at an Indiana public university or an equivalent amount to cover the cost of attending a private college. The program has resulted in a substantial increase in college attendance by low-income youth (St. John et al. 2002: 1–2; St. John, Hu, and Fisher 2011: 24–27).

While financial aid is a huge factor in college access, it is important to note that the Twenty-First Century Scholars Program also provides support services to students and their families. Edward P. St. John, Shouping Hu, and Amy S. Fisher (2011) find these support services facilitate "the formation of the cultural capital needed to complete high school, prepare for and enroll in college, and experience college success." The researchers note that interventions like the Twenty-First Century Scholars Program and the Washington State Achievers Program (to be described next) provide "a catalyst to alter cultural capital or overcome barriers associated with it."

The constraining role of cultural capital is deliberately challenged by certain aspects of the Twenty-First Century Scholars Program. The scholars come from low-income families and have few, if any, relatives who have attended college. Initially, the students served by the program have limited knowledge of college. Picturing themselves participating in higher education and pursuing professional careers is difficult if not impossible. Yet through participation in the program, by both students and parents, their cultural capital is transformed "from a discouraging force into a form of encouragement" (St. John, Hu, and Fisher 2011: 74). Scholars begin to see themselves as college students. Formal visits to college campuses, arranged through the program, help students construct images of themselves being academically successful (St. John, Hu, and Fisher 2011: 105). For the students, and for their families, the possibility of college attendance becomes real.

Washington State Achievers Program. This program combines guarantees of financial aid to low-income students and funding for reforms in the high schools the students attend (St. John and Hu 2007: 351–352). The overall intent is to improve college access. The Washington State Achievers Program is funded by the Bill and Melinda Gates Foundation.

Five hundred juniors per year from 16 high schools receive college scholarship guarantees immediately after being accepted into the program. The 16 high schools attended by the students have also received funding to implement comprehensive reforms, including the development of small schools within larger high schools and the addition of more college preparatory courses into the curricula.

An important aspect of the Washington State Achievers Program is the mentoring students receive throughout high school into college. As St. John, Hu, and Fisher (2011) explain:

> Cultural capital functions as student and family knowledge transmitted through human systems of support and trust. The most natural human system to transmit cultural capital is the family. But if the family is dysfunctional, broken or lacks role models who have completed college, it is more difficult to acquire this knowledge. (92)

In the Washington State Achievers Program, mentors within the schools serve as role models, as would be expected. What St. John, Hu, and Fisher (2011: 93) find to be more novel is that "the culture of a high school can help form an inner image that functions like a role model." Supportive cultures in high schools, cultures that encourage college attendance, can be created through programs like the Washington State Achievers.

St. John, Hu, and Fisher (2011: 126) note that while some cultural capital is formed through early experiences in the family, as students move through school they begin to "form their own cultural capital....School counselors and mentors were the major sources of information that empowered them to overcome the odds by taking personal responsibility for navigating a life course." Contact with more experienced students, staff, and faculty expands students' knowledge about higher education and increases their chances of attending college. As Alexander Jun (2001: 26) advises, "The challenge for educators is to create opportunities for youth to gain access to various forms of cultural capital through counselors, mentors and family members in order to achieve their educational pursuits."

Success Academy's Countdown to College Program

As already discussed, Flandreau Indian School seniors participating in Success Academy take two three-credit courses at South Dakota State University. One course meets in the fall, the other in the spring, once per week at FIS and once per week at SDSU. The course schedule allows for regular contact between SDSU staff and FIS seniors throughout their final year of high school. As students attending an off-reservation federal Indian boarding school, most of these seniors are far separated from relatives who might otherwise help them complete the steps necessary for college admission. Consequently Success Academy staff step in to play these roles. In the process, the FIS students acquire some of the capital, both cultural and social, helpful in making a successful transition from high school to college.

The five steps that comprise the year-long Countdown to College program also give SDSU staff, from both the academic and the student affairs sides of the university, an opportunity to build their capacity for more effectively working with Native American students. This in turn creates a more welcoming environment for the students when they graduate from FIS and enroll at SDSU. The five steps, and their relation to cultural capital formation, will be discussed next.

Applying for Admission. One evening each September is set aside for the Success Academy seniors to fill out college applications. As concurrent high school students, taking classes on campus, the seniors apply for admission to SDSU as true freshmen the following fall. The FIS students stay after their regular class on campus and are joined by SDSU Admissions counselors. One of the two senior-year FIS counselors (both American Indian) accompany the students to this session.

The counselors from SDSU work one-on-one with the seniors to complete their applications. The counselors from FIS make sure that all the necessary paperwork from their school, such as official transcripts and immunization records, is provided. Success Academy pays the $20 fee required to submit each application. These are examples of leading students *institutionally* through the murky maze of the college application process (Mehan et al. 1996: 216–217), supplying cultural (and social) capital that might be more readily available to those from privileged backgrounds.

A requirement for participation in senior-year Success Academy is being in the top 60 percent of the FIS graduating class. That is also one of the criteria used for admission to South Dakota State University. Consequently, all the Success Academy seniors who apply for admission to SDSU are, in fact, admitted. This means that early in the fall semester, the seniors receive letters at FIS from SDSU congratulating them on their acceptance. Flandreau Indian School counselors have used the receipt of the acceptance letters as an occasion for celebration. The seniors' names are read during the daily announcements, and the students are warmly congratulated on their admission to SDSU. FIS administrators sometimes host an after-school reception in the seniors' honor. Teachers and staff are invited so that they can commend the seniors on their acceptance into college. Clearly, this is an example of the "culture of a high school" (St. John, Hu, and Fisher 2011: 93) helping students construct "images of success" (St. John, Hu, and Fisher 2011: 105). Cultural capital is formed—not in the family, but rather in *institutions*—as the seniors begin picturing themselves as college students.

Preparing for (and Taking) the ACT. While taking the ACT test is a *prerequisite* for college admission, taking a prep course to prepare for it is a *perquisite* (perk) usually reserved for students who are raised in certain families, live in certain communities, and attend certain schools—in other words, students with certain kinds of cultural capital. The reasons for this are apparent. First, the course costs money, about $75 at the time the first cohort of FIS seniors started preparing for college. Second, schools like the Flandreau Indian School are usually not able to offer such courses on campus. Third, while a course may be offered at a neighboring school, often there is no transportation readily available between the two institutions.

Success Academy hired a retired Flandreau Public School teacher to organize an ACT prep course for seniors at the Flandreau Indian School. A prep book is provided for each of the seniors, so they can study for the ACT not only in class but also in the dorms. Prep course sessions are scheduled a couple of times each week, usually during October and November. The seniors involved are gaining cultural capital from a nonhabitus source. Besides reviewing subject matter in English, mathematics, reading, and science, the seniors acquire test-taking skills essential to academic success.

FIS counselors make sure that all the seniors are signed up for the ACT test well in advance of the deadline. The ACT test itself is held in early December at the Flandreau Indian School.

Financing a College Education. "Concern about college costs is an inhibiting force for low-income families, especially when parents have no personal knowledge of college," write St. John, Hu, and Fisher (2011: 15). "Aid guarantees provide a way to overcome these fears."

Addressing students' and families' concerns about college costs is fundamental to increasing college access. Doing so ensures that students such as the Success Academy seniors who are admitted to SDSU actually enroll.

In mid-December, just before students return to their homes for the holiday break, FIS hosts an assembly for all of its seniors (not just the 10 taking Success Academy classes at SDSU). The assembly's purpose is to allow students to learn about financial aid. Jay Larsen talks about college costs from his perspective as SDSU Financial Aid director. Derek Burshiem, an FIS counselor, focuses on the help available to cover college costs. He shares with students insights he gained as a Native scholar moving through higher education.

Some messages consistently resonate with students attending these December assemblies. The first is the relatively low cost of attending SDSU. Tuition, fees, room, and board amounted to $12,686 for the 2011–2012 academic year.

The second message that consistently resonates with the students is the relatively high amount of financial aid available to them to cover college costs. Larsen tells the students that, through a combination of grants, scholarships, loans, and work-study, they will be able to pay for their higher education expenses. For the

2011–2012 academic year the maximum federal Pell Grant was $5,550. Since many of the FIS students fall into the category of highest need, they are eligible for the maximum grant. In addition, each Success Academy student to date has received a renewable scholarship ranging between $1,500 and $2,000 directly from SDSU.

Students leave the assembly with a handout to review over the holidays and to share with their families. Students are urged to start looking for scholarships and contacting their tribal higher education offices immediately. A final message delivered at the assembly is an important one: No Success Academy student in the history of the program who has wished to attend SDSU has ever been prevented from doing so because of finances.

When the Success Academy seniors return to FIS in January after semester break, they and their counselors come to SDSU for an afternoon of working on FAFSA forms. Eligibility for financial aid is based on completing these Free Applications for Federal Student Aid. FAFSAs are now completed online, so this particular work session is held in one of the university's computer labs.

Even families with vast amounts of college-going experience find the process of completing FAFSAs intimidating. Having SDSU Financial Aid staff members work with them (and, by extension, with their families) one-on-one is a tremendous boon to the Success Academy students. Most of them are geographically separated from their parents much of the school year. The completion of the FAFSAs extends over the remainder of the spring semester, conducted via mail, telephone, fax, and e-mail. The laborious process is greatly aided by the careful attention paid to detail by the Financial Aid staff at SDSU and the counseling staff at FIS.

Knowing that college is affordable creates that "culture of possibility" (Gandara 1995: 112), second nature to many middle-income, white students. Through mechanisms like a financial aid assembly and assistance preparing FAFSAs, the Success Academy program helps Native students "form their own cultural capital" (St. John, Hu, and Fisher 2011: 126) and empowers them to tackle college.

Visiting Academic Departments. "Parental involvement and knowledge of practices that allow high-SES [socioeconomic status] students access to college, such as SAT courses, college prep courses and on-campus visits, are practices that demonstrate higher forms of cultural capital," writes Shawna L. Acker-Ball (2007: 56). William G. Tierney (2002) says that outreach programs need to put greater emphasis on families being involved in college preparatory activities. Yet often inflexible schedules at work and inability to secure transportation make it difficult for low-income parents to be as involved as they would like to be with their children's education.

For most boarding school students, having parents arrange campus visits for them and then accompany them on the visits is impossible. The Countdown to College schedule allows each Success Academy senior to visit SDSU once, during either February or March, for a departmental visit, accompanied by an FIS counselor.

These visits are scheduled in conjunction with what the university calls "Jackrabbit Previews" (formerly called "TGIFs"). Jackrabbit Previews are group programs designed for high school students and their families. Sessions focus on academic planning, student activities, financial aid, university housing, and other aspects of college life.

Also included in the Jackrabbit Previews are campus tours and academic appointments with department representatives from students' chosen fields of study. Success Academy seniors during Jackrabbit Previews visit one-on-one with faculty members in the majors of interest to them. Learning how to talk comfortably with college professors is a form of cultural capital that seniors gain through Success Academy experiences like these.

Success Academy Pre-orientation Day. Pre-orientation day is the capstone experience for Success Academy seniors. The day is usually scheduled in April, just weeks before the FIS seniors graduate from high school and return to their homes for the summer. All of the seniors will attend one of the university-wide New Student Orientation sessions scheduled for June or July. The focus of pre-orientation day, however, is on the academic, cultural, and spiritual resources available at SDSU for this particular group of seniors as Success Academy scholars and Native American students.

We begin by discussing educational resources available to help students make a successful transition from high school to college. The seniors hear first about TRiO Student Support Services and Minority Peer Mentoring, and then they fill out application forms for these programs. Parents with cultural capital, understood in the strict Bourdieun sense, know the benefits of participating in programs like these and help their children apply for them. Success Academy staff members, however, play this role for the students they serve. Beyond that, Success Academy staff members advocate for their students' acceptance into programs like TRiO, which take only a limited number of applicants.

Throughout pre-orientation day, the seniors meet the American Indian Studies program head, the Native American adviser, and the Native American Club president, learning how these individuals work to support American Indian students on campus. Members of the university's Native American Advisory Committee (later renamed the Tiospaye Council) join the seniors for lunch. NAAC members are individuals from throughout the campus who have committed themselves to Native student success. Occasions like these allow Success Academy seniors to acquire social capital. Students become embedded in a network of supportive faculty and staff who promise to "be there" for them when they return to campus in the fall. The luncheon provides an opportunity for FIS seniors to practice talking to SDSU professors and staff, this time in a relaxed, small-group setting. This is an example of cultural capital acquisition made possible by the Success Academy program.

After lunch the seniors hear about the Success Academy living-learning community, of which they will be a part in the fall. (The living-learning community will be discussed in more detail in Chapter 6.) Staff from Residential Life work with students one-on-one to fill out housing applications. The deposit fee for housing is waived for Success Academy students.

The day ends with students filling out applications to attend one of the university's New Student Orientation (NSO) sessions during the summer. All of the Success Academy students attend the same NSO session; fees for room and board are paid by our program.

Many of the Success Academy students will have to travel vast distances to attend NSO. During the final work session, plans are made for the Success Academy program to provide transportation to campus for those students who need it.

Most incoming SDSU freshmen have the economic capital necessary to pay a myriad of what the university considers to be small fees not covered by financial aid. The families of "majority" students usually make sure they have rides to campus when they need them. For many of the Success Academy seniors, however, this kind of financial and logistical support is not available. Consequently our program must step in to fill this gap.

Success Academy strives to be "an educational ladder with every rung in place." As we try to live out that maxim, we come to realize there are many forms of capital needed to successfully navigate from high school to higher education. Taken-for-granted assumptions about these forms of capital are deeply embedded in the university system, creating practices that ease access for some while denying it to others.

Pre-orientation day is a microcosm of the overall Countdown to College program. Both are efforts to supply capital to students who without it might not pass through the university gates.

Some Final Thoughts on Capital

The previous sections of this chapter have discussed cultural capital as it relates to college preparatory programs in general and to Success Academy in particular. It is important to create programs that affirm the cultural wealth of American Indian students, best known as aspirational, familial, resistant, and navigational capital. In addition, effective programs should supply some of the more traditional kinds of cultural capital that Bourdieu identifies as being essential to educational success. As we have seen, cultural capital and social capital are closely related. Cultural capital (what you know) often depends on social capital (who you know).

Bourdieu (1986: 243) distinguishes between three types of capital—cultural, social, and economic. Cultural capital has the most relevance to college preparation and American Indians. That said, a brief discussion of two aspects of economic capital, as they relate to Success Academy, concludes this chapter.

Economic capital is money and material objects used to produce goods and services (Turner 1991: 512). The first aspect of economic capital to be discussed is external funding for senior-year classes. The second is the in-state tuition rate secured for Success Academy students completing Countdown to College.

External Funding for Senior-Year Classes

These words from Tierney (1992) are useful to begin thinking about economic capital and Success Academy:

> A community college that is set up for vocational training, or a public university that emphasizes the liberal arts, or a private college that encourages scientific inquiry—all need to address more straight-forwardly how their institutions might more fully incorporate Native Americans into their institutions rather than assume that students who do not meet specific criteria should look elsewhere. The role for state agencies is of crucial importance here. State education agencies need to encourage, coax, and at times mandate that institutions more clearly address how they will enable minority students such as Native Americans to fully participate in the life of the institution. (156)

By Success Academy's sixth year, it had become apparent that students graduating from the Flandreau Indian School did not "meet specific criteria" (Tierney 1992: 156) established by South Dakota State University for admission. Many of the graduates had extremely low ACT scores in English and mathematics. While they were admitted to the university, their acceptance was on the condition that they take (and pass) Basic Writing and Basic Algebra during their freshman year. SDSU clearly needed to address how it would "enable...Native Americans to fully participate in the life of the institution" (Tierney 1992: 156).

The answer, in part for Success Academy, was to teach these remedial courses as part of the senior-year program. To do this, year after year, Success Academy had to seek external funding.

Funding for senior-year classes amounts to about $22,500, by far the largest single part of Success Academy's annual budget. While exact amounts have changed throughout the years, tuition for 10 students to take two one-semester, three-credit classes runs about $15,000.

Classes meet twice a week, during the last period of the FIS school day. One class meeting a week is at FIS, and the other is at SDSU. SDSU hired a retired teacher from the Flandreau Public Schools to oversee the class when FIS said it could not provide a staff member to do this. The salary of this teacher-mentor is about $5,200 a year.

Books cost about $2,100. Other small miscellaneous expenses, including those for supplies and travel, total about $200.

It would have been impossible to add senior-year classes to the Success Academy program without external funding. This funding comes from two sources, the Citi Foundation and the South Dakota Space Grant Consortium.

Citi Foundation. Starting in 2005, Success Academy applied for and received a $15,000 per year grant from the Citi Foundation to support college classes for Success Academy seniors. The connection between Success Academy and Citi was created by Jerry Nachtigal, an SDSU Journalism graduate and now the senior vice president for public affairs at Citibank, N.A. in Sioux Falls, South Dakota. As Nachtigal (2013) recalls:

> I was sitting next to my dad at an SDSU basketball game, at Frost Arena, and I remember looking up in the stands and seeing all these yellow Success Academy shirts. I grew up in Brookings and remember in the ninth grade going over to the Flandreau Indian School to play basketball. It really opened my eyes. There were four different teams. We spent the whole day there on campus. We had lunch in the cafeteria with hundreds of Native American kids. That was an eye-opener for me as a white kid who had perhaps two or three Native American classmates. I looked up and thought about Success Academy, "what a great idea." Here were two schools just 25 miles apart. Why didn't a partnership start before this? This program fits with Citibank's priorities. (personal communication, January 11)

Under the federal Community Reinvestment Act of 1977, financial institutions like Citibank are required to meet the credit and community development needs of low- and moderate-income individuals in the areas they serve (Nachtigal, personal communication, January 11, 2013). Flandreau Indian School students, involved in a college preparatory program at South Dakota State University, certainly fit into this category. One of the Citi Foundation's focus areas at the time it began supporting Success Academy was increasing college access for low-income and first-generation students.

In 2009 the Citi Foundation increased its annual grant to Success Academy from $15,000 to $25,000, noting that the program had become a national model. "Nothing is easy in Indian Country," Nachtigal concludes. "You start with the odds against you. Success Academy has opened doors for a lot of people."

South Dakota Space Grant Consortium. The South Dakota Space Grant Consortium (SDSGC) is the other external funder of Success Academy senior-year classes. SDSGC, one of 52 similar consortia nationwide, serves as a link between the National Aeronautics and Space Administration and South Dakota citizens. The consortium's mission is to encourage South Dakotans—through education, research, and service—to become more involved in the fields of aerospace and earth science. A particular emphasis is on bringing previously underrepresented individuals into the workforce in the areas of science, technology, engineering, and mathematics (STEM).

The Consortium provides about $7,500 per year to fund college classes in these STEM disciplines for Native students participating in Success Academy. Because of this funding, 101 Success Academy seniors have taken Astronomy, Geography, and Mathematics courses at South Dakota State University. Fifty-two of these seniors enrolled full-time at SDSU the following year, many of them majoring in STEM fields ranging from Engineering and Mathematics to Nutrition and Nursing.

Success Academy has always had a close relationship with the Space Grant Consortium because the two programs shared office space in SDSU's Engineering Resource Center. Former Engineering Resource Center director Kevin Dalsted (2013), now the Consortium's associate director, reflects on the partnership this way:

> FIS-SDSU Success Academy directly supports the consortium's goal of inspiring underrepresented individuals to consider STEM fields of study. The university classes provide an effective means of introducing the FIS students to the requirements they will face as university students. The classes also help the students realize that they can succeed at the next level. (personal communication, February 1)

Since 2003 Success Academy has attracted external funding in the amount of $60,000 from the South Dakota Space Grant Consortium and $160,000 from the Citi Foundation. These grants are important because they enable Success Academy to provide a "best in class" college preparatory experience for Native American high school seniors.

That said, it is also important to note that the senior-year classes were the only component of Success Academy dependent on external funding. Had grant funding for these classes expired, a scaled-down version of the senior-year program would still have continued, as would the rest of Success Academy. Having both SDSU and

FIS support Success Academy institutionally—with substantial investments of money, time, skill, and effort—has kept the program strong and sustainable for the past 12 years.

More often than not college preparatory programs for students of color begin with funding from large external grants. Once the grants expire, the sponsoring universities themselves are then expected to fund the programs. Unfortunately, the universities usually do not do so. Tierney (1992) describes this process in some detail:

> Someone has a good idea and finds funds to implement the idea.... The funding runs out, and the program dies. The cycle begins again when someone gets another good idea and locates a funding source. Universities and tribal colleges need to come to terms with which programs help Indian students and which programs do not, and, when programs are proven successful, the institution needs to incorporate them into its budget, so that the project administrators have the leeway to plan over a longer period of time instead of constantly searching for funds. (157)

In-State Tuition for FIS Seniors

"Academe must do more than officially encourage students to attend college on mainstream society's terms, for when this is done Indian students generally encounter institutional discouragement," Tierney (1992: 165) writes. As mentioned earlier, one discouragement that Flandreau Indian School students faced when they tried to enter South Dakota State University was their lack of preparedness in the basic skills of English and mathematics. This largely resulted from systemic flaws in Indian education that impact federal boarding schools and individual students themselves.

A second discouragement faced by FIS students admitted to SDSU was an unjust residency requirement. To establish residency for tuition purposes, students had to live in South Dakota for the 12 consecutive months immediately preceding their enrollment at a state university. Because most FIS students went back to their homes out of state during the summer months, they did not qualify for in-state tuition at any regental institution, including SDSU. The difference between a year of in-state versus out-of-state tuition is about $2,000, a considerable sum for a low-income student. Before Success Academy, on average only about one student per year had graduated from FIS and enrolled at SDSU. Success Academy increased that number about tenfold—and made the issue of getting in-state tuition for FIS students a top priority.

SDSU staff in offices ranging from Financial Aid to Diversity Enhancement brought the matter first to the attention of the South Dakota Board of Regents.

(The board oversees the state's system of public higher education, including its six universities.) Granting in-state tuition to high school students who had spent four years living in South Dakota and contributing to its economy seemed to be a just and obvious plan. From the perspective of SDSU faculty and administrators, clearly this must have just been an oversight in the establishment of residency requirements, due to the small number of FIS grads previously moving on to higher education. The Board of Regents, however, saw things differently. Because of the expected loss of revenue, the board rejected the idea of granting residency to FIS students. Another approach was needed. Meanwhile, SDSU had already matriculated two cohorts of Success Academy seniors, all of whom had paid out-of-state tuition.

Administrators from FIS approached then State Senator Dan Sutton from Flandreau for help. Sutton drafted legislation that in its final form read, "Any student who is a graduate of an accredited high school operated by the United States Bureau of Indian Affairs in this state is entitled to resident classification for the purposes of postsecondary education at a state supported institution" (South Dakota Legislature 2012). The bill had to pass through a number of Senate and House committees. A contingent of administrators from both FIS and SDSU travelled to the state capitol in Pierre and delivered testimony.

A very important behind-the-scenes player in all of these negotiations was SDSU President Peggy Gordon Miller, who fervently believed in the basic rightness of the proposed legislation. She exemplified the role of "advocate" described by Alice Chandler (1997) this way:

> Presidents have a unique opportunity to influence the elected leaders of our society. Although it goes against the grain of the current trend toward budget cutting, presidents need to be advocates for both the principles and policies (of access, inclusion and equity) and for the resources needed to implement them. (37)

The bill faced its toughest fight in the Senate Appropriations Committee, which narrowly passed it with five yeas and four nays. After that, no one in either the House or the Senate voted against it. Senate Bill 88 was signed into law by Governor M. Michael Rounds, an SDSU alumnus, on February 22, 2006. Shortly thereafter, another group of Success Academy seniors was filling out FAFSA forms and calculating college costs, with a lessened financial burden standing between them and college. The following month Senator Sutton was recognized with a star quilt and an honor song at SDSU's annual *wacipi* (pow wow). It was a fitting recognition for his role in a battle for inclusion and equity.

Summing Up and Looking Ahead

Generating *cultural capital* while maintaining *cultural integrity* are the hallmarks of successful college preparatory efforts for students of color (Tierney 2008: 115). We will briefly review how senior-year Success Academy addresses both of these issues.

Cultural Integrity and Cultural Capital in a College Preparatory Program: What Works?

Maintain Cultural Integrity. "College preparation programs framed by a focus on cultural wealth *and* academic skills development can have a substantial impact on college enrollment rates of underrepresented students" (Villapando and Solorzano 2005: 26). The senior-year classes for Success Academy students are framed exactly this way.

All of the SDSU professors who teach courses for Success Academy seniors do so in ways that honor the community cultural wealth (Yosso 2006) the students bring with them into the classroom. Successful Native students seem to draw most heavily on four forms of capital that constitute community cultural wealth— aspirational capital, familial capital, resistant capital, and navigational capital (Lindley 2009: 144–163). An understanding of students' aspirational, familial, resistant, and navigational capital clearly informs the SDSU professors' decisions about what to teach (curriculum) and how to teach (instructional techniques). The approach taken by the professors is called in the literature a "cultural integrity" framework (Deyhle 1995; Cummins 1997) because it affirms students' identities.

The focus of the senior-year classes has always been on academic skills development. This has been particularly important in the areas of mathematics and English. High academic standards are the clearest indicators of whether children will go on to postsecondary education (Adelman 2002). About one-third of all freshmen entering four-year colleges in South Dakota need some kind of remedial work (Complete College America 2012). Success Academy tries to ensure that its scholars are not among them.

Generate Cultural Capital. Success Academy tries to imbue its students with a form of cultural capital that white, middle-class students take for granted. The kind of cultural capital emphasized in Success Academy is called "academic instrumental knowledge" (AIK) (Rueda, Monzo, and Arzubiaga 2003). AIK is defined as knowledge, skills, and aspirations that are useful for academic success and that facilitate the college-going process (Corwin, Colyar, and Tierney 2005: 6). Those who write about academic instrumental knowledge are quick to point out that correctly incorporating it into college preparatory programs does not impinge on students' cultural backgrounds.

There are numerous kinds of academic instrumental knowledge FIS seniors receive through their participation in Success Academy. These include the "how-tos" of applying for college, taking the ACT, and obtaining financial aid.

Success Academy also gives seniors access to valuable social networks, creating educational opportunities the students otherwise might not have. For example, a campus visit with an academic department head may lead to a scholarship. A conversation with TRiO staff during pre-orientation day may open up a slot in the program for a Success Academy student that might otherwise have gone to someone else.

It is not enough to simply develop initiatives like those just described that increase college access for individual Native students. We must also be aware of the larger, structural constraints, deeply embedded in our universities, that discourage American Indians from fully participating. If Native students who attend under-resourced schools are ill-prepared for college, then preparatory courses must be offered free of charge by the colleges themselves to remedy this situation. If tuition rates for American Indians are discriminatory, then regents and legislators must be challenged to enact change. These are only a few of the confrontations in which Success Academy engaged as our students moved through their last year of high school and into their first year of college. Their postsecondary journey, and what we learned as we accompanied them on it, is the subject of Chapter 6.

6

Counterhegemony and the Scholars' Transition to College

In 2004 the first cohort of Success Academy scholars graduated from the Flandreau Indian School in May and enrolled as true freshmen at South Dakota State University in August. The name *scholars* was chosen deliberately for these special students. That label was intended to help the students *see* themselves as part of a cohort that had successfully finished high school (and senior-year Success Academy) and was now moving on to the next goal of completing college.

Two of the five Success Academy scholars had participated in FIS-SDSU Success Academy since its start during their freshman year of high school. The other three students had enrolled at FIS later in their high school careers.

In all, 52 Success Academy scholars have enrolled as true freshmen at SDSU starting in Fall 2004. Of that group, two have graduated from SDSU and at least 12 have transferred to other institutions. Just as the Flandreau Indian School has had difficulty keeping track of its alumni, so, too, has Success Academy at South Dakota State University. That said, 37 percent of the Success Academy scholars who started school at SDSU as true freshmen either graduated from SDSU or transferred to another college. Overall, for American Indian/Alaska Natives across the United States, the six-year college graduation rate is about 37 percent (Brayboy et al. 2012: 57).

The FIS-SDSU Success Academy partnership ended in 2012 when a final cohort of seven seniors graduated from FIS and enrolled as true freshmen at SDSU. Reasons for ending the partnership are myriad and complex. They will be discussed in more detail later in the chapter. But what one administrator called "limited success with student retention and graduation" at SDSU was a significant factor.

This chapter will examine what Native scholars and critical theorists have to say about questions such as the following:

- What constitutes "success" in Native American higher education? (Pavel and Inglebret 2007: 150)
- Would "stepping out" (McAfee 2000) be a more appropriate term than "dropping out" to describe American Indian students leaving college?
- Is "the problem" Indian students, or is "the problem" the institutions that purport to serve them? (Tierney 1992)

Conventional approaches to college access and student success are hegemonic in that they often exclude indigenous understandings (Pidgeon 2008–2009: 339). Broadening notions of success and considering alternate theories of student retention are examples of counterhegemony.

This chapter will begin by defining hegemony and counterhegemony as they relate to Native education. Then the chapter will address more specifically counterhegemony and Native retention in higher education.

The chapter's focus, however, will be on Success Academy student retention at South Dakota State University. We will use a framework developed by William G. Tierney (1992: 36) called the "critical theory/empowerment approach to American Indian student retention." Most discussions of Native American retention focus on the individual student. "What is it with them anyway?" (McDermott 1987: 362) becomes the central question. Our discussion, organized around Tierney's framework, is counterhegemonic in that it focuses on the institution's role in Native student success.

The chapter will end where the book began, by looking back at systemic change throughout the 12-year history of the Flandreau Indian School-South Dakota State University Success Academy. We will reflect on successes and challenges, what worked and what didn't.

We will then look ahead to how K–16 partnerships and college access programs, like Success Academy, might adapt to a "new normal" (Bruininks, Keeney, and Thorp 2010) to meet the demographic and economic challenges facing universities in the future.

Hegemony and Native Education

Italian social theorist Antonio Gramsci (1992) uses the term "hegemony" to describe the domination of ideas in the major institutions of capitalist society, for example, in the education system. Hegemony can describe the "oppressive structures inherent in schools" (Wink 2000: 82). Power is used in subtle ways, hard to see, because the dominated groups may partially support the process.

Janine Pease-Windy Boy (Crow Tribe of Indians of Montana), former president of Little Big Horn College, gives this example. She points out that, for decades, large groups of Indian students have been vocationally tracked. Since admission to college often depends on high school classes completed and grade point averages earned, tracking is especially damaging to underrepresented students like Native Americans. The educational selection processes are "powerful and political sifters of human potential" (Pease-Windy Boy 1995: 406). As Pease-Windy Boy (1995) explains:

> In the fall of 1992, the college and university admissions officers in Montana met to discuss admission waivers. The author was present. Each unit retold how they were granted a number of admission waivers based on the total enrollment ceiling. Alas, none of these institutions had used their waivers, for few if any students (Indian and non-Indian) had applied for a waiver. Although convenient for the schools, this explanation indicated to the author that students in Montana have self-selected—that is, sorted and sifted themselves out of the system's reach. The political message of education's "sort and sift" has apparently been internalized and then been personally applied to themselves. (406–407)

Hegemony occurs when dominant groups come together and sustain leadership over subordinate groups (Apple 1996: 14). Clearly, tracking as it is applied to American Indian students is a hegemonic process. To be completely true to a definition of hegemony, however, the dominated group has to at least partially support the process. Then voices are silenced, and identities are diminished. This is what happens when students decide not to apply for waivers, waivers designed in principle to make college more accessible.

Counterhegemony and Native Education

The term *counterhegemony*, as it is used in the context of schools, describes situations in which "power relationships are reconstructed to make central the voices and experiences of those who have historically existed at the margins of public institutions" (Darder, Baltodano, and Torres 2009: 12). Brazilian Paulo Freire is considered the father of critical scholarship in education, and his work centers around issues of power, culture, and oppression within schools. "His most important contribution has to do with the mind-set of individuals within school systems, which appears to be both unfair and hegemonic," writes Kitty Kelly Epstein (2006: 8). Freire (1994: 8) views schools as places where people should struggle for justice with "critical hope." In other words, Freire urges progressive educators to actively engage in counterhegemony in their classrooms.

Geneva Gay (1995: 173) says that those teachers who refuse to allow students to learn in styles congruent with their cultures engage in "pedagogical hegemony." She points out that Native American cultures tend to be highly communal, group-based, and action-oriented.

Counterhegemonic teaching for Native students should then, by extension, involve strategies that are "participatory, cooperative and collaborative" rather than "competitive, individualistic and passive" (Gay 1995: 173). A good example of counterhegemonic teaching is the Kamehameha Early Education Program (KEEP) for Native Hawaiian students. By matching methods of teaching language arts to Native Hawaiian cultural styles, the program dramatically increased academic achievement among its students (Kawakami 2003a, 2003b).

Counterhegemonic writing is called "counternarrative" (discussed in more detail in Chapter 5). Counternarratives can challenge the hegemonic master narratives that are so pervasive and so damaging to American Indian identity. Caskey Russell (Tlingit of Alaska) reminds us that while the notion of the counternarrative is now closely associated with Critical Race Theory, CRT simply "reached back to a long-standing practice of storytelling…common to oppressed groups like American Indians" (Russell 2011: 132).

Lisa K. Neuman (2008) presents a fascinating account of counterhegemonic writing that occurred at a school for American Indians in Muskogee, Oklahoma, in the early 20th century. Neuman (2008: 196) says that at Bacone College "students took hegemonic cultural ideas about Indianness that were known but were often left unsaid and articulated them through Indian play, thereby making them open to negotiation and contestation." Neuman (2008) gives the example of students writing humorous headlines in the school newspaper, declaring they had gone "savage" or implying they were "uncivilized":

> Students seized the opportunity to bring such hegemonic cultural meanings out in the open, to confront them in the public forum of their campus peer culture. Moreover, this public peer culture was possible because of the specific historical, financial, legal, and social forces at Bacone College that created an environment in which ideas about Indianness could be openly expressed. (196)

Neuman makes an important point: Hegemonic cultural meanings, like those surrounding Indian identity, draw their power largely from being unconscious. Once people become aware of them, they are then transformed into either "the iteration of overt dominant ideologies" or "rebellious counterhegemonic cultural forms" (Neuman 2008: 196).

Counterhegemony and Native Retention in Higher Education

To repeat an important point made earlier, conventional approaches to college access and student success often exclude indigenous understandings (Pidgeon 2008–2009: 339). Supposedly commonsense, taken-for-granted assumptions, largely developed around white students, can become hegemonic when applied to American Indians. Those with power may assume (and convince others to assume) that a one-size-fits-all approach to retention will serve equally well students who are Native American as well as students from other cultural groups.

Counterhegemony "deconstructs what is deemed normative by hegemonic discourse" (Pascarella 2007: 46). Again, as mentioned earlier, the words *success*, *dropout*, and *problem* are all contested terms for critical theorists writing about Native retention in higher education. The issues surrounding each of these words will be discussed in more detail as we examine the Success Academy scholars' transition from the Flandreau Indian School to South Dakota State University.

What Is "Success"?

How Native students define success is often far different from how it is defined by non-Native students and predominantly white universities. "The way that success is conceptualized is grounded in one's individual and collective identity," writes Skokomish scholar D. Michael Pavel and his coauthor Ella Inglebret (Pavel and Inglebret 2007: 150). "For American Indian and Alaska Native students, Native identity will provide the framework through which success is defined."

Each of the 52 Success Academy scholars who attended South Dakota State University has his or her own view of the world. Here we present two real stories of American Indian success. The first is by Daniel "Dino" Johns, Success Academy's first college graduate. The next is by Alaina Hanks, the program's second college graduate.

Daniel "Dino" Johns: "Don't Give Up!" It is important for college preparatory programs such as Success Academy to create their own success stories. Each year, as a new cohort of students graduates from high school and moves into college, our program has more scholars to call on for stories of inspiration. Every FIS-SDSU Success Academy commencement is a celebration, but none more so than the one held on May 5, 2010. That was the day that Success Academy, then 10 years old, recognized its first scholar to graduate from college.

The commencement speech was delivered by that graduate. Dino is a Gila River Pima from Sacaton, Arizona. He came to the Flandreau Indian School when he was a sophomore. He participated in Success Academy for three years before enrolling full-time at SDSU in Fall 2005. Dino was raised by his grandmother, Ruth Johns, who attended Success Academy commencement and listened to Dino's words, addressed to the younger students:

> I'd like to encourage you all to go on to higher education. It's not the easiest thing you'll ever do, but it's definitely not the hardest either. I struggled at times, but I just kept with it even when I felt like giving up. It took me awhile, but I did it, and I'll be graduating this weekend with a Bachelor of Science in Electronics Engineering Technology. I remember I used to call home, complaining about classes and how tough it is. Then my grandma would be telling me about all her doctors' appointments. Also at that time she was on dialysis. So I really didn't have anything to complain about. We've all been through tough times in our lives before, and we made it through those, so taking a few college classes should be nothing. It's only a few years out of your life, and you can still have a life when you are going to college. A lot of people get the misconception that when you're in college, it's all school all the time. You'll still have time to hang out with your friends and do fun stuff. I wanted to go to college not only for myself, but for my family, too. We all could probably think of at least one person, if not more, that we would want to have a better life than ours. Think about that person when times are tough and you feel like giving up. I have a lot of nieces, nephews, cousins and other family that look up to me, so I have plenty of reasons to stay motivated. I also wanted to get a college degree to change the question in my family from "Are you going to college?" to "Where are you going to college?" I'm glad to say that it seems to have happened, and I was part of the reason why.

Success Academy has been blessed by having scholars like Dino and Alaina, generous and willing to tell their stories. These scholars provide inspiration, advice, and motivation for younger students just starting on their educational journeys.

Alaina Hanks: "Education Is Important to Bring About Change." Alaina, a member of the White Earth Anishinabbe Tribe, plans to graduate from SDSU in May 2013. She attended FIS and participated in Success Academy during her last three years of high school.

After moving to SDSU in fall 2007, Alaina became the first recipient of the Jack and Marty Marken Scholarship for Native American Students. She was also the first Success Academy scholar to study abroad. She won a highly competitive Turkish Coalition of America scholarship that allowed her to spend the

Spring 2010 semester studying at Balikesir University. When she returned, Alaina shared her experiences with younger students, exciting them about previously unimagined possibilities.

Throughout her years at SDSU, Alaina continued to work with Success Academy and its students. In 2009 she wrote these words to share with the Success Academy juniors:

> Right now I'm working on getting my bachelor's degree in English with minors in American Indian Studies and Spanish. I plan on eventually going to law school and going back to Minnesota to work on various reservations or in the Twin Cities as a public defender. I think it's important for Native students to attend college because you can't change anything by doing nothing. People will always talk about what's wrong and complain, but there's nothing you can do, unless you get your education. It's the one thing that people can't take away from you. Education is so important, not only to bring about change, but also for yourself. It's something that helps you grow into the person you're supposed to be. Whether you go to a tech school, a community college, a university like SDSU, or a job-training program, it's just important that you keep learning.

So what is "success" to our Native students? It is finishing what you have begun, being a role model, developing a voice, serving one's tribal community, and so much more. We learn from students, like Alaina and Dino, that we all must be willing to share our stories. Only then can we teach each other what is possible.

Should "Dropping Out" Be Called "Stepping Out"?

A majority of Native students have at least one "stepping out" experience sometime during their college careers (Brayboy et al. 2012: 59). "Stepping out" is a term coined by Mary E. McAfee (2000) based on a qualitative study involving 43 Native undergraduates attending four-year institutions. "Stepping out" captures the dynamic nature of American Indian students moving into, out of, and back again into higher education. McAfee (2000) identifies eight "stepping stones" that affect students' paths toward eventual graduation: cultural identity, academic preparation, financial resources, motivation, family support, academic performance, alcohol and drug use, and institutional interface.

Statistics about Native student retention and graduation, couched in traditional terms such as "dropping out," may be unreliable, says Lumbee scholar Bryan McKinley Jones Brayboy and his co-authors (Brayboy et al. 2012: 59). As McAfee writes, "It is essential to understand that stepping out does not imply the departure from the broad system of higher education, indeed, it implies continuation at a later time." She ties her work to that of Tierney (1992) titled *Official Encouragement,*

Institutional Discouragement: Minorities in Academe—the Native American Experience. "Without an understanding of institutional discouragement that fails to recognize and support the phenomenon of stepping out, there is a serious lack of systemic commitment to the spirit and intent of increasing diversity on campuses," McAfee (2000) writes. "Without widespread institutional change, American Indians will continue to be underrepresented in higher education."

Following are three stories of Success Academy scholars who left SDSU between 2007 and 2010. Each story illustrates, in a slightly different way, the phenomenon of "stepping out."

Stepping Out to Be Closer to Family. Alyandra Aday (White Mountain Apache) was a Success Academy scholar during the 2009–2010 academic year. She majored in Pre-Dental while at South Dakota State University. With assistance from SDSU staff, she transferred to Northern Arizona University at the end of the spring semester to be closer to her family in Fort Apache, Arizona.

Success Academy scholars often keep in close touch with SDSU faculty even after moving on to finish school elsewhere. Alyandra is now majoring in Forestry with a certificate in Wildland Fire Ecology and Management. Her co-curricular activities include involvement in the Forestry Club, the Student Association for Fire Ecology, Native Americans United, the Society of American Foresters, and the National Society of Leadership and Success (Northern Arizona University 2012).

Alyandra plans to graduate in May 2014. She recently received the Virgil Masayesva Native American Environmental Education Scholarship. Shortly thereafter this quote from Alyandra appeared on the university's website (Northern Arizona University 2012):

> I chose the certificate in Wildland Fire Ecology and Management because I have a strong desire to work with fire in a positive way to help better our forest or just to stop it from harming our tribal land....I have a strong passion for the outdoors and really enjoy doing all the outdoor recreation. Making a career out of it is something I always wanted to do. I am able to become knowledgeable within the field, enjoy the outdoors, better our forest, and enjoy my future job.

Stepping Out to Attend Tribal College. For some students, attending tribal college brings them not only closer to home but also closer to culture. Jillian Pappan (Omaha Tribe of Nebraska) was a Success Academy scholar and SDSU Journalism major during the Fall 2006 and Fall 2007 semesters. In a recent telephone conversation, Jillian said she "thoroughly enjoyed classes" at SDSU, particularly her Honors Speech course.

Jillian, who is from Sioux City, Iowa, left SDSU to attend Nebraska Indian Community College in South Sioux City, Nebraska. Jillian is a published author—her poem, "If I Could See the Sky," appeared in an anthology compiled by the National Museum of the American Indian (Pappan 1999: 24). She has also received national recognition (including a story in the *Washington Post*) for being one of six Native Americans to legally challenge the Washington Redskins name and logo as "racist" (Weiss 2006). Her political activism has continued as she travelled with other Nebraska Indian Community College students to Washington, D.C., to lobby Congress on climate change (Power Shift 2007).

Stepping Out to Another Academic Track. "Institutional interface" is one of the eight factors that can prevent "stepping out" of college temporarily from becoming "dropping out" permanently (McAfee 2000). The term "institutional interface" covers a wide range of activities by faculty and administrators, all aimed at supporting American Indian students. In its simplest form, "institutional interface" could mean keeping in touch with students—via mail, e-mail, and telephone—while they are transitioning from one school to the next.

Brennon Lyons (Omaha Nation) was a Success Academy scholar and an SDSU Nutrition/Food Science major during the 2005–2006 academic year. He left to attend Nebraska Indian Community College during the Fall 2006 semester and returned to SDSU for the Spring 2007 semester.

Before leaving SDSU in May 2007, Brennon was mentored by faculty and staff from TRiO, Native American Student Advising, the College of Family and Consumer Sciences, Success Academy, and many other offices throughout the university. Between 2007 and 2012, some of these individuals continued to keep in touch with Brennon. In April 2012 I received this e-mail from him:

I am now living in Las Vegas, working as a Certified Nursing Assistant as well as a personal caregiver. I just wanted to tell you that all is well. I have never had the opportunity to thank you for all that you have done for me. I always remember your words, "Find something that you are good at, and something that you are passionate about." At that time I did not know the meaning behind those wise words, but today I do. It was those words that stuck with me all these years. Here's what I have been up to. I am working for a company here in Las Vegas in an inclusive Alzheimer's home, a ten-bed house. It is a wonderful job. I graduated from Tri-State Nursing about two years ago and just finished up at a six-month program to be a personal caregiver about a month ago. I was referred to the company by my instructor. I just wanted to let you know that I am doing really well and that I have not forgotten about you…as well as the awesome staff at SDSU. I am eventually going to go back and further my education to become an LPN and then a nurse. I am working really hard to get to that point. (personal communication, April 27, 2012)

Retention statistics, as they are currently maintained, would count the three Native American students just described as SDSU "dropouts." But each of the three is moving toward degree completion, in large part because of the Success Academy program and South Dakota State University.

Distinguished Professor of English Charles L. Woodard, who serves on Success Academy's steering committee and who has been working closely with SDSU American Indian students for nearly 40 years, reflects on the situation this way:

> I believe that the graduation rates for this invaluable program will eventually be much higher. All of the Success Academy students who participated in it, whether or not they chose to attempt college after they graduated from high school, will carry with them for the rest of their lives the idea that higher education is important and possible. I believe that some of them, perhaps even significant numbers of them, will eventually act upon that idea, and obtain their degrees.

Is "the Problem" Indian Students—or the Institutions They Attend?

Most research on college student persistence is based on Vincent Tinto's highly acclaimed model of student departure (Tinto 1993). The model's premise is that social and academic integration into the university are essential to student retention. But as Tierney (2000: 218) explains, "The onus in such a model is on the individual. The individual integrates; the individual undergoes the ritual; the individual finds ways to fit into the academic and social milieu of the institution." The model assumes that students must fit into an alien culture. Those who do not become "the problem" for the institution.

A critical theory/empowerment approach to American Indian student retention turns Tinto's model on its head (Tierney 2000: 219). Such an approach recognizes that "the problem" is the institution itself. Tierney (1992: 36) says that predominantly white institutions must create within themselves "the organizational conditions for empowerment" of Native students.

Tierney knows whereof he speaks. He served as academic dean at Fort Berthold Community College, a tribal college in New Town, North Dakota, before moving on to the Pennsylvania State University and the University of Southern California. Tierney's ideas on organizational adaptation, organizational voice, organizational bridges, organizational effectiveness, and organizational culture were covered in detail in Chapter 3. In this chapter we focus on "the organizational conditions for empowerment" (Tierney 1992: 36) that relate specifically to student retention.

Before proceeding, it should be noted that Success Academy was created to be, first and foremost, a college preparatory program for American Indian students; soon after it became recognized as a social change agent for a predominantly white university. The intent was not the recruitment of more American Indian students to South Dakota State University, although the Success Academy scholars who did take SDSU classes and ultimately enrolled were warmly welcomed to campus. Nor was the intent to create a retention program for these students once they started college. It was assumed, until May 2005, that the university as a whole would provide the support needed to retain the Success Academy scholars.

Of the first group of five Success Academy scholars to enroll full-time at SDSU in Fall 2004, four had left the university and one had transferred to another institution by the end of their freshman year. Clearly steps needed to be taken to improve retention. Charles R. Colbert, Joseph J. Saggio, and Dawn Tato (2004: 146) note that "institutions serious about retaining American Indian/Alaska Native students should seriously consider forming a retention task force." This is exactly what SDSU did. A Success Academy steering committee was formed specifically to address retention. As a committee, a "critical theory/empowerment approach" (Tierney 1992: 36) guided our work. In explaining this approach Tierney (1992: 49) says, "Failure exists in postsecondary institutions before students are admitted, enrolled, or take classes. Failure, or leave taking, or departure does not come in the door when the students enter." If that is so, then what could we as educators do about it?

On the one hand, we initially had no additional funding available for student retention. On the other, we knew we had a responsibility to nurture the Success Academy scholars we had encouraged to attend our university. And, our steering committee included people with power to enact change—the SDSU provost, two academic deans, the FIS principal, the school's superintendent, and a senior vice president at Citibank.

The strategies implemented were counterhegemonic because they took several taken-for-granted, business-as-usual practices, once considered sufficient for student retention, and turned them on their heads. Certainly all our attempts were not successful. That said, we did make serious efforts to change aspects of the institution that seemed to disempower Success Academy scholars. Many practices implemented by Success Academy are now being used throughout the university to improve the retention of Native and non-Native students alike.

Counterhegemonic Strategies and Success Academy Retention

Transportation

Financial resources play an important role in shaping college plans (Stuber 2011: 36). When FIS students began attending SDSU full-time, the first assumption we confronted was that they could afford to get to campus for New Student Orientation in June and for first-semester classes in August, like most other new freshmen.

Throughout the years, Success Academy scholars have come to SDSU from states as distant as Arizona and Wisconsin. Even scholars coming from neighboring states have had transportation issues. The Turtle Mountain Indian Reservation, where two Success Academy scholars (twin sisters) lived, is located close to the Canadian border. Another scholar came from Iowa but needed transportation not only for herself but also for her baby and for her sister who would be caring for her baby.

In May 2004, our first cohort of five Success Academy seniors graduated from the Flandreau Indian School and returned to their homes—in Minnesota, North Dakota, and Wisconsin. In June 2004 the seniors needed to be back on the South Dakota State University campus for New Student Orientation.

Eastern South Dakota, where SDSU is located, has no passenger rail lines and extremely limited bus service. Also we soon learned that transporting students in rental cars was problematic due to liability issues. Out of options for transporting the three Wisconsin students, we called on the colleges in which the students would be majoring for help. College of Family and Consumer Sciences Dean Laurie Stenberg Nichols (who is now SDSU's provost) had an idea—why not fly the students back and forth to campus on the university's airplane?

On June 17, 2004, SDSU's six-person, twin-engine plane made its descent onto a remote airstrip in Keshena, Wisconsin, in the heart of the Menominee Indian Reservation. Those of us on the plane—the pilot, an FIS counselor, and I—were uncertain if we would find any students there to meet us. Those on the ground were equally uncertain if they would be met. The plane taxied to a stop, and the door opened. We saw not only our three students but also a huge crowd of family and friends who had come to see them off to college. We ran over to the fence and were greeted with smiles, hugs, and warmth. After ensuring the students' relatives that we would take good care of their children, we packed the airplane tight with sleeping bags, suitcases, food, and everything else the students thought they could possibly need for New Student Orientation, and we headed back to Brookings.

Throughout Success Academy's history, I have often thought of that day. It set the tone for what an institution can do, officially and institutionally (to use Tierney's terms), to truly encourage Native American participation in higher education.

Orientation

Finances can influence far more than students' ability to travel back and forth to campus. Many seemingly small fees, like those charged for mandatory events, are really not so small for students and their families living below the poverty line.

New Student Orientation. New Student Orientation is a two-day event held every summer for all incoming SDSU freshmen. Attendance is required because students register for classes, tour the university, meet with faculty in their majors, and engage in myriad other activities critical to success in college.

The two-day New Student Orientation is reasonably priced for most students. Fees are typically about $25 per person for meals and about $10 per person per night for rooms. Families are encouraged to attend.

It is important to remember, however, when discussing issues such as fees, that hegemonic practices draw their power from being largely unconscious. We, as a Success Academy steering committee, had to first become aware that many of our students and their relatives could not afford to attend New Student Orientation. Next we had to set about making sure that these fees were paid for the students and their families by the Success Academy program.

SDSU offers several New Student Orientation sessions throughout the summer, each with a couple of hundred attendees. Success Academy asks all of its scholars to sign up for the same session. Respectful planning in this regard is necessary because many tribes have ceremonies such as Sun Dance in which students participate during the summer months.

New Student Orientation can actually be somewhat *dis*orienting for the Success Academy scholars. Despite years of visits to SDSU, it is the first time the scholars have truly experienced the university as a predominantly white institution. At most Success Academy events held at SDSU, American Indians are in the majority. By having all of the Success Academy scholars attend the same orientation session we move toward creating something of a "critical mass." Barbara Astone and Elsa Nunez-Wormack (1990: 65) say that critical mass means having enough students around who are like oneself so as not to feel isolated, uncomfortable, and alone. As one student explains, "There are other minorities there, so I don't have to feel like a Martian" (Loo and Rolison 1986: 69).

We encourage Success Academy scholars to bring family members with them to New Student Orientation. We have a meal for scholars and families right before the first orientation session. This allows relatives to become acquainted with each other and with Success Academy staff and steering committee members who will be working with the scholars. Throughout that day and the next, these staff members are continuously circulating throughout the Student Union where New Student Orientation is held, assisting as needed and being "familiar faces" for the Native students and their families.

Success Academy Orientation. Success Academy orientation is held the last week of August, just before the start of fall classes. This event is patterned after a similar one at the University of North Dakota, a school noted for its exemplary support of American Indian students. As described by Donna L. Brown (Turtle Mountain Chippewa), formerly of UND, the orientation "is an opportunity for students to find out about…programs for American Indian students and more importantly to connect with the Native American community" (Brown 2005: 89).

The first Success Academy orientation was in August 2005, shortly after the formation of the retention/steering committee. That orientation involved Success Academy scholars as well as Multicultural scholars (students involved in the university's 2+2+2 program described in detail in Chapter 1). While specific orientation activities and schedules change from year to year, the overall intent remains the same—to make the transition from high school to college as seamless as possible for Native American students. The Family Education Model, developed by Iris HeavyRunner and Richard DeCelles (2002), is the foundation upon which the orientation is built—the scholars' relatives are deliberately engaged as partners working toward their students' educational success.

On Saturday Success Academy orientation begins with Native American Club members on hand to welcome scholars and their families as they arrive on campus. After helping with the move into the residence halls, the club hosts a cookout at a nearby church. Over the years several parents have said how comforting it is to leave campus that evening, seeing their children surrounded by a supportive community of Native and non-Native faculty, staff, and students.

On Sunday the scholars meet in the Lakota/Dakota Conference Room for "Real Life 101." It is an afternoon of hands-on activities, aimed at providing students with an "academic toolkit" of skills needed for a successful first semester. SDSU deans, faculty, staff, and students all participate.

On Monday Success Academy scholars are paired with Native peer mentors. First the teams print out class schedules. Next they find the locations of all of the scholars' classes. Then they purchase needed books and supplies. A final stop is made at the office of each scholar's academic adviser. Classes begin the following day.

In 2009 the Citi Foundation increased its annual grant to Success Academy by $10,000. These additional monies were used to enhance the three transition-to-college activities (pre-orientation day in April, New Student Orientation in June, and Success Academy orientation in August). In 2010, with the help of a recently acquired College Access Challenge Grant from the South Dakota Board of Regents, these activities were made available to all incoming Native freshmen. Success Academy orientation was expanded into an intensive, four-day event called SAIGES (Strengthening American Indian Generational Educational Success).

Living-Learning Community

Living-learning communities (LLCs) are defined as "an academic strategy to create an environment in which more intellectual interaction will occur among students, faculty and staff by linking the core curriculum to on-campus living" (University of San Diego 2011). The Success Academy living-learning community was one of the early LLCs on the South Dakota State University campus.

Research has been done on the effects of LLCs on underrepresented and underprepared students. Findings shows that LLCs enhance students' perceptions of their own learning and help them avoid academic failure (Stassen 2003; Smith 2010).

Living Community. Most years the Success Academy living-learning community has been in Pierson Hall. It is a centrally located residence hall that houses both male and female students in separate wings or on separate floors, depending on the year.

Pierson Hall was chosen as a good fit for the Success Academy scholars. The Hobo Hangout on the lower level includes a big-screen television and games ranging from Wii and air hockey to foosball and table tennis. Many out-of-state students are housed in Pierson because it has a full complement of weekend and holiday activities for those who remain on campus.

Having a Native living-learning community is certainly not unique to South Dakota State University. Native American House at Dartmouth College is one of the oldest and most well known. Others include the American Indian Cultural House at the University of Minnesota–Twin Cities, Kanonhsesne Native American Student Community at the University of Massachusetts–Amherst, and the Native American Living-Learning Community at the University of California–Davis.

Learning Community. By definition the Success Academy LLC is a "curricular learning community" (Lenning and Ebbers 1999: 17). Curriculum coordination is the link that defines the community.

For most of the program's history, three first-semester classes for Success Academy scholars were block scheduled—Intermediate Algebra, Composition I, and Mastering Lifetime Learning Skills. (A fourth block-scheduled class, Success Academy Study Table, will be discussed later.) Because of the small number of Success Academy freshmen, block scheduling was relatively easy most years. By registering the Success Academy scholars early in the summer, we were able to block schedule them into class sections taught by faculty known to be especially supportive of Native students.

A hegemonic view of cultural living-learning communities is that they equate to "racial segregation." A counterhegemonic position (and one borne out by numerous studies) is that "ethnic clustering" in residential and academic settings is highly valued by minority students (Loo and Rolison 1986: 72). As one Native graduate assistant, who works closely with the Success Academy scholars, observes, "The students feel a lot of support from the community and from one another." The students always have readily accessible study partners—and they do not quite so often have that "feeling like a Martian" experience (Loo and Rolison 1986: 69) of walking into class and being the only Native student. Chalsa M. Loo and Garry Rolison (1986: 72) identify two institutional factors that can counter the alienation of minority students and promote their academic success. The first factor is "the presence of a residential, sociopolitical, academic community on campus that provides cultural support where the larger university seems ethnically unsupportive." The second factor is "supportive and accessible faculty who impart a sense of academic and personal worth to students." Success Academy has tried to address both of these factors through the creation of its living-learning community.

The College Access Challenge Grant from the South Dakota Board of Regents, mentioned earlier, made possible the transformation of what was once the "Success Academy living-learning community" into what has become the "Tioti living-learning community." "Tioti" is a combination of the words "tiospaye" (family) and "tipi" (dwelling). The new community was named by former Native American student adviser Ron McKinney (Choctaw Nation). It is open to all incoming Native freshmen.

Culture-Based Strategies for Native Student Success

Historically the United States has used its educational system as an instrument to eradicate traditional Native culture and remake Natives according to the image of dominant society. Federal Indian boarding schools have been part of this "hegemonic agenda" (Jester 2002).

Certainly many changes have occurred in the federal Indian boarding school system since the time of Captain Richard Pratt and the Carlisle (Pennsylvania) Indian School. That said, the Flandreau Indian School students who come to South Dakota State University experience high school in far different ways than other incoming college freshmen.

"Our students need more academic preparation," says FIS counselor Zonya Tantype (Crow Creek Sioux), who has worked in Indian boarding schools for more than 30 years. She mentions the lack of upper-level classes and insufficient "rigor" in existing classes as problems confronting FIS and its students.

Since 2000 when the Success Academy partnership began there have been numerous "Reductions in Force" at FIS, "RIFs" that have drastically decreased the number of teachers and staff. Insufficient funding affects many areas of school operation. For example, a limited number of textbooks means that those available have to stay in the classrooms. Throughout their high school careers, FIS students have little to no homework to complete after school hours. "Part of the students' problems when they go to college is our fault," Tantype says. "They need to learn time management."

In fact, the many committed administrators, teachers, and staff at the Flandreau Indian School do an amazing job of educating their students under very challenging circumstances with extremely limited resources. Closure of the school has been discussed not once, but several times during the history of our partnership. The situation at FIS and many similar schools exists despite the federal government's obligations—through laws, treaties, and policies established over hundreds of years—to provide adequate funding for Indian education.

It is important to note that many students, both Native and non-Native, graduate from high school unprepared for college. About 35 percent of all freshmen entering four-year colleges in South Dakota need some kind of remedial work (Complete College America 2012). Only 53 percent of all entering freshmen graduate from South Dakota State University within six years (Complete College America 2011).

That said, starting and finishing college present special challenges for Native students. "The U.S. dominant culture's values and ways of knowing depicted in college curriculum assume that American Indian/Alaska Native college students will assimilate to dominant cultural beliefs and values in order to acquire a degree in higher education," writes Nanci M. Burk (2007). She calls this the "hegemonic pedagogical paradigm."

Mainstream institutions such as SDSU, which officially encourage American Indians to enroll, must lead the way in developing culture-based strategies for Native student success. Success Academy regards this as a necessary and appropriate counterhegemonic practice. The following four sections outline the specifics of how this is done.

Two of the strategies to be discussed—the employment of Native American "success coaches" and a study room decorated with American Indian art—are clearly culture-based. These strategies, drawing as they do on the notions of "community cultural wealth" (Yosso 2006) explained in Chapter 5, affirm and honor students' identities.

The other two strategies—study table and laptop computers—align more closely with culture as it is used in the term "cultural capital." "Cultural capital" can come from a state-sponsored source (Mehan et al. 1996), also as explained in Chapter 5. Students who have attended a federal Indian boarding school may understandably come to the university unaccustomed to structuring their own study time or lacking the technology to be academically successful. By making available study tables and laptop computers, programs like Success Academy can supply students with certain kinds of "cultural capital" they may not have received from their families.

Success Coach. A recent article in *The Chronicle of Higher Education* defines a "success coach" as someone who can "motivate and counsel students, many of whom need more than positive reinforcement and time-management tips" (Farrell 2007: A25). During the 2005–2006 academic year, Success Academy employed its first-ever success coach for the six scholars then enrolled. At that time Success Academy was headquartered in the SDSU College of Engineering. The Engineering college decided that retaining Native students was an important enough goal to commit a graduate assistant position to achieving it.

Success Academy has had three Native success coaches during its 12-year history. All were pursuing master's degrees in Counseling at SDSU. Their job was to help the younger Success Academy scholars navigate mainstream university culture, without losing their Native identity. Jean E. Ness (2002: 39) stresses the importance of hiring Native American staff to promote a welcoming atmosphere and provide needed role models for students.

The success coaches, all young and female, had to walk a careful line between that of "academic adviser" and "elder sister." During study tables, they could be strict and demanding. Through the years they learned they could accomplish more by rewarding than by punishing. For example, perfect attendance at study table for a certain amount of time was recognized with a treat for all the scholars, such as going bowling or having pizza.

Through their work, the success coaches lived out the values of bravery, fortitude, generosity, and wisdom (Marshall 2002). Those of us around them grew because of that.

Less than one half of one percent of all staff in higher education are Native American (Fox 2005: 51). Providing Native graduate students with opportunities to hone their professional skills while working with Native undergraduates is an example of empowerment. The first success coach, Jill Kessler (Cheyenne River Sioux Tribe), became a school counselor at the Cheyenne-Eagle Butte (South Dakota) Primary School. The second success coach, April Eastman (Sisseton-Wahpeton Oyate), moved into the position of Native American student adviser at SDSU. The third success coach, Eliza Yellow Bird Johns (Mandan, Hidatsa, and

Arikara/Muscogee Nation), is earning a doctorate in Higher Education at the University of Arizona.

Study Table. Success Academy scholars meet with their success coach two hours a day, three days a week, for a regularly scheduled class called Study Table. Study Table is mandatory for all first-year Success Academy scholars. Many other study tables, with mandatory attendance, operate across campus, for example, those involving student athletes and fraternity/sorority members.

Success Academy study table sessions reinforce what is covered in the schol-ars' first-semester Mastering Lifetime Learning Skills course. Students set long- and short-term goals, which they review periodically with the success coach. Each study table begins with students checking their academic planners and noting what has to be accomplished that particular day or week. Then students set to work on their assignments, with the success coach assisting as needed.

Student issues, addressed by the success coach during study table, often extend far beyond academics. For students who have attended a federal Indian boarding school for four years, college life presents special challenges. The Flandreau Indian School has myriad rules that govern student life. Dormitory lights go out at 10:30 p.m., and sleeping after 7:45 a.m. is not allowed. The campus is closed, which means students cannot leave without being "checked out."

Programs like Success Academy that serve special populations of Native stu-dents have a particular obligation to assist them as they transition to college. "Do not assume that mainstream teaching methods are appropriate for Native American students," Comanche scholar Mary Jo Tippeconnic Fox (2005: 55) says. Her reminder guides our work. In reflecting on the Success Academy scholars' first semester at SDSU, one former success coach explains:

> A majority of the students struggled with the freedom that college offered. They all came from a very structured school system at the Flandreau Indian School and the transition into college life was new to them. They were having to hold themselves responsible for their actions and getting what they needed done for the most part on their own. In some cases it was a matter of getting to bed at a reasonable hour so that they would wake up for early classes. In other cases it was learning to structure their time to turn in assignments on time and not procrastinate.

Students connecting with other adults, like the success coaches who mentor them throughout college, is important. Sherrie A. Bosse and her colleagues at the University of South Dakota say this about successful Native students: "They found someone and connected at the college...and that somebody helped them stay strong....A connection needs to be made, preferably with another Native American"

(Bosse et al. 2011: 33). Success Academy study table is all about making connections at the same time and place, week after week, throughout the scholars' first year of college.

Mandatory study hours and success coaches are becoming far more commonplace on campuses nationwide, despite some objections to them as "handholding for students who are supposed to be learning to live on their own" (Farrell 2007: A26). Corporations like Complete College America and InsideTrack specialize in selling remediation and retention services to universities across the United States. "In every form of organizational life, both before and after college, you get more immediate feedback, whether it's from teachers in high school or bosses in jobs," says Alan Tripp, InsideTrack's founder. "It's time for colleges to give a lot more thought to what they can do to motivate students to be engaged and successful" (Farrell 2007: A26).

Study Room. "Students must have some place where they feel they belong," writes Navajo scholar Shelly C. Lowe (2005: 37). The Success Academy study room is just such a place for the Success Academy scholars.

Both Success Academy study table and the senior-year classes meet in the room. Its decorations include a star quilt and Native art.

Since its creation four years ago, the room has moved from its first location, in the College of Engineering's Harding Hall, to its second, in the new American Indian Education and Cultural Center. The room's purposes remain the same, and they are to affirm the identities of SDSU's Native students to whom it is dedicated and to provide a space for gathering to work on shared academic assignments.

On December 10, 2009, Success Academy dedicated the study room with a smudging and prayers by Native elders. Three fortuitous circumstances had coincided during the previous year, making the study room possible.

First, the Electrical Engineering and Computer Science Department moved to a new building, and the conference room on the first floor of Harding Hall, next to two preexisting Success Academy offices, was vacated. Second, some funding became available through the Citi Foundation grant, monies originally requested for senior-year classes but left unspent. Third, an upper-level Interior Design class was studying Lakota culture and looking for a hands-on project.

With the help of the students and their professor, an old conference table was restored and 12 new chairs purchased. Fresh paint and new flooring, supplied by the Physical Plant, helped the room further take shape.

Once finished, it quickly became a popular gathering place for Native students outside of class hours. Non-Native faculty and staff also frequently asked to use the room, and these requests were granted whenever possible.

The room attracted students for several reasons. In its original location the room was near the Success Academy living community, but air-conditioned, which the dormitory was not. Harding Hall opened at 6 a.m. and closed at 10 p.m., so the room was available as a cool, quiet study haven almost around the clock. Snacks and drinks were next door in the Success Academy offices. Best of all the room had wireless access, a printer, and paper, which Native scholars could use free of charge.

Laptop Computers. Lack of access to "educational resources" such as computers can be a barrier to college access for students living in rural and impoverished areas (Bosse et al. 2011: 34). American Indian students are more likely than other ethnic groups to come from such areas.

Initially none of the Success Academy scholars came to SDSU owning computers. This became a problem for our program and our students as more and more SDSU classes went online.

In Spring 2009 Success Academy began purchasing laptops for use by both the scholars and the FIS seniors. The number of laptops acquired eventually reached 14. From the start the laptops were stored in the success coach's office right across the hall from the Success Academy study room.

The Success Academy seniors use the laptops when they come to campus for their English class in the fall and for their Math class in the spring. The Success Academy scholars use the laptops during their study table sessions. If they wish, the scholars can check out the laptops between study tables.

The laptop purchase was made possible by the Citi Foundation grant, which supports the senior-year classes. The grant was written to cover the salary of a teacher-mentor. Some years the College of Engineering was able to cover part of the teacher-mentor's salary. Consequently, the unused grant money began to accumulate. The Citi Foundation approved the purchase of the laptops, noting that this was a critical need to ensure student success.

In concluding this section on Success Academy and student retention, one particular strategy deserves consideration: "Perceive and treat each Native student as able to succeed" (Lowe 2005: 39). Every Native student on campus is already a success. They have overcome many obstacles to get where they are now. Native students in college have not only graduated from high school, but they have also been accepted into college. Not every student is accepted, but these students were. They all have what it takes to succeed. Some may just need a little more help from us to realize that.

Systemic Change: Successes and Challenges

It is August 2012. Seven more Flandreau Indian School graduates are starting their freshman year at South Dakota State University. The FIS-SDSU Success Academy partnership is ending, just as this book is being completed.

While there have certainly been challenges during the past 12 years of Success Academy, the successes have been pronounced—and noted. Stories on the program have appeared in many local and national media, including Keloland Television, National Public Radio, *The Houston Chronicle*, *Indian Country Today*, and *Ikce Wicasta Journal*. Nationally syndicated columnist Tim Giago has written about Success Academy. The national publication, *Native Village News*, headlined its story "Success Academy a Model for Native American Education." This book is an opportunity to tell about Success Academy's successes and challenges to an even wider audience.

It is significant that the FIS-SDSU Success Academy has existed for 12 years, in some senses an eternity in Indian education. That said, 12 years is only a moment in time, when we consider that mainstream education has been used to suppress the culture, language, and spirituality of American Indians for the past 500 years.

This book, illustrating critical theory in action, has focused on systemic change. In the end, as we reflect on where we have been and where we are going, these words by Hugh Mehan and his colleagues at the University of California, San Diego (Mehan et al. 1996) are worth considering:

> Before we celebrate the transformation of schools from settings for the reproduction of social inequality into instruments of social equity, we must, of course, determine if the actions we have observed are *substantial, long-term institutional changes*. For, if we have only revealed changes on the margin, then we do not have genuine mobility patterns, but a cynical affordance—a process of allowing a precious few members of the underclass through the gates so as to legitimate achievement ideology, while the great masses are kept down. (217–218)

Enacting *substantial, long-term institutional change*, the kind that Mehan describes, has been the aim of FIS-SDSU Success Academy. As explained in Chapter 1, Success Academy was created with two goals in mind. The first was to help more American Indian students prepare for and succeed in college. The second was to make South Dakota State University into the kind of place where that could happen. In the next two sections we will examine these goals in more detail as well as some indicators of success. Then we will look at the challenges faced along the way.

Success in Increasing College Access for American Indian High School Students

Preventing students from dropping out of high school and making sure they are academically prepared for college are early and important steps in increasing access to higher education for Native Americans.

Keeping More American Indian Students in High School. Before Success Academy only about five FIS graduates per year had attended the school since they were freshmen. By 2004, when the first cohort of Success Academy freshmen graduated, 47 seniors had attended FIS for all four years of high school.

Helping Boost Academic Achievement. Stanford Achievement Test scores in reading increased from 31 to 40 for FIS ninth graders, when comparing figures from the year before the start of Success Academy to the year after the start of Success Academy. A similar jump from 36 to 48 was seen in ninth graders' math scores.

Increasing the Number of American Indian High School Students Going to College. Before Success Academy, only a handful of FIS students each year attempted higher education. Year by year this number has increased. Among the 59 seniors who graduated from FIS in 2012, 50 said they planned on pursuing postsecondary education of some kind.

Increasing the Number of FIS Students Attending SDSU. Since the start of Success Academy, 101 Success Academy scholars have enrolled in SDSU as concurrent high school students (FIS seniors taking SDSU classes). Between Fall 2004 and Fall 2012, 52 Success Academy scholars have enrolled at SDSU as true freshmen. Before Success Academy on average one FIS graduate per year enrolled at SDSU.

Success in Transforming the University in Ways That Have Long-Term Impact for American Indians

While Success Academy's first goal just discussed deals directly with college access for Native students, the second goal addresses broader issues of institutional change, as this relates to American Indians.

Building the Capacity of SDSU Faculty and Staff to Effectively Serve American Indian Students. About 300 SDSU faculty and staff have been involved with planning and presenting Success Academy activities over the past 12 years. "Success Academy was not only SDSU's best diversity effort ever, but it is a model for college and university campuses everywhere," said Distinguished Professor of English Charles L. Woodard. "It was invaluable in introducing SDSU students and faculty members to indigenous presence and cultures and for creating relationships and program possibilities which will extend far into the future."

Preparing SDSU Students for a Diverse World. About 4,000 SDSU students have worked one-on-one with FIS students, as co-planners and co-presenters of Success Academy events, throughout the years. In addition, multiple service-learning projects have taken SDSU students in the fields of Education, Nursing, English and Health, into the Flandreau Indian School. These projects all grew out of contacts made as a result of Success Academy. For non-Indian college students attending an overwhelmingly white university, the importance of working closely with Indian people—and learning from them—cannot be overstated. As one SDSU dean put it:

> I just visited with an undergraduate student who is helping conduct a Success Academy workshop. I asked her how it was going and if she was enjoying it. She told me that this has been one of the greatest learning experiences of her life. It has opened her eyes to working with students from different backgrounds from her own. In addition, she has learned that not all students are naturally motivated and that it is our job to help them see the value of a learning experience. She said that she has grown immensely from this experience.

Strengthening SDSU's American Indian Student Community. About 20 different Native American Club members each year have hosted dinners and otherwise assisted with Success Academy events. As one former NAC adviser explained, "Success Academy encourages SDSU Native American Club students to be better role models and better students. Our Native American Club students feel good about giving something back to the younger students."

Affirming, Honoring, and Incorporating American Indian Identity Into All Aspects of SDSU's Culture. Programs like Success Academy are a way for the institution to rethink how best to work with American Indians. To succeed, Native students should not have to leave their identities parked outside the university gates. Rather, the university needs to develop a broad range of programs, activities, events, and curricula that celebrate Indian ways of life.

This point, while closely intertwined with the three just discussed, deserves special emphasis because it goes to the heart of the kind of *substantial, long-term institutional change* that Mehan advocates. Consider the following three examples.

Almost every Friday during spring semester for 12 years, SDSU professors in all the academic colleges have organized freshman Success Academy workshops for Native students. Workshop titles have ranged from "Wokunze—A Life Pathway in

Nursing" to "Caring for Community and Mother Earth Through Civil Engineering." As they worked to create culturally relevant workshops for American Indian students, non-Native faculty had to rely heavily on Native faculty, staff, students, and volunteers as resources. What was learned in the process has extended far beyond Success Academy. As this sociology professor reflected:

> I would say that one of the effects of Success Academy on SDSU faculty is a rethinking of the relevance of our disciplines to the real-life problems of these students, and a critical assessment of the relevance of what they will learn from us that will help them help their home communities.

Besides presenting workshops, Success Academy has sponsored many cultural activities, such as "Three Voices: Speaking From the Past" (about the Wounded Knee massacre) and hoop dancing by Jackie Bird (Sisseton-Wahpeton Dakota). Many of these activities have subsequently been repeated year after year and incorporated into the university's diversity calendar. They have attracted substantial audiences from across campus, far beyond those simply participating in freshman and sophomore Success Academies. In addition, because of their involvement with Success Academy, many SDSU faculty, staff, and students have attended Native events and had cultural experiences they might otherwise have missed. As this former Nutrition, Food Science and Hospitality professor explained:

> It was so nice for me to attend the recent Pow Wow at SDSU and see an FIS freshman male student who recognized me and spent time talking with me. (I had eaten dinner with him.) I also had a nice conversation with a female teacher who was with the students. Just getting to know people and to build relationships can have innumerable, far-reaching impacts. Success Academy also gave me an opportunity to know members of the Native American Club and other faculty, grad students and administrators at SDSU who are interested in this type of activity.

Success Academy has had an impact on both the academic and the student affairs sides of the university. Many professional staff members from offices such as Residential Life, Admissions, Financial Aid, New Student Orientation, and TRiO Student Support Services have worked consistently and respectfully over the years with the Success Academy juniors and seniors. Since 2004 when our first Success Academy cohort graduated from high school, SDSU staff have taken seriously their job of making the scholars' transition from FIS to SDSU a smooth and welcoming one. Once on campus, the scholars find that they know a wide range of student affairs professionals, people they feel comfortable approaching for assistance when needed. Asked about the benefits of Success Academy to the institution, one staff member said:

> SDSU gains an obvious and better insight into the needs and challenges facing the Flandreau Indian School and its students. We also gain an awareness of how we might better serve FIS and its students. It teaches us that one university, one group, even one individual can make a difference in the lives of students.

Steering committee member and Honors College Dean Tim Nichols mentions a final and important way that Success Academy has helped the university affirm American Indian identity. "The American Indian Education and Cultural Center would not have happened without Success Academy," Nichols says. The Success Academy coordinator, together with several other campus leaders, was instrumental in advocating for the establishment of a first-ever American Indian Center at SDSU. When the Center opened in Fall 2010, the Success Academy program relocated there. From its former home in the College of Engineering, Success Academy brought to the Center two staff members, a generous budget, a study room, 14 laptop computers, and a vibrant schedule of activities.

FIS-SDSU Success Academy's successes—in increasing college access for American Indian students and in helping the university better serve Native peoples—are significant. The past 12 years, however, have not always been easy. The next three sections outline some of the challenges the program has endured. While the formal partnership between the Flandreau Indian School and South Dakota State University ended in August 2012, the Success Academy model is continuing to evolve, and that process will be discussed at the book's end.

Challenges Involving Partners

Much of this book has been devoted to discussing "what works" in designing programs for underrepresented students. In this section and the next we return to two key ideas introduced in Chapter 3. The first was "The importance of having people in power backing programs that benefit students of color cannot be overestimated."

By August 2012, all of the key administrators at the Flandreau Indian School, those people who had been so supportive in backing the partnership during its early years, had retired—Superintendent Betty Belkham (Cherokee), Principal Stuart Zephier (Cheyenne River Sioux Tribe), and Assistant Principal Sandra Koester. A new set of administrators had replaced them. With changing personnel came changing priorities.

Institutional priorities are frequently shaped by outside forces. This certainly was the case at the Flandreau Indian School. The federal No Child Left Behind Act of 2001 (NCLB) has had a profound effect on Indian education generally and on the Flandreau Indian School particularly. NCLB, with its emphasis on standardized testing and the use of a one-size-fits-all approach to education, has not served American Indian children well (Lee 2012).

No Child Left Behind requires schools to show that a substantial number of their students are making Adequate Yearly Progress (AYP) toward state standards for proficiency in reading and mathematics (Education Week 2004). Schools such as FIS that fail to meet AYP year after year face increasingly stringent penalties, ending with firing the staff and closing the school. AYP is determined by student performance on standardized tests. Critics of "high-stakes testing" say it results in many negative consequences including narrowing the curricula to what is tested, teaching to the test, and producing heightened test-taking skills without the actual learning of content (Dworkin 2005).

A consequence of high-stakes testing at FIS was the school cutting back on its commitment to Success Academy so that students and teachers could spend more time in class. In 2010 a new Flandreau Indian School administrator decided that the number of SDSU visits and the number of FIS students participating in them would need to be dramatically reduced. In addition, Success Academy visits would be shortened by eliminating FIS student attendance at SDSU co-curricular events. Success Academy students would no longer be routinely accompanied to the SDSU campus by FIS teachers, as they could not be spared from their classrooms.

These changes were cause for concern at South Dakota State University. A major commitment of university resources had been made to create (and for many years sustain) a model college preparatory program. Success Academy had been expressly designed to be an *early* and *intensive* college preparatory effort, one that promoted postsecondary education for *all* students at the Flandreau Indian School.

At that same time SDSU, just like FIS, was also experiencing some major changes, involving but not limited to personnel. As mentioned earlier, SDSU's American Indian Education and Cultural Center opened in Fall 2010. Four professional staff members—the Native American student adviser, the American Indian Studies head, the Service-Learning associate, and the Success Academy coordinator—moved from disparate locations across campus into the Center. Success Academy, which had been headquartered in the College of Engineering for 10 years, began reporting to the university's director for diversity enhancement.

Between 2009 and 2011, three different individuals held the diversity director's position. By Fall 2012, three of the four professional staff members at the American Indian Center (all except the Success Academy coordinator) had left for positions elsewhere. Again, just as at FIS, with changing personnel came changing priorities. Institutional priorities are reflected in institutional budgets.

Challenges Involving Budgets

Another key idea, introduced in Chapter 3, was that "money matters." A university's commitment to diversity can be judged by the willingness of its leaders to invest in the education of students of color.

In January 2011, South Dakota Governor Dennis Daugaard proposed a budget that cut $127 million, or about 10 percent, from the state's general fund (Ellis 2011). Every corner of state government was hit, none harder than education.

By April 2011, SDSU President David Chicoine had devised a plan to cut 90 jobs and multiple programs in order to counter the $1.8 million loss in state funding the university would undergo. When interviewed, Chicoine said the mood on campus reflected the weather—"gloomy, overcast, windy, rainy" (Businessweek 2011).

A new fiscal era had begun for SDSU. Success Academy was not immune to the changes. "SDSU needs to see improved results in terms of student retention and graduation from the most generously funded program in its portfolio of diversity activities," one administrator commented.

Challenges Involving Structure

"Structure" is that which constrains or determines the actions of individuals. It is important to remember that administrators who make decisions about resources at the micro level operate within a larger, macro-structural environment. Just like FIS, SDSU found its institutional priorities shaped by outside forces. Two of these are described in the following sections.

Board of Regents. SDSU's environment is profoundly influenced by the South Dakota Board of Regents, which oversees the state's six public universities. In the early years of Success Academy, there was a clear regental focus on recruiting. That emphasis later shifted to retention. As this October 2012 article by Sioux Falls *Argus Leader* reporter Josh Verges (2012) explained:

> University officials acknowledge they historically have been too focused on recruiting new students and haven't done enough to help those recruits succeed once they get to college. Spurred on by a spring 2011 conference featuring a national expert on student retention (Vincent Tinto), all six Board of Regents schools have put a range of plans in place to make students feel like they belong on campus and get academic or social help when they need it....For all their efforts, however, the regental system showed no improvement in freshman retention last year. Of every seven students who went straight from high school to a South Dakota public university full time last year, two did not return this fall; that 72 percent

retention rate was the same the previous year. That's well behind the national average for four-year public universities, which was 79 percent in 2010, the most recent year for which data was available. (1A, 12A)

Two aspects of the article require comment. First, Vincent Tinto, the "national expert" hired by the Board of Regents, has been extensively critiqued for what has been called his "acculturation/assimilation" approach to retention as it applies to underrepresented students (Rendon, Jalomo, and Nora 2000). Second, the "range of plans in place to make students feel like they belong on campus" is remarkably similar to the retention strategies put into place for the Success Academy scholars years earlier, strategies that were decried by some as "handholding" when offered to Native students. Now as these supports are being extended to non-Native students, they are applauded as "intrusive advising" techniques (Verges 2012: 12A).

Citi Foundation. In the early years of Citi Foundation funding for FIS-SDSU Success Academy, grants were awarded under a focus area called "college access." By 2011 Citi had renamed this focus area "college success." The message was clear. It suggested that the problem of access to higher education for underrepresented students had been solved. Henceforth the awarding of funds would be dependent upon retention and graduation rates for low-income students and students of color.

A senior Citibank officer, one who helped secure the initial funding for Success Academy, expressed our collective frustration this way:

> There are those in Citi who would say, "How many kids have gotten degrees?" If you are sitting in a skyscraper in Manhattan you could say that, but you don't go from zero to sixty right away. My belief is that there are success stories. Hundreds of students never would have set foot on a college campus or thought of a college degree without Success Academy. It will have an impact on them a lot later in life. It is not fair to judge by the number of college degrees. Only a small percentage of these students' relatives have gone to college. These kids in Success Academy have had that experience. They got here.

In Fall 2000 Success Academy was created to be a college preparatory program for American Indian students. As a result, many Flandreau Indian School students went on to postsecondary education, and 101 of these students enrolled at South Dakota State University.

By fully embracing Success Academy with a rich array of resources, the university got to know intimately its backyard neighbor, FIS—and grew immensely from that experience. Success Academy became a systemic change initiative for a predominantly white institution.

"Persistence is in keeping with Lakota philosophy, which considers not only what is good for today and tomorrow but also what will be good for seven generations into the future," wrote 2+2+2 founders Laurie Stenberg Nichols and Tim Nichols (1998: 41). Success Academy is still in its first generation.

Looking Ahead: What Worked—and Didn't

The practice of introducing a proven intervention, like Success Academy, into a new setting, with the goal of producing similarly positive effects in larger or more diverse populations, is called in the educational literature "scale-up" (McDonald et al. 2006: 15). As an institution, South Dakota State University would like to take the lessons learned from the FIS-SDSU Success Academy partnership and use them to further increase college access for underserved students.

SDSU is in the process of preparing a progress report on institutional diversity for the Higher Learning Commission of the North Central Association of Colleges and Schools. An early draft of that report calls Success Academy a "signature project" of the university. The report further suggests that there will be an expansion of the Success Academy model to additional high schools serving tribal students.

This book has focused on "what works" in a good partnership aimed at college access for Native students. It is also important to discuss "what didn't work" or perhaps "what could work better" in the future. The five factors discussed below are significant to consider as we look toward new collaborations.

Strong Ties (Between College Access Efforts and High School Curriculum)

In the early years of Success Academy, an FIS course called Freshman Seminar regularly brought discussions of college and careers into the classroom. This was important because it reinforced the messages about higher education the FIS students received when they came to SDSU.

Committed Educators

A college preparatory program on the scale of Success Academy requires a substantial investment of institutional resources. All partners must continue to be serious in their commitment of time, effort, skill, and money for the undertaking to be sustainable. Persistence is key.

Family Involvement

One of Success Academy's shortcomings has been its failure to involve Native families in the education of their children. Numerous attempts were made to do so, but none were very successful. Vast physical and psychological distances separated college preparatory efforts at SDSU from the students' relatives back home. Working with boarding school students did present challenges. In the future, however, such obstacles should not be considered insurmountable.

Continuous Participation

Ample research on college preparation points to the importance of early interventions and long-term support (Bonous-Hammarth and Allen 2005). That said, many boarding school students, like those at FIS, return to their home communities to finish their education. Such changes in students' lives complicate participation and make program continuation impossible. When students move in and out of school, it has presented challenges to Success Academy.

Academic Preparation

The academic rigor of a student's high school curriculum is the single best predictor of college success (Brayboy et al. 2012: 34). Studies have shown that Native high school graduates are the least likely of all student groups to have completed core courses necessary for college entrance (Brayboy et al. 2012: 35). Furthermore, students who come to college needing remedial classes are much less likely to graduate. In South Dakota, only 38 percent of all students who attend four-year colleges and take remedial classes graduate within six years of enrolling (Complete College America 2012). The historic underfunding of American Indian education seriously impacts students like the Success Academy scholars and their readiness for college. Perhaps the answer lies, in part, with developing more K–16 partnerships and ones that address academic preparation more explicitly.

The "New Normal": Implications for College Access and K–16 Partnerships

"Changing demographics and spending priorities coupled with increasing competition and demands for accountability mean that universities face a 'new normal' in which they must embrace a clear vision of the future, including access and opportunity for all learners," Robert H. Bruininks, Brianne Keeney, and Jim Thorp (2010) of the University of Minnesota explain. A willingness to embrace innovation will be the key to success. Following are two examples of innovative programs involving K–16 partnerships and college access for underrepresented students.

Community-University-School Partnerships

A community organization can play an important role as an "intermediary" and "facilitator" among postsecondary institutions and school districts (Collins et al. 2009: 395). Between 2005 and 2009 eight community-university-school partnerships were created in cities nationwide. Their purpose was "to influence systemic change in both K–12 and higher education institutions to improve access and attainment for underrepresented students" (Collins et al. 2009: 410).

Foundation funding for these innovative initiatives came from the now defunct Partnerships for College Access and Success. Foundations such as the W. K. Kellogg Foundation (Native American Higher Education Initiative) and the Bill and Melinda Gates Foundation (Washington State Achievers Program) often fuel the development of partnerships more egalitarian than those that have existed previously. These partnerships frequently use an approach called "collaborative inquiry," "a process consisting of repeated episodes of reflection and action," to answer questions of importance to them (Bray et al. 2000: 6).

Community-university-school partnerships bring different kinds of stakeholders to the table to address educational equity. These partnerships, which involve business, political, civic, and educational leaders, have many advantages. High school reform, postsecondary access, and college success all become tied into workforce development. Data on students—as they move (or do not move) through high school, college, and jobs—can be easily shared. Another "plus" to such partnerships, say those who study them, is "avoiding the blame game" (Collins et al. 2009: 405).

The lead organization usually enters into the community-university-school partnership with an established track record in a field such as college access. Consequently, "the levers for change already exist" (Collins et al. 2009: 411). Engaging in the partnership then allows for the reform work to expand into other areas such as college preparation, remediation, and retention. Donald Earl Collins et al. (2009: 411) conclude, "This work is for leaders willing to take a long-term approach to P–20 education reform, leaders willing to tend this garden until it yields students ready for and successful in postsecondary education."

Does the work surrounding community-university-school partnerships have implications for Success Academy? Success Academy has already made substantial progress in college preparation and access. Could the program now move toward expanding its focus to include college success and retention? And could we partner with community organizations, not yet engaged, to achieve these ends?

Community-university-school partnerships are one innovative idea that has been advanced to help universities face the "new normal." The "educational field station" is another new concept that also involves access, opportunity, and K–16 linkages.

An "Educational Field Station"

CREATE is the Center for Research on Educational Equity, Access, and Teaching Excellence at the University of California, San Diego. CREATE was established in the wake of a 1995 decision by the Regents of the University of California to eliminate "affirmative action," the practice of using race, ethnicity, and gender explicitly as factors in admission. The decision had "disastrous consequences" (Mehan 2007: 67) on the diversity of the student body throughout all of the campuses in the University of California system.

CREATE's purpose is to build college-going cultures in schools with large populations of underrepresented students. CREATE is an "educational field station" for the San Diego region (Mehan 2007: 67). Educational field stations are analogous to agricultural field stations. They develop and disseminate research, in this case, research on college access for minority students.

Just as importantly, educational field stations contribute to economic development. By making higher education accessible to those previously excluded by race or income, educational field stations increase the number of college graduates entering the workforce. As Mehan (2007) explains:

> Just as the University has risen to the challenges confronting the state from previous *economic* and *industrial* shifts in our society, now the University must rise to the challenges facing us from the recent *cultural* and *demographic* shifts in our society....The question facing policy makers, researchers, citizens now is: How do we forge a Civil Society in the face of ethnic, cultural, and socio-economic diversity? That is a question for public debate to be sure; but more importantly, we think that diversity is a *research* question that our University, because it is a public university, has the obligation to confront seriously. (67)

CREATE developed the Preuss School on the University of California, San Diego campus. It is a single-track, college-preparatory public charter school, established expressly for the purpose of preparing low-income students for college. CREATE takes the principles developed at the Preuss School and adapts them to help other schools improve. Mehan (2007: 78) describes the Preuss School as "a model for institutions of higher education to collaborate with their K–12 colleagues in order to strengthen the academic programs of elementary and secondary schools and address the overwhelming lack of diversity on college and university campuses."

Could South Dakota State University develop an "educational field station" similar to CREATE? Could the Success Academy model—for K–16 partnerships that increase college access for Native Americans—be disseminated to other universities in the regental system and beyond? The possibilities for affecting higher education and economic development are intriguing.

Afterword

This book is about critical theory in educational practice. It is about the "doing" of critical theory in the education of American Indians. One shortcoming of critical theory has always been its separation from the real-life problems of students and from the daily pursuit of social justice. This book tries to address that shortcoming.

Systemic change, as it relates to Success Academy, is about constant and complex struggles against oppression and inequality. It is about ongoing fights and permanent revolution. It is about a continuing and continual potential for transformation.

For many of us Success Academy is also about having a passion, about finding a sense of joy in what we do in the places where we find ourselves.

Who can we be, institutionally and personally in the future, because Success Academy once was? In 2013, we tell our story. And we welcome a new year, full of things that have never been.

Appendix: FIS-SDSU Success Academy Enrollment by Class and Year

	2000–2001	2001–2002	2002–2003	2003–2004	2004–2005	2005–2006	2006–2007	2007–2008	2008–2009	2009–2010	2010–2011	2011–2012
Freshman	87	99	125	91	71	89	72	58	90	71	63	53
Sophomore		77	77	69	63	116	81	70	70	71	81	37
Junior			74	52	32	26	25	19	18	17	20	17
Senior				17	24	13	7	13	13	13	10	15
Scholar					5	6	2	6	6	3	8	9

References

Acker-Ball, Shawna L. 2007. "A Case Study of the Influence of Family on First-Generation College Students' Educational Aspirations Post High School." PhD dissertation, Department of Education, Policy and Leadership, University of Maryland, College Park, MD.

Adelman, Clifford. 2002. "The Relationship Between Urbanicity and Educational Outcomes." Pp. 35–63 in *Increasing Access to College: Extending Possibilities for All Students,* edited by W. G. Tierney and L. S. Hagedorn. Albany: State University of New York Press.

Alliance for Excellent Education. 2011. "Accelerating the College and Career Readiness of South Dakota's Students." Retrieved August 16, 2012 (http://search.ebscohost.com/login.aspx?direct=ture&db=eric&AN=ED520677&site=ehost-live).

Alva, Sylvia Alatorre. 1991. "Academic Invulnerability Among Mexican-American Students: The Importance of Protective Resources and Appraisals." *Hispanic Journal of Behavioral Sciences* 13(1): 18–34.

American Indian College Fund. 1999. *Developing Your Vision While Attending College.* Denver: American Indian College Fund.

——. 2011. "Facts About American Indian Education." Retrieved August 15, 2012 (http://www.col legefund.org/userfiles/2011_FactSheet.pdf).

American Indian Graduate Center. 2011. "Welcome." Retrieved December 6, 2012 (http://www.aigc.com/Home.aspx).

Anzaldúa, Gloria. 1987. *Borderlands/La Frontera: The New Mestiza.* San Francisco: Aunt Lute Books.

Apple, Michael W. 1982. *Education and Power.* Boston: Routledge & Kegan Paul.

——. 1986. *Teachers and Texts: A Political Economy of Class and Gender Relations in Education.* New York: Routledge & Kegan Paul.

———. 1996. *Cultural Politics and Education.* New York: Teachers College Press.

Astin, Alexander W., and Helen S. Astin. 2000. *Leadership Reconsidered: Engaging Higher Education in Social Change.* Battle Creek, MI: W. K. Kellogg Foundation.

Astone, Barbara, and Elsa Nunez-Wormack. 1990. *Pursuing Diversity: Recruiting College Minority Students.* Washington, DC: School of Education and Human Development, George Washington University.

AVID. 2013. "Decades of College Dreams." Retrieved January 26, 2013 (http://www.avid.org/index/html).

Bauske, Gloria. 2003. "An Old Church That's New Again." *Argus Leader,* August 26, p. 2B.

Bonous-Hammarth, Marguerite, and Walter R. Allen. 2005. "A Dream Deferred: The Critical Factor of Timing in College Preparation and Outreach." Pp. 155–172 in *Preparing for College: Nine Elements of Effective Outreach,* edited by W. G. Tierney, Z. B. Corwin, and J. E. Colyar. Albany: State University of New York Press.

Bosse, Sherrie A., Kelly Duncan, Susan C. Gapp, and Lisa A. Newland. 2011. "Supporting American Indian Students in the Transition to Postsecondary Education." *Journal of the First-Year Experience & Students in Transition* 23(2): 33–51.

Bourdieu, Pierre. 1977. "Cultural Reproduction and Social Reproduction." Pp. 487–511 in *Power and Ideology in Education,* edited by J. Karabel and A. H. Halsey. New York: Oxford University Press.

———. 1986. "The Forms of Capital." Pp. 241–258 in *Handbook of Theory and Research for the Sociology of Education,* edited by J. G. Richardson. New York: Greenwood Press.

Bourdieu, Pierre, and Jean-Claude Passeron. 1990. *Reproduction in Education, Society and Culture.* Newbury Park: Sage.

Brandt, Carol B. 2008. "Scientific Discourse in the Academy: A Case Study of an American Indian Undergraduate." *Science Education* 92(5): 825–847.

Bray, John N., Joyce Lee, Linda L. Smith, and Lyle Yorks. 2000. *Collaborative Inquiry in Practice: Action, Reflection, and Meaning Making.* Thousand Oaks: Sage.

Brayboy, Bryan McKinley Jones. 2005. "Toward a Tribal Critical Race Theory in Education." *The Urban Review* 37(5): 425–446.

Brayboy, Bryan McKinley Jones, Amy J. Fann, Angelina E. Castagno, and Jessica A. Solyom. 2012. *Postsecondary Education for American Indian and Alaska Natives: Higher Education for Nation Building and Self-Determination.* Hoboken: John Wiley & Sons.

Breneman, David W. 2006. "Institutional Perspectives on Student Success." Pp. 145–155 in *College Success: What It Means and How to Make It Happen,* edited by M. S. McPherson and M. O. Schapiro. New York: Macmillan.

Bridges Transitions. 2011. "Choices Planner: Overview." Retrieved December 9, 2012 (http://www.bridges.com/us/prodnserv/choicesplanner_hs/index.html).

Brooks, Trevor, Mike McCurry, and Donna Hess. 2008. *South Dakota State and County Demographic Profiles.* Brookings, SD: South Dakota Rural Life and Census Data Center.

Brown, Donna L. 2005. "American Indian Student Services at UND." Pp. 87–94 in *Serving Native American Students,* edited by M. J. T. Fox, S. C. Lowe, and G. S. McClellan. San Francisco: Jossey-Bass.

Bruininks, Robert H., Brianne Keeney, and Jim Thorp. 2010. "Transforming America's Universities to Compete in the 'New Normal.'" *Innovative Higher Education* 35. Retrieved February 13, 2013 (http://link.springer.com/article/10.1007%2Fs10755–009–9135-y?LI=true).

Bureau of Indian Education. 2009. "Introduction." Retrieved August 13, 2012 (www.bie.edu/cs/groups/xbie/documents/text/idc-008174.pdf).

Burk, Nanci M. 2007. "Conceptualizing American Indian/Alaska Native College Students' Classroom Experiences: Negotiating Cultural Identity Between Faculty and Students." *Journal of American Indian Education* 46(2). Retrieved February 26, 2013 (jaie.asu.edu/v46/46_2_%202007%201%20Burk.pdf).

Businessweek. 2011. "South Dakota State University Outlines Budget Cuts." April 14. Retrieved March 3, 2013 (http://www.businessweek.com/ap/financialnews/D9MJOAA00.htm).

Chandler, Alice. 1997. *Access, Inclusion and Equity: Imperatives for America's Campuses.* Washington, DC: American Association of State Colleges and Universities.

Chavers, Dean. 1999. *Exemplary Programs in Indian Education.* Albuquerque: Native American Scholarship Fund.

Child, Brenda J. 1998. *Boarding School Seasons: American Indian Families, 1900–1940.* Lincoln: University of Nebraska Press.

Clark, Patricia, and Norma Sherman. 2011. "The Importance of Elders and Family in Native American Culture." *Horizons*, March/April, pp. 14–16.

Colbert, Charles R. Joseph J. Saggio, and Dawn Tato. 2004. "Transforming the First-Year Experience for American Indians/Alaska Natives." Pp. 137–160 in *Transforming the First Year of College for Students of Color,* edited by L. I. Rendon, M. Garcia, and D. Person. Columbia, SC: National Resource Center for the First-Year Experience and Students in Transition.

Collins, Donald Earl, Alexandra T. Weinbaum, Gilberto Ramon, and Debra Vaughan. 2009. "Laying the Groundwork: The Constant Gardening of Community-University-School Partnerships for Postsecondary Access and Success." *Journal of Hispanic Higher Education* 8(4): 394–417.

Colyar, Julia E. 2006. "Neighborhood Academic Initiative: Connecting Culture and College Preparation." Pp. 39–56 in *Ethnicity Matters: Rethinking How Black, Hispanic and Indian Students Prepare for and Succeed in College,* edited by M. B. Lee. New York: Peter Lang.

Complete College America. 2011. "South Dakota." Retrieved March 10, 2013 (http://www.completecollege.org/docs/South_Dakota.pdf).

———. 2012. "Remediation: Higher Education's Bridge to Nowhere." Retrieved March 10, 2013 (http://www.completecollege.org/docs/CCA-Remediation-final.pdf).

Connected Mathematics Project. 2009. "Overarching Goal of CMP." Retrieved January 14, 2013 (http://connectedmath.msu.edu/).

Corwin, Zoe B., Julia E. Colyar, and William G. Tierney. 2005. "Introduction: Engaging Research and Practice—Extracurricular and Curricular Influences on College Access." Pp. 1–9 in *Preparing for College: Nine Elements of Effective Outreach,* edited by W. G. Tierney, Z. B. Corwin, and J. E. Colyar. Albany: State University of New York Press.

Crazy Bull, Cheryl. 1997. "A Native Conversation About Scholarship." *Tribal College Journal* 9(1): 17–24.

Cummins, Jim. 1993. "Empowering Minority Students: A Framework for Intervention." Pp. 101–117 in *Beyond Silenced Voices: Class, Race, and Gender in United States Schools,* edited by L. Weis and M. Fine. Albany: State University of New York Press.

———. 1997. "Minority Status and Schooling in Canada." *Anthropology & Education Quarterly* 28(3): 411–430.

Darder, Antonio, Marta P. Baltodano, and Rodolfo D. Torres. 2009. "Critical Pedagogy: An Introduction." Pp. 1–20 in *The Critical Pedagogy Reader,* edited by A. Darder, M. P. Baltodano, and R. D. Torres. New York: Routledge.

Davis, Julie. 2001. "American Indian Boarding School Experiences: Recent Studies from Native Perspectives." *Organization of American Historians Magazine of History* 15 (Winter). Retrieved April 19, 2003 (http://www.oah.org/pubs/magazine/deseg/davis.html).

Delgado-Gaitan, Concha, and Henry Trueba. 1995. *Crossing Cultural Borders: Education for Immigrant Families in America.* Philadelphia: Falmer Press.

Desimone, Laura. 2002. "How Can Comprehensive School Reform Models Be Successfully Implemented?" *Review of Educational Research* 72(3): 433–479.

Devoe, Jill Fleury, Kristen E. Darling-Churchill, and Thomas D. Snyder. 2008. *Status and Trends in the Education of American Indians and Alaska Natives: 2008.* Washington, DC: U.S. Department of Education.

Deyhle, Donna. 1995. "Navajo Youth and Anglo Racism: Cultural Integrity and Resistance." *Harvard Educational Review* 65(3): 403–444.

Deyhle, Donna, and Karen Swisher. 1997. "Research in American Indian and Alaska Native Education: From Assimilation to Self-Determination." Pp. 113–194 in *Review of Research in Education 22*, edited by M. W. Apple. Washington, DC: American Educational Research Association.

Dworkin, A. Gary. 2005. "The No Child Left Behind Act: Accountability, High-Stakes Testing, and Roles for Sociologists." *Sociology of Education* 78(2). Retrieved March 3, 2013 (http://www.jstor.org/stable/414890310.2307/4148903).

Education Week. 2004. "No Child Left Behind." September 19. Retrieved March 2, 2013 (http://www.edweek.org/ew/issues/no-child-left-behind/).

Ekman, Richard, Russell Garth, and John F. Noonan. 2004. "Introduction." Pp. 1–6 in *Powerful Partnerships: Independent Colleges Share High-Impact Strategies for Low-Income Students' Success*, edited by R. Ekman, R. Garth, and J. F. Noonan. Indianapolis: Lumina Foundation for Education.

Ellis, Jonathan. 2011. "Daugaard Budget Calls for 10% Cuts." *Argus Leader*, January 19. Retrieved March 3, 2013 (http://www.argusleader.com/article/20110120/NEWS/101200304/Daugaard-budget-calls-10-cuts).

Epstein, Joyce L. 2003. "A New Model for Comprehensive School Reform: Results of the Partnership Schools—CSR Pilot Study." Paper presented at the Annual Meeting of the American Sociological Association, August, Atlanta, GA.

Epstein, Kitty Kelly. 2006. *A Different View of Urban Schools: Civil Rights, Critical Race Theory, and Unexplored Realities.* New York: Peter Lang.

Faircloth, Susan C., and John W. Tippeconnic III. 2010. *The Dropout/Graduation Crisis Among American Indian and Alaska Native Students: Failure to Respond Places the Future of Native Peoples at Risk.* Los Angeles: Civil Rights Project at UCLA.

Farrell, Elizabeth F. 2007. "Some Colleges Provide Success Coaches for Students." *The Chronicle of Higher Education*, July 20, pp. A25–A26.

Flandreau Indian School Archives, Chronology of Events—Flandreau Indian School, December 8, 1995. Prepared by Jack Belkham, Superintendent.

Flandreau Indian Vocational High School. 1936? *Bulletin of the Flandreau Indian Vocational High School.* Sioux Falls, SD: Will A. Beach Printing Co.

Foley, Douglas. 2005. "Enrique Trueba: A Latino Critical Ethnographer for the Ages." *Anthropology & Education Quarterly* 36(4): 354–366.

Fox, Mary Jo Tippeconnic. 2005. "Voices From Within: Native American Faculty and Staff on Campus." Pp. 49–59 in *Serving Native American Students*, edited by M. J. T. Fox, S. C. Lowe, and G. S. McClellan. San Francisco: Jossey-Bass.

Freire, Paulo. 1990. *Pedagogy of the Oppressed*. New York: Continuum.

———. 1994. *Pedagogy of Hope*. New York: Continuum.

Gandara, Patricia. 1995. *Over the Ivy Walls: The Educational Mobility of Low-Income Chicanos*. Albany: State University of New York Press.

Gardner, Howard. 1983. *Frames of Mind: The Theory of Multiple Intelligences*. New York: Basic Books.

Garrod, Andrew, and Colleen Larimore, eds. 1997. *First Person, First Peoples: Native American College Graduates Tell Their Life Stories*. Ithaca: Cornell University Press.

Gartman, David. 2013. *Culture, Class, and Critical Theory: Between Bourdieu and the Frankfurt School*. New York: Routledge.

Gay, Geneva. 1995. "Mirror Images on Common Issues: Parallels Between Multicultural Education and Critical Pedagogy." Pp. 155–189 in *Multicultural Education, Critical Pedagogy, and the Politics of Difference*, edited by C. E. Sleeter and P. L. McLaren. Albany: State University of New York Press.

Gilbert, W. Sakiestewa. 1992. *School, College and University Partnership Program (SCUP)*. U.S. Department of Education Final Report, 1988–1991. P204A80062–90. Flagstaff: Northern Arizona University Center for Excellence in Education.

———. 2000. "Bridging the Gap Between High School and College." *Journal of American Indian Education* 39(3): 36–57.

Gillespie, Diane, Gillies Malnarich, and George Woods. 2006. "Critical Moments: Using College Students' Border Narratives as Sites for Cultural Dialogue." Pp. 99–115 in *Ethnicity Matters: Rethinking How Black, Hispanic and Indian Students Prepare for and Succeed in College*, edited by M. B. Lee. New York: Peter Lang.

Giroux, Henry A. 1988. "Border Pedagogy in the Age of Postmodernism." *Journal of Education* 170(3): 162–181.

———. 1992. *Border Crossings: Cultural Workers and the Politics of Education*. New York: Routledge.

Glaser, Barney G., and Anselm L. Strauss. 1967. *The Discovery of Grounded Theory: Strategies for Qualitative Research*. New York: Aldine de Gruyter.

Gramsci, Antonio. 1992. *Prison Notebooks*. New York: Columbia University Press.

Greene, Maxine. 1995. *Releasing the Imagination: Essays on Education, the Arts, and Social Change*. San Francisco: Jossey-Bass.

Grinnell, Frederick. 1987. *The Scientific Attitude*. Boulder: Westview Press, quoted in *Revolutionizing Higher Education in Agriculture: Framework, Principles, and Agenda for Action*, by H. O. Kunkel and C. L. Skaggs. 2001. Ames: Iowa State University Press.

Guajardo, Miguel A., and Francisco J. Guajardo. 2002. "Critical Ethnography and Community Change." Pp. 281–304 in *Ethnography and Schools: Qualitative Approaches to the Study of Education*, edited by Y. Zou and H. T. Trueba. Lanham, MD: Rowman & Littlefield Publishers.

Hayes, Elisabeth, and Sondra Cuban. 1997. "Border Pedagogy: A Critical Framework for Service-Learning." *Michigan Journal of Community Service Learning* 4: 72–80.

HeavyRunner, Iris, and Richard DeCelles. 2002. "Family Education Model: Meeting the Student Retention Challenge." *Journal of American Indian Education* 41(2). Retrieved February 10, 2013 (http://jaie.asu.edu/v41/V41I2A4.pdf).

Heiss, Jerold. 1981. *The Social Psychology of Interaction*. Englewood Cliffs, NJ: Prentice-Hall.

Hodges, Carolyn R., and Olga M. Welch. 2003. *Making Schools Work: Negotiating Educational Meaning and Transforming the Margins*. New York: Peter Lang.

hooks, bell. 1994. *Teaching to Transgress: Education as the Practice of Freedom*. New York: Routledge.

Hoover, Eric. 2006. "Study Finds School-College 'Disconnect' in Curricula." *The Chronicle of Higher Education*, February 24, pp. A1, A37.

Howarth, Rea. 1999. "Reaching New Heights: Native Kids Get a Toehold on a College Degree." *American Indian Report* 15(3): 12–15.

Huffman, Terry E. 1999. *Cultural Masks: Ethnic Identity and American Indian Higher Education*. Buckhannon, WV: Stone Creek Press.

———. 2008. *American Indian Higher Educational Experiences: Cultural Visions and Personal Journeys*. New York: Peter Lang.

———. 2010. *Theoretical Perspectives on American Indian Education: Taking a New Look at Academic Success and the Achievement Gap*. New York: AltaMira Press.

Huffman, Terry E., Maurice L. Sill, and Martin Brokenleg. 1986. "College Achievement Among Sioux and White South Dakota Students." *Journal of American Indian Education* 25(2). Retrieved September 24, 2012 (http://jale.asu.edu/v25/V25S2col.html).

Jester, Timothy E. 2002. "Healing the 'Unhealthy Native': Encounters with Standards-Based Education in Rural Alaska." *Journal of American Indian Education* 41(3). Retrieved February 26, 2013 (jaie.asu.edu/v41/V41I3A1.pdf).

Johnson, Kyle. 2012. "Tatonka!" *STATE*, Summer 2012, p. 11.

Jordan, Will J., James M. McPartland, Nettie E. Legters, and Robert Balfanz. 2000. "Creating a Comprehensive School Reform Model: The Talent Development High School With Career Academies." *Journal of Education for Students Placed at Risk* 5(1&2): 159–181.

Jun, Alexander. 2001. *From Here to University: Access, Mobility, and Resilience Among Urban Latino Youth*. New York: RoutledgeFalmer.

Kanpol, Barry. 1999. *Critical Pedagogy: An Introduction*. Westport, CT: Bergin & Garvey.

Kappler, Charles J. 1904. *Indian Affairs: Laws and Treaties*. Washington, DC: Government Printing Office.

Kawakami, Alice J. 2003a. "Talking Story: A Virtual Interview with Christine Tanioka and JoAnn Wong-Kam." *Amerasia Journal* 29(2): 81–90.

———. 2003b. "Where I Live, There Are Rainbows: Cultural Identity and Sense of Place." *Amerasia Journal* 29(2): 67–79.

Kayongo-Male, Diane, Laurie Stenberg Nichols, and Timothy Nichols. 2003. "Developing an Engaged Institution: South Dakota State University's 2+2+2 Project and American Indian Students." *Journal of Higher Education Outreach and Engagement* 8(1): 205–218.

Kellogg Commission on the Future of State and Land-Grant Universities. 1999. *Returning to Our Roots: The Engaged Institution*. New York: National Association of State Universities and Land-Grant Colleges.

Keloland. 2008. "The Little Bird Band." Retrieved November 11, 2012 (http://www.keloland.com/News/EyeonKELOLAND/newsdetail6403.cfm/the-little-bird-band/?id=67948).

———. 2009. "Flandreau Indian School to Receive $23 Million." Retrieved March 9, 2013 (http://www.keloland.com/newsdetail.cfm/flandreau-indian-school-to-receive-23-million/?id=84002).

Kemple, James J., Corinne M. Herlihy, and Thomas J. Smith. 2005. *Making Progress Toward Graduation: Evidence From the Talent Development High School Model.* New York: MDRC.

Kidwell, Clara Sue. 1994. "Higher Education Issues in Native American Communities." Pp. 239–257 in *Minorities in Higher Education*, edited by M. J. Justiz, R. Wilson, and L. G. Bjork. Phoenix: Oryx Press.

Kim, Young M. 2011. *Minorities in Higher Education: Twenty-Fourth Status Report 2011 Supplement.* Washington, DC: American Council on Education.

King, John T. 2004. "Service-Learning as a Site for Critical Pedagogy: A Case of Collaboration, Caring, and Defamiliarization Across Borders." *Journal of Experiential Education* 26(3): 121–137.

King, Martin Luther, Jr. 1958. *Stride Toward Freedom: The Montgomery Story.* New York: Harper.

Kingston, Paul W. 2001. "The Unfulfilled Promise of Cultural Capital Theory." *Sociology of Education* Extra Issue 2001: 88–99.

Kizer, William M. 1940. "History of the Flandreau Indian School, Flandreau, South Dakota." Master's thesis, Department of Education, University of South Dakota, Vermillion, SD.

Koester, Sandra. 2004. "Flandreau Indian School Success Academy: A Transition From Eighth Grade to College." Presented at the National Meeting of the Bureau of Indian Affairs–Office of Indian Education Programs, August, Denver.

Kohli, Sonali, and Joe Sneve. 2012. "S.D. Colleges Earn Low Marks." *Argus Leader*, June 25, pp. 1A, 4A.

Kunkel, H. O., and C. L. Skaggs. 2001. *Revolutionizing Higher Education in Agriculture: Framework, Principles, and Agenda for Action.* Ames: Iowa State University Press.

Lal, Barbara Ballis. 1995. "Symbolic Interaction Theories." *American Behavioral Scientist* 38(3): 421–444.

Landrum, Cynthia Leanne. 2002. "Acculturation of the Dakota Sioux: The Boarding School Experience for Students at Flandreau and Pipestone Indian Schools." PhD dissertation, Graduate College, Oklahoma State University, Stillwater, OK.

Learning Forward. 1998a. "Advancement Via Individual Determination (AVID)." *Tools for Schools*, April. Retrieved January 26, 2013 (http://ed.gov/pubs/ToolsforSchools/avid.html).

———. 1998b. "Talent Development High School with Career Academies." *Tools for Schools*, April. Retrieved November 27, 2011 (http://www2.ed.gov/pubs/ToolsforSchools/tdhs.html).

Lee, MaryJo Benton. 2001. *Ethnicity, Education and Empowerment: How Minority Students in Southwest China Construct Identities.* Burlington, VT: Ashgate.

———, ed. 2006. *Ethnicity Matters: Rethinking How Black, Hispanic and Indian Students Prepare for and Succeed in College.* New York: Peter Lang.

———. 2007. "Turning the Notion of 'Community' on Its Head: SDSU-Flandreau Indian School Success Academy." Pp. 99–116 in *Peril and Promise: Essays on Community in South Dakota and Beyond*, edited by C. L. Woodard. Brookings, SD: South Dakota Agricultural Heritage Museum.

Lee, Tanya. 2012. "No Child Left Behind Act: A Bust in Indian Country." *Indian Country Today*, March 7. Retrieved March 2, 2013 (http://indiancountrytodaymedianetwork.com/article/no-child-left-behind-act%3A-bust-in-indian-country-101597).

Legters, Nettie E., Robert Balfanz, Will J. Jordan, and James M. McPartland. 2002. *Comprehensive Reform for Urban High Schools: A Talent Development Approach.* New York: Teachers College Press.

LeMay, Konnie. 2012. "A Brief History of American Indian Military Service." *Indian Country Today*, May 28. Retrieved August 10, 2012 (http://indiancountrytodaymedianetwork.com/2012/05/28/a-brief-history-of-american-indians-military-service-115318).

Lengerich, Ryan. 2012. "Nation's Top Three Poorest Counties in Western South Dakota." *Rapid City Journal,* January 22. Retrieved July 3, 2012 (http://rapidcityjournal.com/news/nation-s-top-three-poorest-counties-in-western-south-dakota/article_2d5bb0bc-44bf-11e1-bbc90019bb2963f4.html).

Lenning, Oscar T., and Larry H. Ebbers. 1999. *The Powerful Potential of Learning Communities: Improving Education for the Future.* Washington, DC: School of Education and Human Development, George Washington University.

Lindley, Lorinda S. 2009. "A Tribal Critical Race Theory Analysis of Academic Attainment: A Qualitative Study of Sixteen Northern Arapaho Women Who Earned Degrees at the University of Wyoming." PhD dissertation, Program of Curriculum and Instruction, University of Wyoming, Laramie, WY.

Loo, Chalsa M., and Garry Rolison. 1986. "Alienation of Ethnic Minority Students at a Predominantly White University." *Journal of Higher Education* 57(1): 58–77.

Lowe, Shelly C. 2005. "This Is Who I Am: Experiences of Native American Students." Pp. 33–40 in *Serving Native American Students,* edited by M. J. T. Fox, S. C. Lowe, and G. S. McClellan. San Francisco: Jossey-Bass.

Lysne, Mark, and Gary D. Levy. 1997. "Differences in Ethnic Identity in Native American Adolescents as a Function of School Context." *Journal of Adolescent Research* 12(3): 372–388.

Marshall, Joseph M. 2002. *The Lakota Way: Stories and Lessons for Living.* New York: Penguin Compass.

Mashek, Carol Martin. 1988. "An Historical Building Study of Ten Buildings at the Flandreau Indian High School." Historical Research Services, Sioux Falls, SD. Unpublished manuscript.

Maynard, Eileen, and Gayla Twiss. 1970. *That These People May Live: Conditions Among the Oglala Sioux of the Pine Ridge Reservation.* Pine Ridge, SD: U.S. Public Health Service.

McAfee, Mary E. 2000. "From Their Voices: American Indians in Higher Education and the Phenomenon of Stepping Out." *Research News on Graduate Education* 2(2). Retrieved February 13, 2013 (http://ehrweb.aaas.org/mge/Archives/5/Macafee.html).

McDermott, R. P. 1987. "The Explanation of Minority School Failure, Again." *Anthropology & Education Quarterly* 18(4): 361–364.

McDonald, Sarah-Kathryn, Venessa Ann Keesler, Nils J. Kauffman, and Barbara Schneider. 2006. "Scaling-Up Exemplary Interventions." *Educational Researcher* 35(3): 15–24.

McDonough, Patricia M. 1997. *Choosing Colleges: How Social Class and Schools Structure Opportunity.* Albany: State University of New York Press.

McLaren, Peter. 1989. *Life in Schools: An Introduction to Critical Pedagogy in the Foundations of Education.* New York: Longman.

McNamee, Stephen J., and Robert K. Miller Jr. 2004. *The Meritocracy Myth.* Lanham, MD: Rowman & Littlefield.

McPartland, James, Robert Balfanz, Will Jordan, and Nettie Legters. 1998. "Improving Climate and Achievement in a Troubled Urban High School Through the Talent Development Model." *Journal of Education for Students Placed at Risk* 3(4): 337–361.

McPartland, James, Will Jordan, Nettie Legters, and Robert Balfanz. 1997. "Finding Safety in Small Numbers." *Educational Leadership,* October 1997, pp. 14–17.

Mehan, Hugh. 2007. "Inter-organizational Collaboration: A Strategy to Improve Diversity and College Access for Underrepresented Minority Students." *Actio: An International Journal of Human Activity Theory* 1: 63–91.

Mehan, Hugh, Irene Villanueva, Lea Hubbard, and Angela Lintz. 1996. *Constructing School Success: The Consequences of Untracking Low-Achieving Students.* New York: Cambridge University Press.

Meriam, Lewis. 1928. *The Problem of Indian Administration.* Baltimore: Johns Hopkins Press.

Merton, Robert K. 1968. *Social Theory and Social Structure.* New York: Free Press.

Moeller, Mary. 2012. "Enhancing Cross-Cultural Competencies Through Online Social Networking." Presented at the Conference for the Scholarship of Teaching & Learning, March 7, Georgia Southern University.

Moeller, Mary, Carla Anderson, and Linnea Grosz. 2012. "Six Elements of Diversity: Teacher Candidate Perceptions After Engaging Native American Students." *Journal of Invitational Theory and Practice* 18: 3–10.

Moeller, Mary, and Darla Bielfeldt. 2011. "Shaping Perceptions: Integrating Community Cultural Wealth Theory Into Teacher Education." *Journal of Applied Learning in Higher Education* 3: 81–97.

Moeller, Mary, and Dianne Nagy. 2013. "More Questions Than Answers: Assessing the Impact of Online Social Networking on a Service-Learning Project." *International Journal for the Scholarship of Teaching and Learning* 7(1). Retrieved February 3, 2013 (http://academics.georgiasouthern.edu/ijsotl/v7n1.html).

Montecinos, Carmen. 1995. "Culture as an Ongoing Dialog: Implications for Multicultural Teacher Education." Pp. 291–308 in *Multicultural Education, Critical Pedagogy, and the Politics of Difference*, edited by C. E. Sleeter and P. L. McLaren. Albany: State University of New York Press.

Morse, Jodie. 2001. "The New College Try." *Time,* January 8, pp. 48–50.

National Congress of American Indians/National Indian Education Association. n.d. "National Tribal Priorities for Indian Education." Retrieved August 15, 2012 (http://www.ncela.gwu.edu/files/uploads/18/NCAI_NIEA_jointESEAreauth.pdf).

Ness, Jean E. 1998. "Creating a Path to the Future: The Circle of Learning Project." *Winds of Change* 13(1): 16–17.

———. 2002. "Crossing the Finish Line: American Indian Completers and Non-Completers in a Tribal College." *Tribal College Journal* 13(4): 36–40.

Neuman, Lisa K. 2008. "Indian Play: Students, Wordplay, and Ideologies of Indianness at a School for Native Americans." *American Indian Quarterly* 32(2): 178–203.

Nichols, Laurie Stenberg, and Tim Nichols. 1998. "2+2+2: Collaborating to Enhance Educational Opportunities for Native Americans." *Journal of Family and Consumer Sciences* 90(1): 38–41.

Nichols, Tim, and Laurie Stenberg Nichols. 2006. "2+2+2: An Equation for Native American Student Success." Pp. 57–80 in *Ethnicity Matters: Rethinking How Black, Hispanic and Indian Students Prepare for and Succeed in College*, edited by M. B. Lee. New York: Peter Lang.

Nixon, Lance. 2002. "SDSU Professor and Tribal Elders Teach Course About the Traditional Uses of Native Plants." *AgBio,* Spring, p. 6.

North Dakota Studies Project. 2011. "Traditional Tribal Government." Retrieved October 30, 2012 (http://www.ndstudies.org/resources/IndianStudies/standingrock/government_traditional.html).

Northern Arizona University. 2012. "The Virgil Masayesva Native American Environmental Education Scholarship Fund." Retrieved February 20, 2013 (http://www4.nau.edu/itep/virgil/scholarship_recipient.asp).

Oakes, Jeannie. 2005. *Keeping Track: How Schools Structure Inequality.* New Haven: Yale University Press.

Oak Lake Writers. 2012. "Retreat." Retrieved November 14, 2012 (http://www.oaklakewriters.org/retreat/).

Ogbu, John U. 1978. *Minority Education and Caste.* New York: Academic Press.

———. 1985. "Research Currents: Cultural-Ecological Influences on Minority School Learning." *Language Arts* 62(8): 860–869.

———. 1992. "Understanding Cultural Diversity and Learning." *Educational Researcher* 21(8): 5–24.

Ogunwole, Stella U. 2006. *We the People: American Indians and Alaska Natives in the United States.* Washington, DC: U.S. Census Bureau.

Oliver, Mary. 2008. *Red Bird: Poems by Mary Oliver.* Boston: Beacon Press.

Oyserman, Daphna, Larry Gant, and Joel Ager. 1995. "A Socially Contextualized Model of African American Identity: Possible Selves and School Persistence." *Journal of Personality and Social Psychology* 69(6): 1216–1232.

Oyserman, Daphna, Kathy Harrison, and Deborah Bybee. 2001. "Can Racial Identity Be Promotive of Academic Efficacy?" *International Journal of Behavioral Development* 25(4): 379–385.

Pappan, Jillian. 1999. "If I Could See the Sky." P. 24 in *When the Rain Sings,* edited by National Museum of the American Indian. New York: Simon & Schuster.

Pascarella, John. 2007. "The Manufacture of Intent." Pp. 31–47 in *Useful Theory: Making Critical Education Practical,* edited by R. A. Goldstein. New York: Peter Lang.

Pavel, D. Michael. 1999. "American Indians and Alaska Natives in Higher Education: Promoting Access and Achievement." Pp. 239–258 in *Next Steps: Research and Practice to Advance Indian Education,* edited by K. G. Swisher and J. W. Tippeconnic III. Charleston, WV: ERIC Clearinghouse on Rural Education and Small Schools.

Pavel, D. Michael, and Ella Inglebret. 2007. *American Indian and Alaska Native Student's Guide to College Success.* Westport, CT: Greenwood Press.

Pease-Windy Boy, Janine. 1995. "Cultural Diversity in Higher Education: An American Indian Perspective." Pp. 399–413 in *Multicultural Education, Critical Pedagogy, and the Politics of Difference,* edited by C. E. Sleeter and P. L. McLaren. Albany: State University of New York Press.

Phelan, Patricia, Ann Locke Davidson, and Hanh Thanh Cao. 1991. "Students' Multiple Worlds: Negotiating the Boundaries of Family, Peer, and School Cultures." *Anthropology & Education Quarterly* 22(3): 224–250.

Pidgeon, Michelle. 2008–2009. "Pushing Against the Margins: Indigenous Theorizing of 'Success' and Retention in Higher Education." *Journal of College Student Retention* 10(3): 339–360.

Pottinger, Richard. 1989. "The Quest for Valued Futures: Steps on a Rainbow Journey." *Journal of Navajo Education* 6(3): 2–11.

Power Shift. 2007. "Power Shift: Then & Now." Retrieved February 21, 2013 (http://www.wearepowershift.org/category/tags/power-shift-2007).

Pozo, Michael. 2003. "Toward a Critical Revolutionary Pedagogy: An Interview With Peter McLaren." *St. John's University Humanities Review* 2(1). Retrieved July 28, 2011 (http://facpub.stjohns.edu/~ganterg/sjureview/vol2–1/mclaren.html).

Putnam, Robert D. 2000. *Bowling Alone: The Collapse and Revival of American Community.* New York: Simon & Schuster.

Reese, R. Neil. 2012. "Native Plant Research and Teaching Programs at SDSU." Retrieved October 1, 2012 (http://www.docstoc.com/docs/114765565/Native-Plant-Research-and-Teaching-Programs).

Reimer, Jaimi. 2000. "Hands-on Science, Math Excites Students, Teachers." *The South Dakota State University Observer,* Fall, p. 3.

Rendon, Laura I., Romero E. Jalomo, and Amaury Nora. 2000. "Theoretical Considerations in the Study of Minority Student Retention in Higher Education." Pp. 127–156 in *Reworking the Student Departure Puzzle,* edited by J. M. Braxton. Nashville: Vanderbilt University Press.

Rick, Lynn Taylor. 2012. "District Still Dealing With High Native Dropout Rates." *Rapid City Journal,* July 8. Retrieved August 16, 2010 (http://rapidcityjournal.com/article_d34007a7-bb40–57d2-b1b9–1af66bd41410.html).

Riordan, Cornelius. 2004. *Equality and Achievement.* Upper Saddle River, NJ: Pearson Education.

Ritzer, George. 1992. *Sociological Theory.* St. Louis: McGraw-Hill.

Rosaldo, Renato. 1989. *Culture & Truth: The Remaking of Social Analysis.* Boston: Beacon Press.

Rosenthal, Robert, and Lenore Jacobson. 1968. *Pygmalion in the Classroom: Teacher Expectation and Pupils' Intellectual Development.* New York: Holt, Rinehart and Winston.

Ross, Kathleen A. 2004. "Heritage University: President as Tour Guide." Pp. 79–88 in *Powerful Partnerships: Independent Colleges Share High-Impact Strategies for Low-Income Students' Success,* edited by R. Ekman, R. Garth, and J. F. Noonan. Indianapolis: Lumina Foundation for Education.

Rueda, Robert, Lilia D. Monzo, and Angela Arzubiaga. 2003. "Academic Instrumental Knowledge: Deconstructing Cultural Capital Theory for Strategic Intervention Approaches." *Current Issues in Education* 6(14). Retrieved January 26, 2013 (http://cie.asu.edu/volume6/number14/).

Russell, Caskey. 2011. "American Indian Counter Narratives: On Survival and Free Money." Pp. 129–135 in *Critical Race Theory Matters: Education and Ideology,* edited by M. M. Zamudio, C. Russell, F. A. Rios, and J. L. Bridgeman. New York: Routledge.

San Juan School District. 2003. "San Juan Heritage: Manuelito." Retrieved July 6, 2012 (http://dine.sanjuan.k12.ut.us/heritage/people/dine/biographies/manuelito.htm).

Schmidt, Peter. 2006. "A Tough Task for the States." *The Chronicle of Higher Education,* March 10, pp. B6–B8.

SDSU University Relations. 2012. "SDSU to Celebrate Morrill Act on Monday." *The Brookings Register,* June 26, pp. A1–A2.

Seib, Gerald F. 2008. "In Crisis, Opportunity for Obama." *The Wall Street Journal,* November 21. Retrieved February 5, 2013 (http://online.wsj.com/article/SB122721278056345271.html).

Seyfrit, Carole L., Lawrence C. Hamilton, Cynthia M. Duncan, and Jody Grimes. 1998. "Ethnic Identity and Aspirations Among Rural Alaska Youth." *Sociological Perspectives* 41(2): 343–365.

Smith, Rachel A. 2010. "Feeling Supported: Curricular Learning Communities for Basic Skills Courses and Students Who Speak English as a Second Language." *Community College Review* 37(3): 261–284.

Snow, David A., and Leon Anderson. 1987. "Identity Work Among the Homeless: The Verbal Construction and Avowal of Personal Identities." *American Journal of Sociology* 92(6): 1336–1371.

Sorenson, Barbara Ellen. 2012. "The Art of Storytelling." *Tribal College Journal* 24(1): 15–18.

South Dakota Art Museum. 2012. "Oscar Howe Biography." Retrieved November 16, 2012 (http://www.sdstate.edu/southdakotaartmuseum/explore/Collections/Howe/oscar-howe-biography.cfm).

South Dakota Board of Regents. 2011. *Fact Book: Fiscal Year 2011.* Pierre, SD: South Dakota Board of Regents.

South Dakota GEAR UP. n.d. "What Is GEAR UP?" Retrieved July 27, 2012 (http://www.sdgearup.org/index.php?page=about).

South Dakota Legislature. 2012. "South Dakota Codified Laws." Retrieved December 31, 2012 (https://legis.state.sd.us/statutes/DisplayStatute.aspx?Type=Statute&Statute=13–53–41.1).

South Dakota Office of Indian Education. 2012. "SD GEAR UP Project." Retrieved August 14, 2012 (http://indianeducation.sd.gov/sdgearup.aspx).

South Dakota State University Catalog. 2012. "Affiliations and Accreditations." Retrieved October 29, 2012 (http://catalog.sdstate.edu/content.php?catoid=2&navoid=199).

South Dakota State University-Flandreau Indian School. 2000. *Memorandum of Understanding*. Brookings, SD and Flandreau, SD.

South Dakota Voices for Children. 2012. "Poverty Hitting S.D. Children Hard." Retrieved July 5, 2012 (http://www.sdvoicesforchildren.org/news_detail.php?iNWSID=110).

Spencer, Velva-Lu. 1994. "Survey of Native American Students Who Attended South Dakota State University, Fall '89–Spring '93." Office of Native American Student Advisement, South Dakota State University, Brookings, SD. Unpublished manuscript.

Stassen, Martha L. A. 2003. "Student Outcomes: The Impact of Varying Living-Learning Community Models." *Research in Higher Education* 44(5): 581–613.

Steele, Claude M. 1997. "A Threat in the Air: How Stereotypes Shape Intellectual Identity and Performance." *American Psychologist* 52(6): 613–629.

St. John, Edward P., Glenda Droogsma Musoba, Ada B. Simmons, and Choong-Geun Chung. 2002. *Meeting the Access Challenge: Indiana's Twenty-First Century Scholars Program*. Indianapolis: Lumina Foundation for Education.

St. John, Edward P., and Shouping Hu. 2007. "School Reform, Scholarship Guarantees, and College Enrollment: A Study of the Washington State Achievers Program." Pp. 351–385 in *Confronting Educational Inequality: Reframing, Building Understanding, and Making Change*, edited by E. P. St. John. New York: AMS Press.

St. John, Edward P., Shouping Hu, and Amy S. Fisher. 2011. *Breaking Through the Access Barrier: How Academic Capital Formation Can Improve Policy in Higher Education*. New York: Routledge.

Stuber, Jenny M. 2011. *Inside the College Gates: How Class and Culture Matter in Higher Education*. Boulder, CO: Lexington Books.

Swann, Brian, and Arnold Krupat, eds. 2005. *I Tell You Now: Autobiographical Essays by Native American Writers*. Lincoln: University of Nebraska Press.

Swanson, Mary Catherine, Hugh Mehan, and Lea Hubbard. 1995. "The AVID Classroom: Academic and Social Support for Low-Achieving Students." Pp. 53–69 in *Creating New Educational Communities: Ninety-Fourth Yearbook of the National Society for the Study of Education*, edited by J. Oakes and K. H. Quartz. Chicago: The University of Chicago Press.

Swidler, Ann. 1986. "Culture in Action: Symbols and Strategies." *American Sociological Review* 51(2): 273–286.

Szasz, Margaret Connell. 1999. *Education and the American Indian: The Road to Self-Determination Since 1928*. Albuquerque: University of New Mexico Press.

Thomas, William I., and Florian Znaniecki. 1927. *The Polish Peasant in Europe and America*. Vol. 1. New York: Alfred A. Knopf.

Thompson, Harry F. 2005. *A New South Dakota History*. Sioux Falls, SD: Pine Hill Press.

Tierney, William G. 1991. "Native Voices in Academe: Strategies for Empowerment." *Change* 23(2): 36–44.

———. 1992. *Official Encouragement, Institutional Discouragement: Minorities in Academe—the Native American Experience.* Norwood, NJ: Ablex Publishing.

———. 1993a. *Building Communities of Difference: Higher Education in the Twenty-First Century.* Toronto, Ontario: OISE Press.

———. 1993b. "The College Experience of Native Americans: A Critical Analysis." Pp. 309–323 in *Beyond Silenced Voices: Class, Race, and Gender in United States Schools,* edited by L. Weis and M. Fine. Albany: State University of New York Press.

———. 2000. "Power, Identity and the Dilemma of College Student Departure." Pp. 213–234 in *Reworking the Student Departure Puzzle,* edited by J. M. Braxton. Nashville: Vanderbilt University Press.

———. 2002. "Parents and Families in Precollege Preparation: The Lack of Connection Between Research and Practice." *Educational Policy* 16(4): 588–606.

———. 2008. *The Impact of Culture on Organizational Decision Making: Theory and Practice in Higher Education.* Sterling, VA: Stylus.

Tierney, William G., and Linda Serra Hagedorn. 2002. *Increasing Access to College: Extending Possibilities for All Students.* Albany: State University of New York Press.

Tinto, Vincent. 1993. *Leaving College: Rethinking the Causes and Cures of Student Attrition.* Chicago: University of Chicago Press.

Torres, Carlos Alberto. 1998. *Education, Power, and Personal Biography: Dialogues With Critical Educators.* New York: Routledge.

Tribal College Journal. 2010. *Touching Home: Stories and Poems by Tribal College Students.* Mancos, CO: Tribal College Journal.

Trueba, Henry T. 1988. "Culturally Based Explanations of Minority Students' Academic Achievement." *Anthropology & Education Quarterly* 19(3): 270–287.

———. 1999. *Latinos Unidos: From Cultural Diversity to the Politics of Solidarity.* Lanham, MD: Rowman & Littlefield Publishers.

———. 2004. *The New Americans: Immigrants and Transnationals at Work.* Lanham, MD: Rowman & Littlefield Publishers.

Trueba, Henry T., Lila Jacobs, and Elizabeth Kirton. 1990. *Cultural Conflict and Adaptation: The Case of Hmong Children in American Society.* London: Falmer Press.

Trueba, Henry T., and Yali Zou. 1994. *Power in Education: The Case of Miao University Students and Its Significance for American Culture.* London: Falmer Press.

Turner, Jonathan H. 1991. *The Structure of Sociological Theory.* Belmont, CA: Wadsworth.

University of San Diego. 2011. "Living-Learning Communities: A Model for USD." Retrieved February 25, 2013 (http://www.sandiego.edu/documents/wasc/effectiveness/attachments/LLC.pdf).

University of Texas at Austin. 2005. "In Memoriam: Enrique (Henry) T. Trueba." Retrieved August 14, 2012 (http://www.utexas.edu/faculty/council/2004–2005/memorials/trueba/trueba.html).

U.S. Census Bureau. 2011. "American Indian and Alaska Heritage Month: November 2011." Retrieved August 15, 2012 (http://www.census.gov/newsroom/releases/archives/facts_for_fea tures_special_editions/cb11-ff22.html).

U.S. Commission on Civil Rights. 2003. *A Quiet Crisis: Federal Funding and Unmet Needs in Indian Country.* Washington, DC: U.S. Commission on Civil Rights.

U.S. Congress. 2012. House Interior Appropriations Subcommittee on Native American Issues. *Statement of Eugene "Ribs" Whitebird:* Public Witness Hearing. 112th Congress.

Venezia, Andrea, Michael W. Kirst, and Anthony L. Antonio. 2003. *Betraying the College Dream: How Disconnected K–12 and Postsecondary Education Systems Undermine Student Aspirations.* Stanford, CA: Stanford Institute for Higher Education Research.

Vergara, Derek, and Len Hightower. 2006. "First Generation Student Success Program: Latino/a Students and Families Working Together." Pp. 81–98 in *Ethnicity Matters: Rethinking How Black, Hispanic and Indian Students Prepare for and Succeed in College,* edited by M. B. Lee. New York: Peter Lang.

Verges, Josh. 2012. "College Retention Rates Slip in S.D." *Argus Leader,* October 7, pp. 1A, 12A.

Villapando, Octavio, and Daniel G. Solorzano. 2005. "The Role of Culture in College Preparation Programs: A Review of the Research Literature." Pp. 13–28 in *Preparing for College: Nine Elements of Effective Outreach,* edited by W. G. Tierney, Z. B. Corwin, and J. E. Colyar. Albany: State University of New York Press.

Wagner, Jon. 1998. "Power and Learning in a Multi-Ethnic High School: Dilemmas of Policy and Practice." Pp. 67–111 in *Ethnic Identity and Power: Cultural Contexts of Political Action in School and Society,* edited by Y. Zou and E. T. Trueba. Albany: State University of New York Press.

Weiss, Eric M. 2006. "Indians Fight Redskins Name." *Washington Post,* August 12. Retrieved February 20, 2013 (http://www.washingtonpost.com/wp-dyn/content/article/2006/08/11/AR2006081101045.html).

What Works Clearinghouse. 2007. "Talent Development High Schools." Retrieved March 8, 2013 (http://ies.ed.gov/ncee/wwc/pdf/intervention_reports/WWC_Talent_Development_071607.pdf).

White Shield, Rosemary. 2004–2005. "The Retention of Indigenous Students in Higher Education: Historical Issues, Federal Policy, and Indigenous Resilience." *Journal of College Student Retention* 6(1): 111–127.

Wink, Joan. 2000. *Critical Pedagogy: Notes From the Real World.* New York: Longman.

Wright, Bobby, and William G. Tierney. 1991. "American Indians in Higher Education: A History of Cultural Conflict." *Change* 23(2): 11–18.

Yosso, Tara J. 2005. "Whose Culture Has Capital? A Critical Race Theory Discussion of Community Cultural Wealth." *Race Ethnicity and Education* 8(1): 69–91.

———. 2006. *Critical Race Counterstories Along the Chicana/Chicano Educational Pipeline.* New York: Routledge.

Zephier, Stuart. 2008. "Successful Partnering by an American Indian Boarding School and a Land Grant University." Presented at The Collaboration for the Advancement of College Teaching & Learning Conference, November 22, Bloomington, MN.

Index

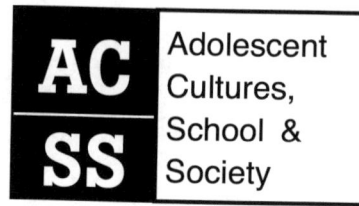

Adolescent
Cultures,
School &
Society

Joseph L. DeVitis & Linda Irwin-DeVitis

GENERAL EDITORS

As schools struggle to redefine and restructure themselves, they need to be aware of the new realities of adolescents. Thus, this series of monographs and texts is committed to depicting the variety of adolescent cultures that exist in today's troubled world. It is primarily a qualitative research, practice, and policy series devoted to contextual interpretation and analysis that encompasses a broad range of interdisciplinary critique. In addition, this series seeks to address issues of curriculum theory and practice; multicultural education; aggression, bullying, and violence; the media and arts; school dropouts; homeless and runaway youth; gangs and other alienated youth; at-risk adolescent populations; family structures and parental involvement; and race, ethnicity, class, and gender/LGBTQ studies.

Send proposals and manuscripts to the general editors at:
Joseph L. DeVitis & Linda Irwin-DeVitis
Darden College of Education
Old Dominion University
Norfolk, VA 23503

To order other books in this series, please contact our Customer Service Department at:
(800) 770-LANG (within the U.S.)
(212) 647-7706 (outside the U.S.)
(212) 647-7707 FAX

or browse online by series at:
WWW.PETERLANG.COM